DATE DUE

American
Catholic Convert Authors

A BIO-BIBLIOGRAPHY

By

BROTHER DAVID, C.S.C., B.L.S., A.M.

Librarian, University of Portland

Introduction by

JOHN MOODY

WALTER ROMIG & COMPANY

14 NATIONAL BANK BLDG.   DETROIT

TYPOGRAPHY, PRINTING, AND BINDING IN THE U. S. A. BY
KINGSPORT PRESS, INC., KINGSPORT, TENNESSEE

TO

MARY IMMACULATE

MOTHER OF CONVERTS

AND TO

LYDIA CORBETT MARTIN

MY MOTHER

CONTENTS

INTRODUCTION

If the full history and background of all American converts to Catholic Christianity could be written, I think it would be found that every one of them had a distinct story to tell. It is sometimes said that "all convert stories are alike, and when we have read one we have read them all." This opinion, however, is never expressed by a convert; it is always the assumption of some one who has never experienced the Great Adventure; who has never traveled the road leading from the desolation of spiritual confusion and despair, to the glorious field of peace and certitude to be found within God's Strong City—the Catholic Church.

Of the eighty to ninety thousand who become converts to Catholicism in this country every year, the vast majority are of course relatively inarticulate, and surely cannot be classed as "American Catholic Convert Authors"; but each has, within his experience, his own vital story, whether long or short. We converts talk with each other about our experiences with a frankness and mutual understanding which other Catholics, of the lifelong variety, not to mention non-Catholics, usually know nothing about. At a certain business men's luncheon, made up of a dozen Catholics, one of the men—a recent convert—remarked that it had taken him thirty years of struggle to finally reach the Catholic Church. I matched that with the story of a woman of my acquaintance, who, with no interest whatever in religion, one weekday afternoon dropped into a Catholic Church, to rest after a long walk. She remained in the church an hour, and while there saw two other women come in and go up to the altar rail and kneel before the Blessed Sacrament. She had no idea why they did this, but when she left the church she went directly to the priest's house next door, rang the bell, and told the priest she wished to become a Catholic. She went under instruction, was received a short time after, and has ever since been a daily communicant.

Now none of the Catholic men at that luncheon could understand how one person could take thirty years to become a Catholic; any more than they could understand how a person could knock at the door of the Church after meditating in the presence of the Blessed Sacrament for but a single hour—not knowing anything about the Blessed Sacrament. Perhaps I was the only person present (aside from the new convert himself) who *did* understand both these cases. But then, you see, I am a convert!

And so it happens that the general public, Catholic or non-Catholic, finds it difficult to understand converts, unless the latter are authors. As authors they are equipped to blazon the truth, not only in regard to the Catholic faith, but their own experiences in finding it. Not only that, but they can defend it against the ignorant or insidious attacks that are made upon it. Not that all Catholic convert authors confine themselves to personal narratives and apologetics, though many of them do (they just can't resist it!); and if they do not, their grounding in the Faith enables them to write "like Catholics," whether it is fiction, fancy or fact that they devote themselves to.

For example, one of the most conspicuous Catholic convert authors of the last century was the famous Orestes Brownson. He did write his own story, and it was an astonishing one, for before he could become a Catholic he had to spend thirty years trying out all the leading Protestant sects, and all the secular philosophies that were rampant in his day. But he wrote many other books on many subjects; and everything he wrote *after* his conversion to Catholicism—whether political, economic, social or religious—was conditioned by his faith in Catholic Christianity.

Thus the studious Catholic, when delving into a new book for the first time, without any knowledge of its author, will quickly see whether the author is a Catholic or not. Whether fiction or fact, a line, a word, a phrase, will enlighten him. Well do I remember being given, years ago, a short Life of Christ, written by a man who, I was told, was a Catholic. Quite perfect until I reached the last chapter—and there the author denied the truth of the Resurrection! Which reminds me of the experience of a non-Catholic friend, deeply prejudiced against *all* Catholic writers. Someone induced him to read *The Everlasting Man* by Chesterton. He did not know that Chesterton was a Catholic, and after reading the book, was enthusiastic about it. When I told him it was fine Catholic literature, he exclaimed, "Catholic? Oh well then, it can't be so good after all!"

This book lists a great galaxy of Catholic convert authors, who have, for the most part, found the Faith in America. And it is a remarkable fact that so many converts are, or have been, authors. Of the total Catholic population in America, which is estimated at over 23,000,000, no one knows how many converts this total includes. It is impossible to know. But taking American Catholic writers as a whole, the percentage of them who are converts is surprisingly high. The same thing is true in England; a large number of English Catholic authors are converts, many of them persons of unusual culture in the literary world.

There is a real reason for this. It is not because converts are necessarily better Catholics than those "who are born that way." We all know many indifferent converts, as well as a host of inarticulate ones. But the convert was *not* "born that way"; he has traveled, often over a very long rough road (though sometimes the road has been short), to enter into a new life, to arrive at a state of spiritual security and peace—to reach what turns out to be a "happy ending." And this great experience, which the lifelong Catholic knows nothing about, is what inspires him to express himself, even if sometimes but crudely. If he has no talent for writing, he will be a speaker, a worker, a debater; in any event he will be certain to give voice to his Faith in some form.

And that, I think, is why we can safely say as converts, regardless as to whether we do it on paper or by word of mouth,

vii

that in the Catholic Church we have found our real and perma-
nent home; and as we go on we are ever impelled to keep aloft
the torch of our Faith. At first blush the typical convert may
be inspired to shout from the housetops—and he writes books,
if he can. Later on, he may no longer shout, but nevertheless his
Faith flowers and goes deeper; as was the case with Cardinal
Newman, who, after more than twenty years in the Church
(during which his sensitive soul suffered much from unmerited
criticism), wrote the following lines:

"There is a depth and power to the Catholic religion, a full-
ness of satisfaction in its creed, its theology, its rites, its sacra-
ments, its discipline, a freedom yet a support also, before which
the neglect or misapprehension about oneself on the part of
living individual persons, however, exalted, is as so much dust,
when weighted in the balance. This is the true secret of the
Church's strength, the principle of her indefectibility, and the
bond of her indissoluble unity. It is the earnest and the beginning of the repose of heaven."

JOHN MOODY

PREFACE

All converts are interesting. Author converts are doubly interesting. Their position as authors has placed them in the public eye and that public regards them as men and women singularly endowed—people who live on a superior intellectual plane. To the non-Catholic an author's conversion commands respect, if not always emulation, but to the Catholic, a writer's conversion enhances his value as an author and gives the Catholic an added reason to thank God for the Faith that is in him. In so far as the convert is important as an author, so it is assumed, he is an important acquisition to the Church. For besides the honest satisfaction the Catholic feels, there is this new piled-up evidence, if it were needed, to support his own belief. Moreover, the conversion of a noted writer has brought to the Catholic a new pride in the ability of the Church to appeal to every stratum of culture and intellect.

While it is true that a given author may not be entitled to the high opinion with which the reader may credit him, nevertheless, it is also true that the medium through which the author expresses himself is a very potent force. It is largely through this medium that the ideas, ideals, and news of the happenings of half the world are brought to the other half. Progress and retrogression are within the power of the writer's pen and his influence is felt directly or indirectly by urbanite and countryman; scholar and illiterate. Hence the conversion of an author is always important.

The ubiquity of the writing guild, the vastly differing qualities of its members, its homogeneous composition, and above all, its tremendous influence, makes the problem of even the discerning reader one of ever increasing difficulty. Few readers have the means of ascertaining a fraction of the facts presented to them through the printed word. They must perforce live by faith—faith in the integrity and competence of the author. For the average reader this faith may be and frequently is a delusion. The reading man is first of all relaxed; his mood is (generally speaking) non-combative; his mind is open for instruction or amusement and hence inclined to follow the line of least resistance. In a word, his acceptance of a printed statement is easier than its rejection. Therefore he accepts it. Over and above this natural vulnerability of the reader, there is besides, a carry-over from earlier days when men could naively accept as authentic such a tale as Gulliver told. Large commercial houses are well aware of the fact that repetition of even the silliest drivel will eventually impress itself upon the reader or hearer—and will sell the goods. What has been established as good trade practice is equally effective in the field of literature, whether it be truth, half-truth, drivel or falsehood.

Writers are frequently the originators as they are certainly the disseminators of new ideas. Moreover, they exert a tremendous influence upon other authors. The same wildfire that was ignited by Malthus' population theory supplied the spark that set the Darwinian forest afire. Darwin himself admits the debt. And through the whole field of literature the great influence exerted by authors upon one another is abundantly evident to the student.

Problems of life, great and small, are the focal points of interest for the maker of literature. But of all the problems that concern man that of religion must be assigned the highest place. All thinking men attempt to solve the eternal riddle in one way or another, and authors are no exception. One chooses atheism, another agnosticism—but the vast majority hold to a belief (sometimes strong, sometimes weak) in Divine Providence. The teachings of the Catholic Church make an indelible impression upon intellectuals who take the trouble to inquire into them. Sometimes this impression is negative, producing only antipathy; more often it is positive and productive of the deepest respect, even love. Waves of thinking men forsook the Church of England in the last century when the Oxford Movement, personified in Cardinal Newman, showed the English thinker that he need have no fear of being intellectually shackled by the Church of Rome. Thousands from every profession followed Newman's example, and the makers of literature took a prominent part. The trend still continues.

That the reaction to the Oxford Movement was not greater in America can be assigned to various causes. One reason is the fact that the over-all cultural crop in this country was meager. Men were too busy with their struggle with the wilderness to think of anything else except making a living. Moreover, it was practically impossible for any but top-ranking authors to earn their livelihood by the pen. Many publishers found it more profitable to pirate the works of well known English and foreign names, and so little opportunity or advantage was held out to the new writer.

Of the authors that America did produce in the early days, few of them were Catholic. Not only because there was a scarcity of Catholics, but also because the greater part of the Catholic population was a comparatively recent acquisition from poverty-stricken Ireland and non-English speaking Germany. The vast majority of those having the privileges of education were Protestants who were not expected to be impressed by the religion of the despised Papist. Indeed, freedom of religion was denied to Catholics (except in Pennsylvania and for a time in Maryland) until almost the beginning of the nineteenth century. After that they had to submit successively to Nativism, the so-called American Protective Association, and in our own day, the Ku Klux Klan. Small wonder that Catholic letters did not flourish as they might have, in the surcharged atmosphere of this, our native land.

In spite of all this the Church has produced writers of merit and distinction in America and has successfully beckoned to many thinking men and women once held by the tenets of Protestantism. It is for the purpose of furnishing a tool for the examination of this latter group that the *Bio-Bibliography* is attempted. Up to this time no such means has been available.

It is believed that the arrangement of the data in this work will help in some small way to answer many questions heretofore unanswerable.

The *Bio-Bibliography* proposes *first*, to locate in a single work a comprehensive list of all American Catholic convert authors and their writings (books) since the beginnings of our history; *second*, to show at what phase of his career a given author has entered the Church; *third*, to furnish a means for the study of the influence made by his conversion upon an author's subsequent writings; *fourth*, to supply a tool by which a student may compare the quality and quantity of the writings of convert writers with those authors born into the Church; *fifth*, to show the movement of intellectuals toward the Church through the *Chronological Lists*; and *sixth*, to indicate, as far as has been possible, the church from which the greater number of convert writers have been drawn. It will be noticed in this connection that a number of authors have left no trace of their previous church affiliations. It may be fairly assumed that these writers had no formal connection with any denomination, although in some cases this fact has simply been unrecorded.

Convert editors are outside the scope of the work, even though some of them, notably Reverend Daniel Hudson, C.S.C., of the *Ave Maria*, have made a large contribution to Catholic letters. On the other hand, some authors not born in the United States or Canada have been included, if the evidence indicates that they are Americans by adoption and if their principal work or education was completed in this country.

Although striving for comprehensiveness, I realize that some convert authors may have been omitted. These omissions are unintentional however, as all of the available sources (and these are not many) have been carefully searched. The same excuse is offered for any omissions in the works credited to an author which may be noted. The possibility of omission here, however, is slight if the works have been copyrighted or listed in standard bibliographies, for the catalogues of the Library of

Congress and the Pacific Northwest Bibliographic Center have been diligently consulted.

Certain inconsistencies may appear in the titles listed under a given author's name, for although it is my intention to include only first editions, the dates of certain books are evidently not first issues. The reason for this is that early bibliographers were not always careful about defining titles, and moreover, they did not always have the data available for complete listing. Also, some early publishers had the exasperating habit of printing books without a date. A *Directory of Publishers and Printers* is added to the work to lend authority to the individual titles by completely identifying the publishers of converts' works. Many of these houses, it need hardly be said, no longer exist.

The biographical feature is considered an essential part of the work, for though brief, these details should cast some light upon the author's religious, educational and cultural backgrounds as well as provide a means for inferences to be drawn from the date of conversion. Unfortunately it has not always been possible to obtain this date.

This work would be virtually impossible had it not been for the generous cooperation of many individuals scattered throughout the country who have obligingly checked submitted lists, suggested additional authors, and otherwise helped with the book. It is a pleasure to have this opportunity to acknowledge my very sincere appreciation to all those who have come to my assistance. Particular mention must be made of Reverend John B. Delaunay, C.S.C., Dean of Men at the University of Portland; Mrs. Lydia Corbett Martin and Miss Emily M. Martin of Chicago for material and moral assistance in forwarding the work; of Miss Mary E. Knapp, Assistant Librarian of the University of Portland for help in organizing the material; and of Dr. John VanMale, Director of the Pacific Northwest Bibliographic Center, who personally checked the bibliographies.

Valuable leads and suggestions were made by Reverend Colman J. Farrell, O.S.B., Associate Librarian of St. Benedict's

College, Atchison, Kansas; Reverend Andrew L. Bouwhuis, S.J., Librarian of Canisius College, Buffalo, N. Y.; Sister Marie Cecelia, Director of the Library School, College of St. Catherine; Mr. Walter Romig of Walter Romig & Company, publishers; Reverend Lloyd Teske, C.S.C., Associate Editor of the *Ave Maria*; Mr. Richard Hurley, of the Catholic University of America Library; Miss Eleanor M. Tucker, Secretary of the Catholic Writers Guild of America; Sister M. Canisius, Librarian of Nazareth College; Rev. Christopher O'Toole, C.S.C., Holy Cross College, Washington, D. C.; Mr. Paul R. Byrne, Librarian of the University of Notre Dame; Miss Lucy S. Murphy of the Buffalo Public Library; Mr. Edward J. Heffron, Executive Secretary of the National Council of Catholic Men.

Many other individuals and organizations gave welcome assistance, including Miss Agnes Collins of the National Catholic Welfare Conference; Mr. Phillips Temple, Librarian of Georgetown University; Mr. Frank Bruce of Bruce Publishing Company; the Editors of The Macmillan Company; the Editors of William H. Sadlier, Inc.; Mr. Henry Watts, Editorial Assistant of *America*; Mr. Eugene Willging, Editor of *Best Sellers*; the Editors of Sheed and Ward; Reverend J. F. Kriebs, Secretary of the Catholic Press Association; Reverend John Forest, O.F.M., Director of St. Anthony's Guild; Miss Mary Kiely, Editor of the *Pro Parvulis Herald*; Mr. Mark Sweeny, Education Director of the Knights of Columbus; Sister M. Justina, S.S.N.D., of Milwaukee; Miss Margaret Lynch, Executive Secretary of the National Council of Catholic Women; Miss Mary F. Larkin, of the Catholic Daughters of America; Mrs. Virginia Thoine Lane, Pasadena, California; Reverend Calvert Alexander, S.J., Editor of *Jesuit Missions*, and the Editors of the Peter Reilly Company. To all these and those other friends who have lent practical and moral support to this work I wish to acknowledge my most sincere gratitude.

Feast of the Immaculate Conception B. D.
Portland, Oregon
1943

ADAMS, CHARLES COLLARD, 1836-

Birthplace: Washington, D. C. **Conversion:** 1883. **Former religion:** Episcopalian (minister, 20 years). **Education:** Wesleyan Univ., Middletown, Conn. (A.B., '59); Trinity Coll., Hartford (A.M., '77). **General:** The author, who was a grandson of Samuel Adams, edited a Sunday newspaper, and was a frequent correspondent to the daily journals. **Authorities:** American Catholic Who's Who. 1911.

Works

1908 Middletown upper houses; a history of the north society of Middletown, Connecticut, from 1650 to 1800 with genealogical and biographical chapters on early families and a full genealogy of the Ranney family. Grafton.

ADAMS, ELIZABETH LAURA, 1909-

Birthplace: Santa Barbara, Calif. **Conversion:** 1929. **Former religion:** Protestant (mother, Methodist). **Education:** Santa Barbara and Los Angeles grammar schools; Santa Monica High School; Von Stein's Acad. of Music, Los Angeles; Ross Studio, Santa Barbara; Beattie Dramatic School, Santa Monica; with Mr. Ralph Freud, Director of Drama, Univ. of California at Los Angeles. **General:** Miss Adams is a Negro author who plans to specialize in writing plays of Negro life. She has contributed poetry and prose to Westward; A Magazine of Verse, and to The Torch. **Authorities:** Letter from Miss Adams, May 21, 1943; Adams, E. L.: Dark Symphony. 1942.

Works

1942 Dark Symphony. Sheed and Ward.

ALEXANDER, REV. RICHARD W., pseud., See Gallagher, Sister Mary Antonio, 1846-1916

ALLEN, GEORGE, 1808-1876

Birthplace: Milton, Vt. **Conversion:** 1847. **Former religion:** Episcopalian (minister 1834-   ). **Education:** Early schooling at home; later sent to Canada where he studied French, etc., in home of Father Consigny; Univ. of Vermont (grad., 1827); studied law and admitted to bar (1831); Vermont Episcopal Institute (grad., 1834). **General:** Dr. Allen was a professor of languages in Delaware College in 1837 and later (1845) held the chair of Greek and Latin at the Univ. of Pennsylvania. He was considered one of the first classical scholars of his day. The author wrote many articles for the United States Service Magazine and after his conversion served for a time as counsel for Pius IX in Philadelphia. **Authorities:** Dictionary of American Biography, v. 1; Smith, W. G.: George Allen; An Address to the Society of Alumni of the University of Pennsylvania. 1900; Pennsylvania Monthly, July; August, 1876.

Works

1849 The remains of W. S. Graham.
1858 The novena of nine Tuesdays in honor of St. Anthony of Padua. C. Shermon.
1859 The history of the automaton chess player in America.
1863 The life of Philidor, musician and chess player. P. Miller.
1878 Catalogue of the chess collection of the late George Allen. J. Meichel. (Collection bought by the Philadelphia library company.)

AGUECHEEK, pseud., **See** Fairbanks, Charles Bullard, 1827-1859

ARENT, LEONORA, 1883-
Birthplace: Iowa. **Conversion:** 1922. **Education:** Iowa State Teachers Coll. (B.Di); State Univ. of Iowa (B.A., M.A.); Columbia Univ. (Ph.D., '19). **General:** Miss Arent is a political economist and lecturer on social studies. She taught at Fordham Univ. and the Catholic Summer School of America from 1923-30. She has contributed prose and verse to various periodicals. **Authorities:** American Catholic Who's Who (1942-43); Guide to Catholic Literature, 1888-1940; Arent, L.: The White Light. 1927.

Works

1919 Electric franchises in New York City. Columbia Univ.
1921 In His service. Fort Dodge, Ia.
1927 Poems. Christopher.
1927 The white light. Christopher.

ATKINSON, SAMUEL
Former religion: Baptist; then militant atheist. **General:** Dr. Atkinson found the Faith by consulting Catholic literary sources. His father was an English Baptist clergyman. **Authorities:** Guide to Catholic Literature, 1888-1940; Atkinson, Samuel: My Catholic Neighbors. 1939; Reviews in the following periodicals: Columbia, July, 1939; Commonweal, April 28, 1939; Extension, August, 1939.

Works

1939 My Catholic neighbors. Devin-Adair.

17

AVERY, MARTHA (MOORE), 1851-1929

Birthplace: Steuben, Me. Conversion: 1904. Former religion: Socialist. Education: Public schools; fifteen years under "master of cosmic law." General: Mrs. Avery was an acknowledged authority on socialism and directed the "Karl Marx Class" in Boston for seven years. This association was known later as the Boston School of Political Economy. The author's book, "Socialism: The Nation of Fatherless Children," written after her conversion, made a deep impression upon social thinkers, and was recommended by Theodore Roosevelt. Authorities: American Catholic Who's Who. 1911; Guide to Catholic Literature, 1888-1940; America, August 24, 1929; Catholic World, September, 1929.

Works

1903　(ed.) Socialism: the nation of fatherless children. Edited by Martha M. Avery. Union news league.

1919　Bolshevism, its cure (with David Goldstein). Boston school of political economy.

1924　Campaigning for Christ (with David Goldstein). Pilot.

BAGGER, EUGENE THOMAS SCHOEN, 1892-

Birthplace: Budapest, Hungary. Came to U. S.: 1915. Americanized: 1920. Conversion: 1909. Former religion: None; parents of Jewish origin. Education: Gymnasium (1901-09); Univ. of Budapest (1909-12). General: Beginning his career as a feature writer on a leading Budapest daily in 1912, Mr. Bagger left to become foreign correspondent for journals of that city in England, Ireland and Denmark. After his arrival in New York he was an editorial writer and correspondent for various papers, including the New York Times from 1915 to 1927. In the latter year he left the journalistic field to study philosophy and pursued this activity until 1940 in various cities of Europe. At present the author is completing two books in his temporary home in Nassau (Bahamas) and plans to return to the U. S. when they are finished. Mr. Bagger has contributed to Atlantic Monthly, Harpers, Current History and other periodicals. Recently his articles have appeared exclusively in America and Thought magazines. **Authorities:** Letter from Mr. Bagger, November 11, 1943; Bagger, E. T. S.: For the Heathen Are Wrong. 1941; American Catholic Who's Who (1944-45).

Works

1922   Eminent Europeans; studies in continental reality. G. P. Putnam.
1924   Psycho-graphology, a study of Rafael Schermann. G. P. Putnam.
1927   Francis Joseph, emperor of Austria—King of Hungary. G. P. Putnam.
1941   For the heathen are wrong. Little, Brown.
1944?   Stendhal; a biography. Little, Brown (In preparation).
1944?   The reconquest of Christendom. Sheed and Ward (In preparation).

BALDWIN, CHARLES SEARS, 1867-1935

Birthplace: New York City. **Conversion:** 1934. **Education:** Public schools of Plainfield, N. J.; Columbia Univ. (grad., '88; A.M., '89; Ph.D., '94). **General:** Professor Baldwin spent his entire professional career in the service of Columbia University, New York City. He was editor of the New American Church Monthly from 1917 to 1918. His wife, **Gratia Eaton (Whithed) Baldwin,** whose death occurred in 1937, is the author of a work entitled "The New Beatrice, or, The Virtue that Counsels; a Study in Dante," and published in 1928. Mrs. Baldwin became a Catholic in 1931. **Authorities:** Letter from Marshall W. Baldwin (q.v.) August 12, 1943; American Catholic Who's Who (1938-39); Guide to Catholic Literature, 1888-1940; Universities and Their Sons, v. 2; Who's Who in New England (1909); Columbia Univ. Quarterly, December, 1935; Commonweal, November 8, 1935.

Works

1894   Inflection and syntax of the Morte d'Arthur of Sir Thomas Malory; a study in fifteenth-century English. Ginn.
1895   (ed.) Specimens of prose description. H. Holt.
1896   (ed.) De Quincey's Revolt of the Tartars. Longmans, Green.
1897   The expository paragraph and sentence. Longmans, Green.
1902   A college manual of rhetoric. Longmans, Green.
1904   (ed.) American short stories. Longmans, Green.
1905   How to write; a handbook based on the English Bible. Macmillan.
1905   (ed.) John Bunyan's The pilgrim's progress. Longmans, Green.
1907   Essays out of hours. Longmans, Green.
1908   A summary of punctuation. Longmans, Green.
1909   Composition, oral and written. Longmans, Green.
1909   Writing and speaking. Longmans, Green.
1914   A introduction to English medieval literature. Longmans, Green.
1917   College composition. Longmans, Green.
1920   God unknown, a study of the address of St. Paul at Athens. Morehouse.
1922   Spelling reviewed, for office and school. Columbia univ. press.
1924   Ancient rhetoric and poetic. Macmillan.

1924 The English Bible as a guide to writing (formerly published under title "How to write.") Macmillan.
1928 Medieval rhetoric and poetic (to 1400) interpreted from representative works. Macmillan.
1930 (ed.) Aristotle's Poetics, Longinus, On the Sublime. Macmillan.
1932 Three medieval centuries of literature in England, 1100-1400. Little, Brown.
1939 Renaissance literary theory and practice; classicism in the rhetoric and poetic of Italy, France and England, 1400-1600. Columbia univ. press.

BALDWIN, GRATIA EATON (WHITHED), See Baldwin, Charles Sears, 1867-1935

BALDWIN, MARSHALL WHITHED, 1903-

Birthplace: New Haven, Conn. **Conversion:** 1930. **Former religion:** Anglican. **Education:** Columbia Univ. (B.A., '24); Cambridge Univ. ('24-25); Princeton Univ. (M.A., '26, Ph.D., '34). **General:** Mr. Baldwin was the son of Charles S. and Gratia Eaton Baldwin (qq.v.). He was a member of the history faculties of Yale and Rutgers from 1926 to 1931 and since 1932, of New York University. The author is a contributor to periodicals, including the Catholic Historical Review. **Authorities:** Letter from Mr. Baldwin, August 12, 1943; American Catholic Who's Who (1942-43).

Works

1936 Raymond III of Tripolis and the fall of Jerusalem (1140-1187). Princeton univ. press.
1940 The medieval papacy in action. Macmillan.

BANDELIER, ADOLPH FRANCIS ALPHONSE, 1840-1914

Birthplace: Berne, Switzerland. **Came to U. S.:** 1848. **Conversion:** 1881. **Education:** Wengern School, Berne; later at home in Illinois; Univ. of Berne (1885). **General:** As an historian, anthropologist, and explorer of southwestern United States and Spanish America, Bandelier did much of his work under the direction of the Archaeological Institute of America; later he was associated with the American Museum of Natural History. Besides his many books, the author contributed to scientific reviews and to the Catholic Encyclopedia. **Authorities:** American Authors, 1600-1900; American Catholic Who's Who. 1911; Dictionary of American Biography, v. 1; Guide to Catholic Literature, 1888-1940; Hodge, F. W.: Bandelier's researches in Peru and Bolivia. 1897; Waterman, T. T.: Bandelier's contribution to the study of ancient Mexican social organization. 1917; American Anthropologist, April-June, 1914; Mid-America, April, 1930; New Mexico Historical Review, October, 1932. (Contains biographical sketch and bibliography, by F. W. Hodge).

Works

1877   On the art of war and mode of warfare of the ancient Mexicans. Salem press.

1878   On the distribution and tenure of lands.

1879   On the social organization and mode of government of ancient Mexicans. Salem press.

1884   Report of an archaeological tour in Mexico in 1881. Archaeological institute of America.

1890   The delight makers. Dodd, Mead.

1890   Hemenway southwestern archaeological expedition. J. Wilson.

1890-92   Final report of investigations among the Indians of the southwestern United States. Archaeological institute of America. J. Wilson. 2 v.

1893   The gilded man (El Dorado) and other pictures of the Spanish occupancy of America. D. Appleton.

1904   Aboriginal myths and traditions concerning the island of Titicaca, Bolivia. Washington.

1905   (ed.) The journey of Alvar Nunez Cabeza de Vaca and his companions from Florida to the Pacific, 1528-1536; tr. from his own narrative by Fanny Bandelier. Edited with an introduction by Ad. F. Bandelier. A. S. Barnes.

1910   Documentary history of the Rio Grande Pueblos of New Mexico. Santa Fe (?) N. M.

1910   The islands of Titicaca and Koati. Hispanic soc.

1911   The ruins of Tiahuanaco. American antiquarian soc.

1923-37   Historical documents relating to New Mexico, Nueva Vizcaya and approaches thereto, to 1773, collected by A. F. A. Bandelier and Fanny R. Bandelier. (Ed. by Charles Wilson Hackett). Carnegie inst. 3 v.

1937   Indians of the Rio Grande valley, by A. F. A. Bandelier and Edgar L. Hewett. Univ. of New Mexico press.

1940   Pioneers in American anthropology: the Bandelier-Morgan letters, 1873-1883 (ed. by) Leslie A. White. Univ. of New Mexico press. 2 v.

1942   Unpublished letters . . . concerning the writing and publication of the delight makers. C. Hertzog.

BARBER, DANIEL, 1756-1834

Birthplace: Simsbury, Conn. **Conversion:** 1818. **Former religion:** Congregational Dissenters ("of strict Puritan rule"); later Episcopalian (minister, 1786-1818). **General:** Daniel Barber served two terms in the Continental Army, and after his ordination practiced his ministry for thirty years in the town of Claremont, N. H. The question of the validity of Anglican orders caused him to investigate the claims of the Church, and this resulted in his own and entire family's conversion. His son Virgil became a Jesuit

23

priest and Virgil's wife a Visitation nun. **Authorities:** Catholic Encyclopedia, v. 2; Parsons, Wilfred: Early Catholic Americana. 1939; Shea, J. G.: History of the Catholic Church in the U. S., v. 3, 4.

Works

1821   Catholic worship and piety, explained and recommended in sundry letters to a very dear friend, and others.

1827-32   A history of my own times. Printed for the author by S. C. Ustick. 3 v.

BARNUM, FRANCIS ALOYSIUS, father (S.J.) 1849-1921

Birthplace: Baltimore, Md. **Conversion:** "In youth." **Education:** Loyola Coll.; Georgetown Univ.; also in Europe. **General:** Father Barnum joined the Society of Jesus in 1880 and thereafter held professorships in various Jesuit colleges in the United States. As a geographer he travelled widely. **Authorities:** Guide to Catholic Literature, 1888-1940.

Works

1901   Eskimo grammar and dictionary.

1901   Grammatical fundamentals of the Innuit language as spoken by the Eskimo of the western coast of Alaska. Ginn.

1912   Genealogical record of the Barnum family, presenting a conspectus of the male descendants of Thomas Barnum 1625-1695 (with Eben Lewis Barnum). Meals.

n.d.   Life on the Alaska mission.

BATTLE, JESSE (MERCER) (Elizabeth Laura Lee, pseud.) 1855-

Conversion: 1906. Education: Clayton (N. C.) Academy. General: Mrs. Battle was a zealous supporter of the Church after her conversion, building or helping to build churches in North Carolina and Michigan. Authorities: American Catholic Who's Who. 1911.

Works

1909 Forget-me-nots. A. R. Fleming.

BAYLEY, JAMES ROOSEVELT, abp., 1814-1877

Birthplace: New York City. Conversion: 1842. Former religion: Protestant Episcopal (minister, 1835-41). Ordained priest: 1844. Education: Amherst Coll.; Trinity Coll., Hartford; St. Sulpice, Paris. General: Archbishop Bayley was an early associate of Bancroft, Irving and Richard Storrs Willis, and the nephew of Mother Elizabeth Seton (q.v.). After serving as vice-president of St. John's College, New York, he became secretary to Bishop Hughes. After his consecration in 1853 he was named to the see of Newark. Authorities: Catholic encyclopedia, v. 2; Dictionary of American Biography, v. 2; Shea, J. G.: History of the Catholic Church in the U. S., v. 4.

Works

1853 A brief sketch of the history of the Catholic church on the island of New York. E. Dunigan.
1861 (ed.) Memoirs of The Right Reverend Simon William Gabriel Brute, D.D., first bishop of Vincennes, with sketches describing his recollections of scenes connected with the French revolution. D. & J. Sadlier.

1872 Lectures and addresses of the Very Rev. Thomas N. Burke, O.P., also the discourses of . . . Archbishop Bayley. J. W. O'Brien.

BEACH, CHARLES FISK, 1854-1934

Birthplace: Kentucky. **Conversion:** 1902. **Former religion:** Presbyterian background but he did not join that church. **Education:** Centre Coll., Kentucky (A.B., '77; A.M., '81); Columbia Univ. (LL.B.). **General:** Beach was the son of a Protestant minister, and practiced law in New York from 1881 to 1895. During the period, 1888 to 1892 he was editor of the Railway and Corporation Law Journal. He resided in London from 1896 to 1900. From the latter year until his death he practiced law in Paris, except for a brief period (1902-03) when he returned to St. Paul, Minn., to lecture. Beach then went to France as a lecturer at the Universities of Paris and Lille. All of the French titles in the Encyclopedia American (1920) were edited by him. **Authorities:** American Catholic Who's Who (1934-35); Who's Who Among North American Authors (1933-35); Curtis, G. P.: Some Roads to Rome in America. 1909.

Works

1881-96　(ed.) The American probate reports (with others). Baker, Voorhis. 8 v.

1885　A treatise on the law of contributory negligence. Baker, Voorhis.

1887　Commentaries on the law of receivers. L. K. Strouse.

1888　A manual of the law of wills. Bancroft-Whitney.

1890　Annual digest of railway decisions and statutes, American and English. F. D. Linn.

1890	The modern law of railways. Bancroft-Whitney.
1891	Commentaries on the law of private corporations. T. H. Flood. 2 v.
1892	Commentaries on modern equity jurisprudence. Baker, Voorhis. 2 v.
1893	Commentaries on the law of public corporations. Bowen-Merrill. 2 v.
1894	A treatise on the modern practice in equity. W. H. Anderson. 2 v.
1895	Commentaries on the law of injunctions. H. B. Parsons. 2 v.
1895	Commentaries on the law of insurance. Houghton, Mifflin. 2 v.
1896	A treatise on the modern law of contracts. Bowen-Merrill. 2 v.
1897	A practical treatise on the law of receivers. Baker, Voorhis.
1898	A treatise on the law of monopolies and industrial trusts. Central law journal co.
1900	Modern pleading and practice. W. H. Anderson. 2 v.
1903	The Northern securities company. The author.

BEDIER, JULIE (Sister Mary Juliana, O.P.) 1896-
Birthplace: Near Davis City, Iowa. **Conversion:** 1914. **Former religion:** Attached to no particular church. **Education:** Public schools in Fruitvale, Colo., and Greenriver, Utah; Sacred Heart Acad., at Ogden, Utah; Maryknoll Teacher Training Coll., Maryknoll, N. Y. **General:** Sister Juliana entered the Maryknoll Foreign Mission Sisterhood in 1921 and then spent thirteen years in Korea, China, and Manchuria. At present she is engaged in mission educational work at Maryknoll, N. Y. **Authorities:** Letter from Sister M. Juliana, August 6, 1943; Book of Catholic Authors. 1st ser.; Guide to Catholic Literature, 1888-1940; the American Catholic Who's Who (1944-45).

1941 Long road to Lo-Ting . . . pictures by Louise Trevisan. Longmans, Green. 31 p.

1942 The important pig . . . pictures by Louise Trevisan. Longmans, Green. 32 p.

1942 Thomas the good thief . . . pictures by Louise Trevisan. Longmans, Green. 31 p.

1943 Chinese Macbeth; a puppet play in three scenes. Maryknoll. pa.

1943 Horse for Christmas; pictures by Louise Trevisan. Longmans, Green.

1943 Little Miss Moses . . . pictures by Louise Trevisan. Longmans, Green. 31 p.

BEEBE, CATHERINE (HERMAN), "Mrs. Robb Beebe," 1896-

Birthplace: Cleveland, O. **Conversion:** 1923. **Former religion:** Unitarian. **Education:** Cleveland public schools; Ursuline Coll., Cleveland (grad., '13); Western Reserve Univ. (Extension); Cambridge Normal School (grad., '15). **General:** All of the Beebe books have been written by Mrs. Beebe and illustrated by her husband Robb. The writing of books for children is an extension of work the couple did before their marriage in 1919. For a time the author taught dramatics and dancing, but the writing field has engaged her since then in the production of plays, short stories, articles, advertising copy, and now, books. The Beebes have three children. **Authorities:** Letter from Mrs. Beebe, October 25, 1943; Book of Catholic Authors. 2d ser.; Guide to Catholic Literature, 1888-1940; the American Catholic Who's Who (1944-45).

1937 Do you like to open packages? . . . Thomas Nelson.
1938 ABC's for Catholic boys and girls . . . Longmans, Green.
1938 Happily ever after . . . Thomas Nelson.
1938 Little patron of gardeners . . . Longmans, Green.
1938 A wish for Timothy. Oxford univ. press.
1939 The children's St. Anthony . . . St. Anthony guild.
1939 Just around the corner . . . Oxford univ. press.
1939 We know the Mass . . . St. Anthony guild.
1940 Calendar . . . Oxford univ. press.
1940 The Christmas story . . . St. Anthony guild.
1940 Our baby's memory book . . . St. Anthony guild.
1941 The children's St. Francis . . . St. Anthony guild.
1942 Bob's bike . . . Oxford univ. press.
1943 Christmas—this way! Oxford univ. press.

BELL, HERBERT CLIFFORD FRANCIS, 1881-

Birthplace: Hamilton, Ontario. **Came to U. S.:** 1903.
Conversion: 1934. **Former religion:** Anglican. **Education:**
Univ. of Toronto (A.B., '03); Paris, France (1906); Univ.
of Penna. (Ph.D., '09). **General:** Mr. Bell was an instructor
at the University of Wisconsin from 1909-12 and professor
of history at Bowdoin College from 1912-26. In 1937 he
received an honorary degree from Bowdoin. During the
World War he was a captain in the U. S. Army; later a
major in the Officers Reserve Corps. At present Mr. Bell
is a contributing editor of the Review of Politics and of the
Commonweal. Since 1926 he also has been a professor at
Wesleyan University. **Authorities:** American Catholic
Who's Who (1942-43); Guide to Catholic Literature, 1888-
1940; Who's Who in America (1942-43).

1917   Studies in the trade relations of the British West Indies and North America, 1763-1773; 1783-1793. Philadelphia.

1926   Guide to British West Indian archive materials, in London and in the islands, for the history of the United States (with others). Carnegie institute.

1936   Lord Palmerston. Longmans, Green. 2 v.

BERRY (ELWOOD) SYLVESTER, father, 1879-

Birthplace: Near Morganville, Ohio; **Conversion:** 1896. **Ordained priest:** 1906. **Education:** Mt. St. Mary's College, Emmitsburg, Md. (A.B., '01; A.M.); Mt. St. Mary's Seminary. **General:** Father Berry engaged in pastoral duties from 1906-22. Since then he has been a professor of theology at Mt. St. Mary's Seminary and of Latin at St. Joseph's College, Emmitsburg. **Authorities:** American Catholic Who's Who (1942-43); Guide to Catholic Literature, 1888-1940.

Works

1911   (tr.) The Eucharistic liturgy in the Roman rite; its history and symbolism adapted from the Italian of Rev. Giovanni Semeria. F. Pustet.

1915   Commentary on the Psalms, Psalms I-L. Benziger.

1921   The Apocalypse of St. John . . . J. W. Winterich.

1921   Archeology series (with Prof. Orazio Marucchi) . . . ed. by Roderick MacEachen, D.D. Catholic book co. 5 v.

1927   The church of Christ; an apologetic and dogmatic treatise. B. Herder.

1928   Theologia fundamentalis.

BLISS, GEORGE, 1830-1897

Birthplace: Springfield, Mass. **Conversion:** 1884. **Educa-**

tion: Harvard Univ. (grad., '51); early schooling at home; later spent eighteen months of study in Europe. **General:** George Bliss was a prominent lawyer and Massachusetts state senator who became an intimate friend of President Arthur. He edited the Annual of Scientific Discovery from 1850-51. Pope Leo XIII made him Commendatore of the Order of St. Gregory in 1895 in recognition for his services to the Church. **Authorities:** American Catholic Who's Who. 1911; Appleton's Cyclopaedia of American Biography, v. 1; Dictionary of American Biography, v. 2; McAdam, D.: History of the Bench and Bar of New York. 1899, v. 2.

Works

1872	Law of life insurance . . . Baker, Voorhis.
1877-80	New York code of civil procedure as amended in 1877. Baker, Voorhis. 2 v.
1880	(joint comp.) The special and local laws affecting public interests in the city of New York . . . C. Van Benthuysen. 2 v.
1882?	Star route conspiracy. United States against Thomas J. Brady and others . . . Govt. print. off.
1884	(ed.) New court rules in force (New York State) March 1, 1884 . . . Baker, Voorhis.

BLYTH, STEPHEN CLEVELAND, 1771-

Conversion: 1809. **General:** Blyth was received into the Church by Bishop Cheverus of Boston. The Library of Congress spells the author's surname as used here; J. G. Shea and the Catholic Encyclopedia spell it "Blythe." **Authorities:** Parsons, Wilfred: Early Catholic Americana. 1939; Shea, J. G.: History of the Catholic Church in the U. S., v. 3. (Reference only).

1806   History of the war between the United States and Tripoli, and other Barbary powers. Printed at Salem Gazette office.

x   1815   An apology for the conversion of Stephen Cleveland Blythe to the Faith of the Catholic, Apostolic and Roman Church. Respectfully addressed to Protestants of every denomination. Desnoues.

BREGY, KATHERINE MARIE CORNELIA, 1888-

Birthplace: Philadelphia. **Conversion:** 1906. **Former religion:** Episcopalian. **Education:** "Studied literature after graduation from Philadelphia Seminary (1899)"; Univ. of Pa. **General:** Lecturer and educator, poet and critic, Miss Bregy is also a regular contributor of essays and poems to various Catholic periodicals. Her works have appeared in several anthologies. **Authorities:** American Catholic Who's Who (1942-43); Book of Catholic Authors. 2d ser.; Guide to Catholic Literature, 1888-1940; Who's Who Among North American Authors (1933-35); Curtis, G. P.: Beyond the Road to Rome. 1914.

Works

1912   Poet's chantry. B. Herder.
1916   (ed.) Juvenile play catalogue (Catholic theatre movement. Philadelphia centre). Wickersham. 36 p.
1919   The little crusaders; a drama of the Children's crusade. P. Reilly. 48 p.
1926   Poets and pilgrims; from Geoffrey Chaucer to Paul Claudel. Benziger.
1930   Bridges, with other verse in varying moods. E. Hartsock.
1930   The stream of English literature (with others). D. C. Heath.
1933   From Dante to Jeanne d'Arc; adventures in medieval life and letters. Bruce.
1936   Ladders and bridges; a book of verse. D. McKay.

BRET HARTE, GEOFFREY

Conversion: 1909. General: Geoffrey Bret Harte is the only living son of the author Bret Harte who was of English, Dutch, and Jewish extraction. He was received into the Church at Rome. Authorities: American Catholic Who's Who. 1911; Guide to Catholic Literature, 1888-1940.

Works

1926   (ed.) The letters of Bret Harte . . . with illustrations. Houghton, Mifflin.

1928   The villas of Pliny; a study of the pastimes of a Roman gentleman . . . with drawings of Max Roeder, and other illustrations. Houghton, Mifflin.

1937   Island in the sun (with Kit Bret Harte); illustrated by Robert Merman. Hodder and Stoughton.

BROUN, HEYWOOD CAMPBELL, 1888-1939

Birthplace: Brooklyn, N. Y. Conversion: 1939. Former religion: Episcopalian; Freethinker. Education: Harvard Univ. (1906-10). General: Mr. Broun was a famous New York journalist, lecturer and columnist. He was with The Nation from 1925-31 and from 1936-39 with the New Republic. Besides his newspaper work he also edited the short-lived Broun's Nutmeg. Authorities: American Catholic Who's Who (1940-41); Current Biography. 1940; Guide to Catholic Literature, 1888-1940; Twentieth Century Authors; American Council on Public Affairs: Heywood Broun; Broun, H.: It seems to me, 1925-1935; Newspaper Guild of N. Y.: Heywood Broun as He Seemed to Us. 1940.

1918 The A.E.F.; with General Pershing and the American forces. D. Appleton.
1918 Our army at the front. C. Scribner.
1921 Seeing things at night. Harcourt, Brace.
1922 The boy grew older. G. P. Putnam.
1922 Nonsenseorship . . . (with others). G. P. Putnam.
1922 Pieces of hate and other enthusiasms. G. H. Doran.
1923 The sun field. G. P. Putnam.
1924 Sitting on the World. G. P. Putnam.
1926 Gandle follows his nose. Boni & Liveright.
1927 Anthony Comstock, roundsman of the Lord (with Margaret Leech). A. & C. Boni.
1931 Christians only; a study in prejudice (with G. Britt). Vanguard.
1935 It seems to me, 1925-1935. Harcourt, Brace.
1941 Collected edition . . . compiled by H. Hale Broun. Harcourt, Brace.

BROWN, BEATRICE BRADSHAW (Michael Kent, pseud.)

Birthplace: New York City. **Conversion:** 1934. **Education:** Univ. of Chicago. **General:** Michael Kent has retired so successfully behind her nom de plume that it is only with certain reservations that the name given in the entry is used. The author has contributed to various periodicals, including the Catholic World. She spent much time in European travel and is now completing the manuscript of a second novel. **Authorities:** Guide to Catholic Literature, 1888-1940; Bruce Pub. Co., Between the Lines, Fall, 1942; Spring, 1943.

Works

1923 A Paris pair, their day's doings, by Beatrice Bradshaw Brown, illustrated by Barbara Haven Brown. E. P. Dutton.

1931   A doll's day, by Beatrice Bradshaw Brown, with illustrations
        by Barbara Haven Brown. Little, Brown.
1942   The Mass of Brother Michael (by) Michael Kent. Illustra-
        tions by Beatrice Bradshaw Brown. Bruce.

BROWN, EDWARD OSGOOD, 1847-1923

Birthplace: Salem, Mass. **Conversion:** 1869. **Former religion:** Protestant of Puritan and English stock. **Education:**
Public schools of Salem; Brown Univ. (A.B.); Harvard
Univ. **General:** Judge Brown presided in the Circuit Court
of Cook County, Illinois, from 1903-09. He contributed
historical essays to various publications. **Authorities:** American Catholic Who's Who. 1911.

Works

1889   De senectute. Chicago literary club.
1914   Two missionary priests at Mackinac. Barnard & Gunthrop.

BROWNE, ANITA MARIA

Birthplace: New York City. **Conversion:** 1939. **Former
religion:** Not affiliated; sang in Protestant Episcopal choir
as a girl. **General:** Miss Browne gave early evidence of
artistic ability by winning scholarships to the New York
School of Fine Arts and the National Academy of Design.
Besides her books and contributions to periodicals, the
author has been editor of Poetry Week Magazine, Current
Events in Poetry and Prose, Literary Shorts, and The
Broadcaster. She is the founder-organizer of Poetry Week
and publisher of The Clubwoman, organ of the New York
State Federation of Women's Clubs. Her radio activities
include that of national broadcasting and radio editor of

the Bulletin of the National League of American Pen Women. **Authorities:** Letter from Miss Browne, October 27, 1943; Who's Who Among North American Authors (1933-35).

Works

1930   (comp.) High dawn; a collection of poems written by club-women of the New York state federation of women's clubs. The Poet's press.

1930   (comp.) A mosaic of muses of the MacDowell club of New York city. The Poet's press.

1933   (ed.) The one hundred best books by American women during the past hundred years, 1833-1933. Associated author's service.

1936   (ed.) Golden jubilee poems of the statue of Liberty. The Poet's press.

1936   (comp.) Homespun; an anthology of poetry by the General federation of women's clubs. American book co.

1940   (ed.) "The year's at the spring," a collection of poems of the earth. The Poet's press.

BROWNE, CHARLES FARRAR (Artemus Ward, pseud.) 1834-1867

Birthplace: Waterford, Me. **Conversion:** 1867. **Education:** Country school until age of 12. **General:** Known best as a humorist, Brown began his active career as a contributor to Carpet Bag in 1852 and from 1858-62 was with the Cleveland Plain Dealer and Vanity Fair. He was constantly on the lecture platform, both here and abroad, and counted Lincoln among his many admirers. The latter read a piece of Browne's shortly before issuing the Emancipation Proclamation. **Authorities:** American Authors, 1600-1900; Dictionary of American Biography, v. 3; Guide to Catholic

Literature, 1888-1940; Haweis, H. R.: American Humorists. 1883; Hingston, E. P.: The Genial Showman. 1871; Seitz, D. C.: Artemus Ward. 1919. (Contains exhaustive bibliography).

Works

1862 Artemus Ward, his book. G. W. Carleton.
1865 Artemus Ward, his travels. (Includes Artemus Ward among the Mormons). G. W. Carleton.
1867 Artemus Ward in London, and other papers. G. W. Carleton.
1868 Sandwiches, by Artemus Ward.
1869 Artemus Ward's panorama, ed. by his executors . . . G. W. Carleton.
1875 Artemus Ward: his works with a biographical sketch by Melville D. Landon. G. W. Carleton.
1900 Letters.
1912 Artemus Ward's best stories, ed. by Clifton Johnson . . . Harper.

BROWNE-OLF, LILLIAN, See Olf, Lillian (Browne)
1880-

BROWNSON, HENRY FRANCIS, 1835-1913

Birthplace: Canton, Mass. **Conversion:** 1844. **Former religion:** Attended an Episcopalian Sunday school. **Education:** Holy Cross Coll., Worcester, Mass.; Georgetown Coll. (grad., '60); studied two years with the Jesuit Fathers in France; also in Munich. **General:** Henry Brownson, son of Orestes A. Brownson and brother of Sara Brownson Tenney (qq.v.) was fluent in eight languages and one of the early colonizers of Brook Farm. He fought in the Civil War, retiring with the rank of major after being wounded in battle. **Authorities:** American Catholic Who's Who. 1911; Guide to Catholic Literature, 1880-1940; Who's Who in America (1901-02); Curtis, G. P.: Some Roads to Rome in America. 1909.

Works

1858   (tr.) Fundamental philosophy. By James Balmes. Translated from the Spanish. D. & J. Sadlier.

1882-07   (ed.) The works of Orestes A. Brownson collected and arranged by H. F. Brownson. T. Nourse. 20 v.

1890   The religion of ancient craft masonry. Detroit, The author.

1891   (tr.) The life of Christopher Columbus, by Francesco Tarducci, after the latest documents. Translated from the Italian . . . Detroit, The translator. 2 v. in 1.

1893   (tr.) John and Sebastian Cabot. Biographical notice with documents. By Francesco Tarducci. Translated from the Italian. Detroit, The translator.

1895   Faith and service; or, How revelation agrees with reason and assists it. The author.

1897   Equality and democracy. Univ. of Notre Dame.

1898-1900   Orestes A. Brownson's . . . life . . . Detroit, H. F. Brownson. 3 v.

BROWNSON, ORESTES AUGUSTUS, 1803-1876

Birthplace: Stockbridge, Vt. **Conversion:** 1844. **Former religion:** Presbyterian; later Universalist (minister, 1826-). **Education:** No formal schooling; wide reading. **General:** Dr. Brownson had an international reputation as scholar, essayist, and philosopher. He edited, and to a great extent wrote, the famous Brownson's Quarterly Review. His active career included that of corresponding editor of the Free Enquirer (early Socialist magazine) and editor, in 1829, of the Gospel Advocate. The Boston Quarterly Review, forerunner of Brownson's Quarterly, was begun by Brownson in 1838 and contiued with the latter title until 1875. **Authorities:** American Authors, 1600-1900; Dictionary of American Biography, v. 3; Guide to Catholic Literature, 1888-1940; Moulton, C. W.: Library of Literary Criticism of English and American Authors. 1935. v. 7; Burton, K.: In No Strange Land. 1942; Sargent, Daniel: Four Independents. 1935; Maynard, T.: Orestes Brownson. 1943.

Works

1836	New views of Christianity. J. Munroe.
1840	Charles Elwood; or, The infidel converted. C. C. Little and J. Brown.
1842	The mediatorial life of Jesus. C. C. Little and J. Brown.
1852	Essays and reviews chiefly on theology, politics and socialism. N. Y.
1854	The spirit-rapper; an autobiography. Little, Brown.
1857	The convert; or, Leaves from my experience. E. Dunigan.
1865	The American republic: its constitution, tendencies and destiny. P. O'Shea.
1876?	Conversations on Liberalism and the Church. Sadlier.
1882-1907	The works of Orestes A. Brownson, collected and arranged by Henry F. Brownson. T. Nourse. 20 v.
1910	Watchwords from Dr. Brownson, chosen and edited by D. J. Scannell O'Neill. Techny, Ill., Soc. of the Divine Word.
1923	Gems of composition from the writings of the late Dr. Orestes A. Brownson, by David Battle. Our Sunday Visitor.

BROWNSON, SARA, See Tenney, Sara (Brownson)
1839-1876

BRYANT, JOHN DELAVAN, 1811-1877

Birthplace: Philadelphia, Pa. **Conversion:** 1842. **Former religion:** Episcopalian. **Education:** Private tutors; later at Episcopalian Acad.; Univ. of Pa. (A.B., '39; M.A., '42); General Theological Sem.; Univ. of Pa. (M.D., '48). **General:** John Delavan (or Delavau) Bryant was the son of an Episcopalian minister. Although he himself studied for the ministry he was not ordained. As a doctor of medicine he was active in the yellow fever epidemic of 1855 in Virginia. During the early sixties he edited the Catholic Herald. **Authorities:** Catholic Encyclopedia, v. 3; American Catholic Historical Records, September, 1904.

Works

1855   The Immaculate Conception of the Blessed Virgin Mary, Mother of God.
1856   The epidemic of yellow fever in Norfolk and Portsmouth, Virginia, during the summer and fall of 1855. T. K. and P. G. Collins. 39 p.
1859   Redemption, a poem. J. Penington.
1867   Pauline Seward: a Catholic story. J. Murphy. 2 v.

BUCK, JACOB REVERDY, father, 1870-

Birthplace: Near St. Peter, Minn. **Conversion:** Ca. 1895. **Former religion:** Presbyterian. **Ordained priest:** 1909. **Education:** Privately educated by parents, with little formal elementary schooling; St. John's Sem., Collegeville, Minn.; Mt. Angel Coll., St. Benedict's, Oregon. **General:** Father Buck taught in country schools in North Dakota and Minnesota for three years. After his ordination he engaged in parish work at Forest Grove, Oregon, and surrounding missions. In 1917 he became pastor of St. Joseph's parish,

Salem, where he remained until retiring in 1934. **Authorities:** Letter from Father Buck, August, 1943; American Catholic Who's Who (1942-43); Buck, J. R.: A Convert Pastor's Autobiography. 1942; Book of Catholic Authors. 3rd ser. 1944.

Works

1929 Convert-pastor explains. 2nd ed. rev. Bruce.
1931 Why do Catholics—? Bruce.
1938 The sage of Exeter. Bruce.
1942 A convert pastor's autobiography. Our Sunday Visitor.

BULL, GEORGE JOSEPH, d. 1911.

Birthplace: Hamilton, Ontario. **Conversion:** 1892. **Education:** The High School (Montreal); McGill Univ. (M.D., C.M., 1869); also the degree, M.D. from Paris, 1889. **General:** Dr. Bull contributed to American and foreign periodicals and while residing in France founded and became president of St. Genevieve's Club for English speaking Catholics. He married the daughter of Howard Hayne Caldwell (q.v.) the poet. **Authorities:** American Catholic Who's Who. 1911; Curtis, G. P.: Some Roads to Rome in America. 1909.

Works

1889 Lunettes et pince-nez. Paris, Masson.
1908 How I became a Catholic. London, Catholic truth soc. (Originally appeared in Paris in 1905 as *Pourquoi je suis devenue Catholique*, and published by Lecoffre)

BURBANK, ADDISON, 1895-

Birthplace: Los Angeles, Calif. **Conversion:** 1941. **Former religion:** Moravian. **Education:** Student, high schools and academies (1907-12); Best's Art School, San Francisco (summers, 1910-11); Chicago Art Institute (1913-14; 19); Santa Clara Univ. (1915); Paris (1925-26). **General:** Mr. Burbank began his career as a journalist with the Winston-Salem, N. C., Sentinel. In 1925 his artistic leanings took him to Europe, Mexico and Central America, where he wrote travel sketches and painted. At present he is engaged in writing a novel—a "life" of a 16th century missionary. His wife, Covelle Newcomb (q.v.) frequently collaborates with him in his works. **Authorities:** Letter from Mr. Burbank, July 25, 1943; American Catholic Who's Who (1944-45); Who's Who in America (Series II—10 Q. 1941).

Works

1939   Guatemala profile, written and illustrated by Addison Burbank. Coward-McCann.

1939   (illus.) Wooden saddles, the adventures of a Mexican boy in his own land, by Marion Lay. W. Morrow.

1940   The cedar deer, written and illustrated by Addison Burbank. Coward-McCann.

1940   Mexican frieze; written and illustrated by Addison Burbank. Coward-McCann.

1942   (illus.) Vagabond in velvet, a story of Miguel de Cervantes, by Covelle Newcomb. Longmans, Green.

1943   (illus.) Silver saddles (by) Covelle Newcomb. Longmans, Green.

BURNETT, PETER HARDEMAN, 1807-1895

Birthplace: Nashville, Tenn. **Conversion:** 1846. **Former**

religion: Disciples church. **Education:** Little formal schooling, but read widely; studied for the bar. **General:** The man who was to become an Oregon and California pioneer and successful lawyer, began his career as a store clerk in Nashville. After unsuccessful efforts in business he turned to law, and in 1839 became prosecuting attorney for the Liberty district. He moved to Oregon two years later as captain of one of the great migrations then moving out West from Independence, Mo. Burnett became judge of the Supreme Court of Oregon in 1845, and three years later was elected to the legislature. He soon left for California however, as leader of an expedition to the gold fields and after becoming established there, was elected to the State Supreme Court. In 1863 he became a founder and first president of the Pacific Bank of San Francisco. **Authorities:** Appleton's Cyclopaedia of America Biography, v. 1; Dictionary of American Biography, v. 3; Guide to Catholic Literature, 1888-1940; Bancroft, H. H.: History of California, v. 6. 1888; Burnett, P. H.: Recollections and opinions. 1880; Hittell, T. H.: History of California (1885-97).

Works

1860 The path which led a Protestant lawyer to the Catholic church. D. Appleton.
1861 The American theory of government considered with reference to the present crisis. D. Appleton.
1880 Recollections and opinions of an old pioneer. D. Appleton.
1884 Reasons why we should believe in God, love God, and obey God.

BURTON, KATHERINE (KURZ), 1890-

Birthplace: Cleveland, O. **Conversion:** 1930. **Former religion:** Episcopalian. **Education:** Western Reserve Univ.

(B.A.). **General:** The author has been a voluminous contributor to the popular periodicals. From 1920-30 she was associate editor of McCalls Magazine and from 1930-33 served Red Book Magazine in the same capacity. Since 1934 Mrs. Burton has been Women's Editor of The Sign. **Authorities:** Letter from Mrs. Burton, July 29, 1943; American Catholic Who's Who (1942-43); Guide to Catholic Literature, 1888-1940; America, July 29, 1939.

Works

1926   Circus lady. Crowell.
1937   Sorrow built a bridge; a daughter of Hawthorne. Longmans, Green.
1939   Paradise planters; the story of Brook Farm. Longmans, Green.
1940   His dear persuasion; the life of Elizabeth Ann Seton. Longmans, Green.
1942   In no strange land. Longmans, Green.
1943   Brother Andre. Ave Maria.
1943   Celestial homespun; the life of Isaac Thomas Hecker. Longmans, Green.

CALDWELL, HOWARD HAYNE, 1831-1858

Birthplace: Newbury, S. C. **Conversion:** ca. 1850. **Education:** South Carolina Coll. (grad., '51). **General:** During his short life Caldwell practiced law in Columbus, and besides bringing out his two books of poetry, contributed to periodical literature. The subject of the poetry in "Oliatta" is the Dismal Swamp, a marshy tract of 150,000 acres in Virginia and South Carolina, originally a part of George Washington's estate. **Authorities:** Thomas, Joseph: Universal Pronouncing Dictionary of Biography and Mythology. 1915, v. 1; Shea, J. G.: History of the Catholic Church in the U. S., v. 4 (Reference only).

Works

1855   Oliatta, and other poems. J. S. Redfield.
1858   Poems. Whittemore, Niles & Hall.

CAMPBELL, THOMAS BOWYER, 1887-

Birthplace: Bedford, Va. **Conversion:** 1931. **Former religion:** Episcopalian (minister, 1913-28). **Education:** Randolph-Macon Acad.; Virginia Polytechnic Institute; William and Mary Coll. (B.D., M.A., '08); Virginia Theological Sem. (grad., '13). **General:** Professsor Campbell was an Episcopal missionary to China from 1913-18 where he taught English, history and theology at St. John's University, Shanghai. Later (1918-28) he served important High Church parishes on the East coast (U. S.) and founded and edited an organ devoted to Catholic re-union. He lived abroad from 1928-31 and is at present a member of the faculty of the University of Notre Dame. **Authorities:** Letter from Mr. Campbell, October 2, 1943.

Works

1928   Black Sadie, a novel. Houghton, Mifflin.
1929   Old Miss, a novel. Houghton, Mifflin.
1931   Far trouble. W. Collins.
1932   White nigger. W. Collins.

CARVER, GEORGE, 1888-

Birthplace: Cincinnati, O. **Conversion:** 1922. **Former re-**

ligion: Presbyterian. **Education:** Univ. of Alabama; Univ. of Chicago; Miami Univ. (B.A., '16). **General:** Professor Carver began his teaching career as instructor of English at Pennsylvania State College in 1916, leaving to serve with the U. S. Army during the World War. He taught English at the University of Iowa from 1919 to 1931 and since then has been professor of English at the University of Pittsburgh. In the short story field the author's best work is "Bread and Soul" which appears in Mary McKenna Curtin's collection of Catholic stories, "Pilgrims All." **Authorities:** Letter from Mr. Carver, July 24, 1943; American Catholic Who's Who (1942-43); Guide to Catholic Literature, 1888-1940; Who's Who in America (1930-31); Who's Who in Education.

Works

1923   Writing and re-writing (with others). Harcourt, Brace.
1924   Minimum essentials of correct writing (with M. F. Carpenter and others). Harcourt, Brace.
1926   (ed.) Catholic tradition in English literature. Doubleday, Page.
1926   (ed.) Representative Catholic essays (with E. M. Geyer). Macmillan.
1928   Points of style; a minimum of correctness in writing English prose. T. Nelson.
1929   Series of six radio talks on essays and essayists (with suggested readings). Univ. of Pittsburgh.
1930   (ed.) Periodical essays of the 18th century. Doubleday Doran.
1930   (ed.) The stream of English literature (with others).
1931   Elements of English composition. Doubleday, Doran.
1932   Paragraph design (with F. P. Mayer). T. Nelson.
1938   Index to sentence essentials. Cordon.
1941   Communicating experience (with E. M. Geyer). T. Nelson.
1944   They live on. Bruce (In preparation).

CARY, EMMA FORBES, 1833-

Birthplace: Boston, Mass. **Conversion:** 1855. **General:** A great part of Miss Cary's life was devoted to social work, particularly in penal institutions. From 1882 to 1892 she was Commissary of Prisons for Boston. She contributed to the Catholic World, Young Catholic, and the Ave Maria. **Authorities:** American Catholic Who's Who. 1911; Curtis, G. P.: Beyond the Road to Rome. 1914; Driscoll, A. S.: Literary Convert Women. 1928

Works

1893   The dayspring from on high. Houghton, Mifflin.

CARY, PHOEBE, 1824-1871

Birthplace: Near Cincinnati, O. **Former religion:** Her sister Alice was a Universalist. **General:** The poetry of this deeply religious author, with that of her sister Alice, was exceedingly popular during the latter part of the nineteenth century. She began publishing verse at the age of thirteen and though her writing was often careless, her work is said to be more poetic in the real sense than that of her older sister. **Authorities:** American Authors, 1600-1900; Dictionary of American Biography, v. 3; Moulton, C. W. Library of Literary Criticism, v. 6; Ames, M. C.: Memorial of Alice and Phoebe Cary. 1873; Bingham, J. M.: The Cary Sisters. 1883; Day, J. M.: The Cary Sisters. 1903; Long, Laura: Singing Sisters. 1941; Musser, B. F.: Outside the Walls. 1914 (Notation on the author's conversion).

Works

1849   Poems of Alice and Phoebe Cary.
1854   Poems and parodies. Ticknor, Reed and Fields.

1861 (ed.) The Josephine gallery (with Alice Cary). Derby & Jackson.
1868 Poems of faith, hope and love. Hurd & Houghton.
1869 (ed.) Hymns for all Christians (with Dr. Charles F. Deems).
1873 The last poems of Alice and Phoebe Cary. Hurd and Houghton.
1874 Ballads for little folk (with Alice Cary). Hurd and Houghton.
1877 The poetical works of Alice and Phoebe Cary; with a memorial of their lives by Mary Clemmer. Hurd and Houghton.
1887 Early and late poems of Alice and Phoebe Cary. Houghton, Mifflin.
1900 One sweetly solemn thought (words & music) F. F. Lovell. 3 p.

CECIL, ELIZABETH FRANCES (NASH)

Birthplace: Powhatan County, Va. **Education:** Principally at home by a governess. **General:** Besides the works listed below, Mrs. Cecil wrote several short stories and certain articles entitled, "Industrial Heroes," "Literary Solons," and "Popular Suffrage and Literature." The author was descended on her mother's side from Elizabeth Washington and on the father's from Robert Cecil, fourth Earl of Salisbury. **Authorities:** National Cyclopaedia of American Biography, v. 3.

Works

1868 Life of Lafayette. P. O'Shea.
1868 Life of Washington. P. O'Shea.

CHAMBERLIN, EDWARD HASTINGS, 1899-
Birthplace: La Conner, Wash. **Conversion:** 1931. **Former**

religion: Methodist. **Education:** Iowa City (Ia.) High School (grad., '16); State Univ. of Iowa (B.S. in Com., '20); Univ. of Michigan (M.A., '22); Harvard Univ. (M.A., '24; Ph.D., '27). **General:** Doctor Chamberlin began his teaching career as an instructor in economics at the University of Michigan in 1920 after serving as 2nd Lieutenant of Infantry in 1918. He left Michigan in 1922 to join the faculty of Harvard University as Assistant Professor of Economics and Tutor in History and Government. Since 1937 the author has been a full professor and tutor, and from 1939 to 1943 he was Chairman of the Department of Economics. Dr. Chamberlin has been on leave from Harvard since 1943, engaged in the activities of the U. S. Office of Strategic Services. **Authorities:** Letter from Dr. Chamberlin, January 9, 1944; America's Young Men (1938-39); Who's Who in America (1942-43); American Catholic Who's Who (1944-45).

Works

1933 The theory of monopolistic competition. Harvard univ. press.
1934 The economics of the recovery program (with others). Mc-Graw-Hill.

CHANDLER, JOSEPH RIPLEY, 1792-1880

Birthplace: Kingston, Mass. **Conversion:** 1849. **Former religion:** Mason. **Education:** Except for common school education, was largely self-taught. **General:** Chandler and his wife taught school after their marriage in 1815. Later (1822-27) he was associated with the United States Gazette and spent a year as minister to the Two Sicilies. From 1848 to 1849 he edited, with J. B. Taylor, Graham's American Monthly, and from 1849 to 1855 he was United States congressman from Pennsylvania. For a time Chandler was Grand Master of the Free Masons. He is remembered particularly for his activities in prison reform. **Authorities:** Appleton's Cyclopaedia of American Biography, v. 1; Biographical Directory of the American Congress, 1774-1927; Catholic Builders of the Nation, v. 3.

Works

1847   A grammar of the English language; adapted to the schools of America. Thomas, Cowperthwait.
1855   Civil and religious equality. J. B. Chandler, printer.
1855   The temporal power of the pope. T. F. McGrath. 32 p.
1875   The Beverly family; or, Home influence of religion. P. F. Cunningham.

CHANLER, MARGARET (TERRY) "Mrs Winthrop Chanler," 1862-

Birthplace: Rome, Italy, of American parents. **Conversion:** 1883. **Former religion:** Episcopalian. **Education:** Privately educated; studied music at Roman Conservatory. **General:** The author had the advantage of a literary and artistic background from her birth. Her half brother was the author, Francis Marion Crawford (q.v.). Nazareth College conferred an honorary degree upon her in 1935. **Authorities:** American Catholic Who's Who (1942-43); Guide to Catholic Literature, 1888-1940; Curtis, G. P.: Beyond the Road to Rome. 1914.

Works

1934   Roman spring; memoirs. Little, Brown.
1936   Autumn in the valley. Little, Brown.

1938 (tr.) Hymns to the church, from the German of Gertrud
      von Le Fort. Sheed and Ward.

CHAPMAN, MICHAEL ANDREW, father, 1884-

Birthplace: Auburndale (Boston), Mass. **Conversion:**
1918. **Former religion:** Episcopalian (minister, 1909-20).
Ordained priest: 1923. **Education:** St. Stephen's College,
Annandale, N. Y.; General Theological Sem., N. Y. C.;
Mt. St. Mary's (Cath.) Seminary, Emmitsburg, Md.; Catholic University of America. **General:** As an Anglican, the
author was rector of Grace Church, Galesburg, Ill., and St.
James Church, Cleveland, O. As a Catholic, he was pastor
of various churches in Indiana, and in 1921, associated editor of Our Sunday Visitor. From 1924-34 Father Chapman
was editor of The Acolyte. He contributes to various periodicals and is a consultant in decoration and liturgical pro-
priety. **Authorities:** Letter from Father Chapman, July 26,
1943; Guide to Catholic Literature, 1888-1940.

Works

1921 The Saviours fountains; a book for children on the seven
      sacraments. Our Sunday Visitor.
1925 Mass of the Cross. Blackwell.
1926 The faith of the gospel; brief sermons for the Sundays of
      the year. B. Herder.
1927 The epistle of Christ . . . B. Herder.
1928 Peregrinus Gasolinus; wandering notes on the liturgy. F.
      Pustet.
1928 The prayer of faith. B. Herder.
1928 Sundays of the saints: sermon outlines . . . B. Herder.
1929 A garland of saints for children. F. Pustet.
1929 Judas (a study of possibilities) and Jude (a study of con-
      trasts). B. Herder.

1930 Open my heart: travel sketches by a pilgrim priest . . .
Bruce.
1931 The heart of the fathers . . . B. Herder.
1931 Peregrinus goes abroad. F. Pustet.
1932 For days and for seasons: notes for occasional sermons. B.
Herder.

CHAUNCEY, SHELTON, pseud., See Nicholls, Charles Wilbur de Lyon, 1854-1924.

CLARK, ELEANOR GRACE, 1895-

Birthplace: Neenah, Wis. **Conversion:** 1925. **Former religion:** Anglican. **Education:** Wayland Acad. (1914-18); Oberlin Coll. (A.B., '18; M.A., '19); Bryn Mawr (Ph.D., '28); post-graduate work at Oxford, London, and Edinburgh universities. **General:** Dr. Clark has been engaged in the teaching profession since 1918. Until 1920 she taught at St. Helen's Hall (Epis.), Portland, Ore. From 1922-30 she was a professor at Friends School, Moorstown, N. Y., and in 1923 at Bryn Mawr. Since 1930 she has been associate professor of English at Hunter College, N. Y. C. **Authorities:** American Catholic Who's Who (1942-43); Guide to Catholic Literature, 1888-1940.

Works

1928 Pembroke plays; a study in the Marlowe canon. Bryn Mawr
Coll.
1937 Elizabethan fustian; a study in the social and political backgrounds of the drama . . . (this work revised as Part I
of Raleigh and Marlowe). Oxford press.
1941 Raleigh and Marlowe, a study in Elizabethan fustian. Fordham univ. press.

COLBY, ELBRIDGE, 1891-

Birthplace: New York City. **Conversion:** 1914. **Former religion:** Episcopalian. **Education:** Barnard School for Boys, N. Y. C.; Proudfit Fellow of Letters; Columbia Univ. (Ph.D., '22); Army schools. **General:** Major Colby taught English at Columbia University and the University of Minnesota from 1914-17. He then joined the U. S. Army, retiring in 1935. He has edited various Army journals and is a contributor to the Dictionary of American Biography, Encyclopedia Britannica and the Encyclopedia of Social Sciences. The author was twice decorated by the Jugo-Slav government and is a member of the Gallery of Living Catholic Authors. **Authorities:** American Catholic Who's Who (1942-43); Guide to Catholic Literature, 1888-1940; Who's Who in America (1942-43).

Works

1918 Small problems for trench warfare.
1920 Echo-device in literature. N. Y. Public Library.
1922 Bibliography of Thomas Holcroft. N. Y. Public Literary.
1922 Education and the army. A. N. Palmer.
1924 (ed) The life of Thomas Holcroft, written by himself. Constable. 2 v.
1924 The profession of arms. D. Appleton.
1924 Swimming soldiers . . . Quartermaster assoc.
1934 American militarism. Soc. of American military engineers.
1936 English Catholic poets, Chaucer to Dryden. Bruce.
1942 Army talk, a familiar dictionary of soldier speech. Princeton univ. press.
1943 Masters of mobile warfare. Princeton univ. press.

COLEMAN (CHARLES) CARYL, 1840-1928

Birthplace: Buffalo, N. Y. **Conversion:** 1868. **Former re-**

ligion: Parents were Unitarian for a time but Charles "grew up a pagan." **Education:** Canisius Coll., Buffalo. **General:** Coleman achieved international fame as a painter besides making important contributions to the fields of archaeology and econography. He contributed regularly to the Architectural Record. The author fought with the Union Army during the Civil War and spent the latter portion of his life on the Island of Capri. **Authorities:** Dictionary of American Biography, v. 4; Guide to Catholic Literature, 1888-1940; Curtis, G. P.: Some Roads to Rome in America; Isham, Samuel: History of American Painting. 1927; Curtis, G. P.: Beyond the Road to Rome. 1914.

Works

1899   Symbolism in religious art. School of applied arts.
1903   A mark of honor. United crafts.
1903   The sacred ciphers. United crafts.
1908   A day with Mary.
1924   Novena in honor of Bl. Therese of the Child Jesus. Benziger.
1926   (ed.) The Little Flower treasury . . . Benziger.

CONVERSE, MARY TERESA EVELYN, 1869-

Birthplace: New Orleans. **Conversion:** 1886. **Education:** Private schools, including the Academy of the Sacred Heart, New Orleans. **General:** The author is a descendant of Benjamin Franklin. She contributed occasionally to the Sacred Heart Review and to Guidon (N. H.). **Authorities:** American Catholic Who's Who. 1911.

Works

1909   Odds and ends. Rumford.

COOK, FREDERICK

Works

1941   Child with folded hands. Saint Anthony guild. 47 p.

COOK, MERCER, 1903-

Birthplace: Washington, D. C. **Conversion:** c. 1930. **Former religion:** Protestant (conversion due to influence of wife). **Education:** Amherst Coll. (B.A., '25); U. of Paris, (diploma, '26); Brown U. (M.A., '31, and Ph.D., '36); studied at the U. of Havana, etc. **General:** Both his parents are Negroes. His father is a composer and his mother an actress. He taught at A. and T. College, Greensboro, N. C. and at Howard U., before becoming head of the department of French at Atlanta U. In the Fall of 1943 he was granted a year's leave of absence to supervise an English teaching project in Haiti, sponsored by the U. S. Office of Inter-American Affairs. His writing is concerned chiefly with French literary and historical subjects. He is a member of the editorial boards of Phylon and the Journal of Negro History as well as a member of the honorary international board of Free World. He contributes to such magazines as Romanic Review, New Republic, Crisis, The Journal of Negro History, French Review, Opportunity, and has edited works in the Heath-Chicago French series, and the Atlanta U. French series. **Authorities:** Negro Catholic Writers (1900-43); The Guide to Catholic Literature, v. 2 (1940-43).

Works

1943   Five French Negro Authors. Associated Publishers.

COOKE, NICHOLAS FRANCIS, 1829-1885

Birthplace: Providence, R. I. **Conversion:** 1875. **Former religion:** Protestant Episcopal. **Education:** Brown Univ. (1846); studied medicine in Providence; toured Europe. **General:** With the organization of Hahnemann Medical College in 1859, Dr. Cooke became associated with it, and until 1870 held the chair of Theory and Practice. Later he was a professor, for a short time, in the Pulte Medical College, Cincinnati. He contributed to many journals, one of his ablest articles being "Pancreas Disease" which appeared in The Clinic, Nov. 15, 1884. **Authorities:** Appleton's Cyclopaedia of American Biography, v. 1; Cooke, N. F.: Satin in Society. 1889.

Works

1866 The pocket doctor. Park City pub. house.
1871 Satin in society. C. F. Vent. The 1889 ed. contains a biographical sketch of the author by Eliza Allen Starr (q.v.).
1882 A treatise on antiseptic medication, or Declat's method. Gross and Delbridge.

COPELAND, CHARLES CARROLL, 1838-

Birthplace: Antwerp, N. Y. **Conversion:** 1865. **Former religion:** Descended from Pilgrim stock (John Alden; Cotton Mather). **Education:** Wilbraham (Mass.) Academy until 17 years old; Albany (N. Y.) Law School (grad.). **General:** Copeland began his law practice in 1859 in Chicago and soon identified himself with the life of the city. He was librarian of the Young Men's Library from 1862-63 and in 1866 organized the Hibernian bank. Copeland was in Rome during the Vatican Council of 1871. Besides the work listed below he wrote several shorter titles including, "The Church Builder," "My Forest in Summer and in Winter," and "To a Fallen Oak," prose poems; "What is Religion?"; and "Why I became a Catholic." **Authorities:** American Catholic Who's Who. 1911; Curtis, G. P.: Beyond the Road to Rome. 1914.

Works

1895   Coming to Kansas in 1869. Smelter.

COPUS, JOHN EDWIN, father (S.J.) (Cuthbert, pseud.)
1854-1915
   Birthplace: Guildford, Eng. **Conversion:** 1876. **Former religion:** Episcopalian (High Church guild). **Ordained priest:** 1899. **Education:** In England. **General:** Father Copus was a journalist before becoming a Jesuit in 1877, and at one time commercial editor of the Detroit Evening News. After finishing his studies he taught in American Jesuit colleges until his death, spending some time on the American Indian missions. Besides the works listed below, the author wrote "Henry White's Conscience," "Lydgate's Call," "The Month of Nisan," and "Sana Teipsum." These novels appeared serially. **Authorities:** American Catholic Who's Who. 1911; Guide to Catholic Literature, 1888-1940; Curtis, G. P.: Some Roads to Rome in America. 1909; America, June 19, 1915.

Works

1903   Harry Russell, a Rockland college boy. Benziger.
1903   Saint Cuthbert's. Benziger.

1904 Shadows lifted. Benziger.
1906 Tom Losely, boy. Benziger.
1908 The son of Siro: a story of Lazarus. Benziger.
1909 The making of Mortlake. Benziger.
1910 Andros of Ephesus: a tale of early Christianity. M. H. Wiltzius.
1910 "As gold in the furnace": a college story. Benziger.

CORBIN, CAROLINE ELIZABETH (FAIRFIELD)
1835-

Birthplace: Pomfret, Conn. **Conversion:** 1907. **Education:** District school of Pomfret; Brooklyn (N. Y.) Female Acad. (grad.). **General:** The author was a charter member of the Daughters of the American Revolution and sometime president of the Chicago Society of Social Purity. In 1897 she was elected president of the Illinois Association Opposed to the Extension of Suffrage to Women. Mrs. Corbin travelled widely in Europe and the United States. **Authorities:** American Catholic Who's Who. 1911.

Works

1860 Our Bible class and the good that came from it. Derby & Jackson.
1867 Rebecca; or, A woman's secret. Clarke.
1874 His marriage vow. Lee and Shepard.
1879 Belle and the boys. Jansen, McClurg.
1886 Letters from a chimney corner. Fergus.
1893 A woman's philosophy of love. Lee and Shepard.
1905 Socialism and Christianity, with reference to the woman question. Chicago. 31 p.

CORSON, GEOFFREY, pseud., See Sholl, Anna McClure

CORY, HERBERT ELLSWORTH, 1883-

Birthplace: Providence, R. I. **Conversion:** 1933. **Former religion:** Congregationalist, etc. **Education:** Brown Univ. (A.B., '06); Harvard Univ. (Ph.D., '10) **General:** Professor Cory, one of the most popular professors ever to teach at the University of Washington, taught English at the University of California from 1909-18. He was lecturer in philosophy at Johns Hopkins University in 1923. Since then he has been professor and head of the College of Liberal Arts at the University of Washington. **Authorities:** American Catholic Who's Who (1942-43); Guide to Catholic Literature, 1888-40; Who's Who Among North American Authors (1933-35); Who's Who in America (1942-43); Cory, H. E.: Emancipation of a Freethinker. 1941.

Works

1911 The critics of Edmund Spenser. Berkeley, The University press.
1912 Spenser, the school of the Fletchers and Milton. Univ. of California press.
1915 (ed.) Essays in exposition (with others). Ginn.
1917 Edmund Spenser, a critical study. Univ. of California press.
1919 The intellectuals and the wage workers. Sunwise Turn.
1941 Emancipation of a freethinker. Bruce.

CRAIGIE, PEARL MARY TERESA (RICHARDS) (John Oliver Hobbes, pseud.), 1867-1906

Birthplace: Boston, Mass. **Conversion:** 1892. **Education:** Privately educated in the U. S.; also in Paris and London. **General:** Much of Mrs. Craigie's work was published in London, and a great deal of her life is identified with that city where she was a prominent figure in literary circles.

She is buried beside the great Catholic poet, Francis Thompson. **Authorities:** British Authors of the Nineteenth Century. 1936; Catholic Encyclopedia, v. 4; Guide to Catholic Literature, 1888-1940; Clarke, I. C.: Six portraits. 1935; Craigie, P. M. T.: Life of John Oliver Hobbes. 1911; Stuart, H. L.: Fenella. 1911; Catholic World, October, 1906; Dublin Review, April, 1897; Thought, September, 1931.

Works

1888-89	The note-book of a diner-out.
1891	Some emotions and a moral. Cassell.
1892	The sinner's comedy. Cassell.
1893	A study in temptations. Cassell.
1894	A bundle of life. J. Selwin-Tait.
1894	Journey's end in lovers meeting.
1895	The gods, some mortals and Lord Wickenham. D. Appleton.
1895	Some good intentions and a blunder. Merriam.
1896	The herb-moon, a fantasia. F. A. Stokes.
1896	A school for saints. T. F. Unwin.
1898	The ambassador; a comedy in four acts. F. A. Stokes.
1899	A repentance.
1900	Osbern and Ursyne, a drama in three acts. J. Lane.
1900	Robert Orange. F. A. Stokes.
1900	The wisdom of the wise, a comedy in three acts. F. A. Stokes.
1901	The serious wooing; a heart's history. F. A. Stokes.
1902	The bishop's move; a comedy in three acts (with Murray Carson). F. A. Stokes.
1902	Love and the soul hunters. Funk and Wagnalls.
1902	Tales about temperament. D. Appleton.
1903	Imperial India; letters from the East. T. F. Unwin.
1903	Letters from a silent study.
1904	The science of life. Scott-Thaw.
1904	The vineyard. D. Appleton.
1905	The flute of Pan. D. Appleton.
1906	The dream and the business. D. Appleton.

1907   Saints in society.
1911   The life of John Oliver Hobbes told in her correspondence with numerous friends. J. Murray.

CRAWFORD, FRANCIS MARION, 1854-1909

Birthplace: Bagni di Lucca, Italy, of American parents. **Conversion:** 1880. **Former religion:** Sent early to Protestant Episcopal school. **Education:** St. Paul's School for boys, Concord, N. H.; Harvard Univ.; Trinity Coll., Cambridge Univ. (England); Heidelberg Univ.; also studied in Rome, Italy. **General:** Crawford began his literary career as a journalist in India, where he had gone to study Sanskrit, one of the many languages of which he was to master. During his career as a novelist his time was spent principally in Europe, coming back to New York during the winters of his later years. Accused by his critics of a diluted faith, Crawford staunchly defended his Catholicity and maintained that his faith had always been firm. **Authorities:** American Authors, 1600-1900; American Catholic Who's Who, 1911; Dictionary of American Biography, v. 4; Guide to Catholic Literature, 1888-1940; Elliott, M.: My Cousin F. Marion Crawford, 1934; Cooper, F. J.: Some American Story Tellers. 1911.

Works

1882   Mr. Isaacs. Macmillan.
1883   Doctor Claudius. Macmillan.
1884   A Roman singer. Macmillan.
1884   To leeward. Houghton, Mifflin.
1885   An American politician, a novel. Houghton, Mifflin.
1885   Zoraster. Macmillan.
1886   A tale of a lonely parish. Macmillan.

1887   Marzio's crucifix. Macmillan.
1887   Paul Patoff. Macmillan.
1887   Saracinesca. Macmillan.
1888   With the immortals. Macmillan.
1889   Greifenstein. Macmillan.
1889   Sant' Ilario. Macmillan.
1890   A cigarette maker's romance. Macmillan.
1891   Khaled, a tale of Arabia. Macmillan.
1891   The witch of Prague, a fantastic tale. Macmillan.
1892   Don Orsino. Macmillan.
1892   Laura Arden ("published as Pietro Ghisleri"). Macmillan.
1892   The three fates. Macmillan.
1893   The children of the king. Macmillan.
1893   Marion Darche. Macmillan.
1893   The novel: what it is. Macmillan.
1894   Casa Braccio. Macmillan. 2 v.
1894   Katherine Lauderdale. Macmillan.
1894   Love in idleness, a Bar Harbor tale. Macmillan.
1894   The Ralstons. Macmillan. 2 v.
1894   The upper berth. G. P. Putnam.
1895   Adam Johnstone's son. Macmillan.
1895   Constantinople. C. Scribner.
1896   Bar Harbor. C. Scribner.
1896   Corleone. Macmillan.
1896   Taquisara. Macmillan. 2 v.
1897   A rose of yesterday. Macmillan.
1898   Ave Roma immortalis. Macmillan.
1899   Via crucis, a romance of the second crusade. Macmillan.
1900   In the palace of the king. Macmillan.
1900   The rulers of the south; Sicily, Calabria, Malta. Macmillan.
        2 v.
1901   Marietta. Macmillan.
1902   Cecilia, a story of modern Rome. Macmillan.
1902   Francesca da Rimini, a play.
1903   The heart of Rome. Macmillan.
1903   Man overboard! Macmillan.
1904   Pietro Ghisleri. See Laura Arden.
1904   Whosoever shall offend. Macmillan.
1905   Fair Margaret. Macmillan.
1905   Salve Venetia: gleanings from Venetian history. Macmillan. 2 v.

1905 Soprano, a portrait.
1906 A lady of Rome. Macmillan.
1907 The little city of hope. Macmillan.
1907 Arethusa. Macmillan.
1908 The diva's ruby. Macmillan.
1908 Prima donna: sequel to Fair Margaret. Macmillan.
1908 The white sister. Macmillan.
1909 Stradella. Macmillan.
1910 Undesirable governess. Macmillan.
1911 Wandering ghosts. Macmillan.
1937 The white sister; a romantic drama in three acts (with Walter Hackett). Dramatist's play service.

CRISS, MILDRED, "Mrs. George Lewis Catlin," 1890- Birthplace: Orange, N. J. Conversion: 1927. Former religion: Episcopalian. Education: Privately educated at home; Mlle. La Salle's school, Geneva, Switzerland; Hollins Coll., Virginia; Columbia Univ.; Paris, France. General: Miss Criss was active in the American Friends of France society from 1939-40. During the rectorship of Dr. Selden P. Delany (q.v.) at St. Mary of the Virgin in New York City, the author was a writer on the staff paper. Authorities: Letter from Miss Criss, November 15, 1943.

Works

1917 In the name of love, by Mildred Criss McGuckin. Knickerbocker.
1922 Wind flower, by Mildred Criss McGuckin. R. G. Badger. 39 p.
1928 Little cabbages, by Mildred Criss McGuckin, illustrated by Nancy Barnhart. Doubleday, Doran.
1929 Malou, a little Swiss, illustrated by Carlotte Lederer. Doubleday, Doran.
1931 Martine and Michel, a story of the Jura mountains . . . illustrated by E. A. Verpilleux. Doubleday, Doran.

1934 The red caravan: the wandering adventures of Francesca . . . illustrated by Pierre Brissaud. Doubleday, Doran.

1938 Madeleine's court on an island in Paris, illustrated by Pierre Brisaud. Dodd, Mead.

1939 Mary Stuart, illustrated by Rose Chavanne. Dodd, Mead.

1941 Isabella, young queen of Spain, illustrated by Marc Simont. Dodd, Mead.

1943 Pocahontas, young American princess, illustrated by Marc Simont. Dodd, Mead.

CURTIS, ALFRED ALLEN, bp., 1831-1908

Birthplace: Pocomoke, Md. **Conversion:** 1872. **Former religion:** Episcopalian. **Ordained priest:** 1874. **Consecrated bishop:** 1886. **Education:** Local public schools; later studied for Episcopalian ministry; after 1872, entered St. Mary's Sem., Baltimore. **General:** Bishop Curtis entered the Church under Newman's guidance and was to become the second bishop of Wilmington. He resigned in 1896 and became titular bishop of Echinus. From 1898 until his death he acted as Cardinal Gibbon's vicar general. **Authorities:** Cyclopaedia of American Biographies, v. 1; Dictionary of American Biography, v. 4; Guide to Catholic Literature, 1888-1940; Allen, Ethan: Clergy in Maryland of the Protestant Episcopal church. 1860; Catholic bishops and archbishops of America. 1899; Sisters of the Visitation: Life and characteristics of Rt. Rev. Alfred A. Curtis. 1913.

Works

1913 Lights and counsels. J. Murphy.

CURTIS, GEORGINA PELL, 1859-1922

Birthplace: New York City. **Conversion:** Before 1909.

Former religion: Protestant Episcopal (?) **Education:** Private schooling, and at St. Mary's (P.E.) school, N. Y.; also attended an art school. **General:** Miss Curtis will be remembered longest as the compiler of American Catholic convert biographies and for her pioneer work in the general field of American Catholic biography. She contributed to various periodicals, including Harper's Bazaar and Harpers Young People. **Authorities:** American Catholic Who's Who. 1911; Curtis, G. P.: Beyond the Road to Rome. 1914; Guide to Catholic Literature, 1888-1940.

Works

1909 Trammelings and other stories. B. Herder.
1909 (ed.) Some roads to Rome in America, being personal records of conversions to the Catholic church. B. Herder.
1911 The American Catholic who's who. B. Herder.
1914 (ed.) Beyond the road to Rome. B. Herder.
1914 The bridge of victory.
1914 The romance of a chap book.
1917 Interdependence of literature. B. Herder.
1921 Faith in the wilderness.

CUTHBERT, pseud., **See** Copus, John Edwin, father (S.J.), 1854-1915

DAHLGREN, MADELEINE (VINTON), 1825-1898
   Birthplace: Gallipolis, O. **Education:** Putnam Female Sem.; School of M. Picot, Philadelphia; Convent of the Visitation, Georgetown, D. C. **General:** Placed in the center of Washington life as hostess to her father, Congress-

man Samuel Finley Vinton, and later as the wife of
Admiral John A. Dahlgren, Mrs. Dahlgren found ample
subject material for her literary and social writings. As a
writer, the author is considered versatile and precise, but
not weighty. **Authorities:** American Authors, 1600-1900;
Cyclopaedia of American Biographies, v. 2; Guide to Catholic Literature, 1888-1940; Vinton, J. A.: The Vinton Memorial. 1858. Ohio Archaeological and Historical Quarterly, v. 4, p. 231-262. 1895.

Works

1859 Idealities.
1861 (tr.) Pius IX, by Montalembert.
1862 (tr.) Essay on Catholicism, liberalism and socialism, by
      Donoso Cortes. J. B. Lippincott.
1871 Thoughts on female suffrage. Blanchard & Mohum. 22 p.
1872 (ed.) Memoir of Ulric Dahlgren. By his father Rear-Admiral
      Dahlgren. J. B. Lippincott.
1873 Etiquette of social life in Washington. J. A. Wineberger.
1874 (tr.) Executive power in the United States, by D. Chamb-
      run. Inquirer print.
1881 South Sea sketches. J. R. Osgood.
1882 Memoir of John A. Dahlgren, rear-admiral. J. R. Osgood.
1882 South mountain magic. J. R. Osgood
1883 A Washington winter. J. R. Osgood.
1886 The lost name; a novelette. Ticknor.
1887 Lights and shadows of a life. Ticknor.
1887 Divorced. Belford, Clarke.
1892 Chim: his Washington winter. C. L. Webster.
1896 The secret directory. H. L. Kilner.
1899 The Woodley Lane ghost, and other stories. D. Biddle.

DAVIS, FOXCROFT, pseud., **See** Seawell, Molly Elliot,
    1860-1916

DAY, DOROTHY, 1899-

Birthplace: New York City. **Conversion:** 1927. **Former religion:** Communism, later Protestant Episcopal. **Education:** Chicago public schools; Univ. of Illinois (1914-16). **General:** Miss Day is a militant convert who began her career as a journalist on the staffs of the New York Call, The New Masses, and The Liberator. Since her conversion she has conducted houses of hospitality for destitute workmen, and since 1933 has been editor of the Catholic Worker, a newspaper. Miss Day has a biography of Peter Maurin (a co-worker) in preparation, which is expected to be published in 1944. **Authorities:** Letter from Miss Day, July 20, 1943; American Catholic Who's Who (1942-43); Guide to Catholic Literature, 1888-1940; Magnificat, June, 1939.

Works

1938   From Union Square to Rome. Preservation of the Faith press.
1939   House of hospitality. Sheed & Ward.

DE COSTA, BENJAMIN FRANKLIN, father, 1831-1904

Birthplace: Charlestown, Mass. **Conversion:** 1899. **Former religion:** Father was Huguenot; mother baptised Catholic but became Episcopalian; author, Episcopalian (minister, 1857-99). **Ordained priest:** 1903. **Education:** Biblical Institute, Concord, N.H. (grad., '56). **General:** De Costa served as an Episcopalian chaplain in the Union Army during the Civil War. As a newspaper man he was a correspondent of the Charlestown Advertiser and from 1865 to 1866 edited the Christian Times. He edited The Churchman for a time and from 1882 to 1883, the Magazine of American History. His writings include fifty-five separately printed works, a great many of which are in the field of history. **Authorities:** Dictionary of American Biography, v. 5; Who's Who in America (1901-02); De Costa, B. F.: The Titles of 55 separately Printed Works. 1899; Catholic World, September, 1900; October, 1902.

Works

1868	Lake George; its scenes and characteristics. A. D. F. Randolph.
1868	A narrative of events at Lake George. New York.
1868	The pre-Columbian discovery of America by the Northmen. J. Munsell.
1868	Scenes in the isle of Mount Desert. New York.
1869	Sailing directions of Henry Hudson. J. Munsell.
1869	Sketches of the coast of Maine and Isles of Shoals. New York.
1870	The Northmen in Maine. J. Munsell.
1871	Notes on the history of Fort George during the colonial and revolutionary periods. J. Sabin.
1873	The Atlantic coast guide; a companion for the tourist. E. P. Dutton.
1880	Verrazano the explorer, being a vindication of his letter and voyage. A. S. Barnes.
1887	The white cross; its origin and progress. Sanitary pub co.
1891-93	The memorial history of the city of New York from its first settlement to the year 1892. New York history co. 4 v.
1902	Whither goest thou. Christian press.
1903	Failure of ritualism. Christian press.

DELANY, SELDEN PEABODY, father, 1874-1935

Birthplace: Fond du Lac, Wisc. **Conversion:** 1930. **Former religion:** Protestant Episcopal (minister, 1899-1930).

Ordained priest: 1934. **Education:** Harvard Univ. (A.B.); Western Theological Sem.; later in Rome. **General:** Dr. Delany was a prominent Episcopalian clergyman of New York City and rector of the Church of St. Mary the Virgin when received into the Catholic Church. His conversion created a considerable stir among non-Catholics. From 1918-29 he edited the New American Church Monthly. **Authorities:** American Catholic Who's Who (1934-35); Guide to Catholic Literature, 1888-1940; Burton, K.: In No Strange Land. 1942; Delany, S. P.: Why Rome? 1930; Delany, S. P.: Rome from Within. 1935; Truth, August, 1930.

Works

1906 Difficulties of faith. Morehouse.
1909 Ideal of Christian worship. Young Churchman.
1914 The value of confessions. Young Churchman.
1919 The religion of the prayer book (with J. G. H. Barry). E. S. Gorham.
1920 Christian practice. E. S. Gorham.
1926 The parish priest (with J. G. H. Barry). E. S. Gorham.
1927 (tr.) A modern plea for Christianity, by Louis de Launay. Macmillan.
1930 Why Rome? Dial.
1935 Married saints. Longmans, Green.
1935 Rome from within. Bruce.

DESHON, GEORGE, father (C.S.P.) 1823-1903

Birthplace: New London, Conn. **Conversion:** 1851. **Former religion:** Parents, Huguenot. **Ordained priest:** 1855. **Education:** West Point Military Acad. (grad., '42) **General:** After leaving West Point, where he was a roommate of the future General Grant, Deshon rose to the rank of captain. Upon his conversion he joined the Redemptorists and with

Father Hecker (q.v.) and others, eventually founded the Congregation of St. Paul. He became Superior General of the Paulists in 1897. **Authorities:** Appleton's Cyclopaedia of American Biography, v. 2; Guide to Catholic Literature, 1888-1940; Extension Magazine, February, 1933.

Works

1860 Guide for Catholic young women, especially for those who earn their own living. Columbus pub. co. ("This book had the most extensive sale of any Catholic book published up to 1860.")

1902 Sermons for all the Sundays of the ecclesiastical year and the principal festivals.

DORSAY, LEWIS, pseud., See Martin, Elizabeth Gilbert (Davis) 1837-

DORSEY, THEODORE HOOPER, 1899-
General: The author is a former Anglican who became a lay street preacher upon his conversion. He tells his story in the work listed below. **Authorities:** Guide to Catholic Literature, 1888-1940.

Works

1939 From a far country; the conversion story of a campaigner for Christ. Our Sunday Visitor.

DORSEY, ANNA HANSON (McKENNEY) 1815-1896
Birthplace: Georgetown, D. C. **Conversion:** 1840. **For-**

mer religion: Her father was a Methodist preacher. **Education**: At home. **General**: Although Mrs. Dorsey began writing while very young, her first noteworthy effort was "The Student of Blenheim Forest," which appeared in 1847. The author wrote more than thirty books during the forty years of her active life, practically all of them reflecting her profound Catholic belief. She received the Laetare Medal from Notre Dame University in 1869. **Authorities**: American Authors, 1600-1900; Catholic Encyclopedia, v. 5; Dictionary of American Biography, v. 5; Guide to Catholic Literature, 1888-1940; Ave Maria, January 16, 1897.

Works

1846 Tears on the diadem. E. Dunigan.
1847 The student of Blenheim forest; or, The trials of a convert. J. Murphy.
1848 The oriental pearl; or, The Catholic emigrants. J. Murphy.
1849 Flowers of love and memory. J. Murphy.
1852 Woodreve manor; or, Six months in town. A. Hart.
1857 The oriental pearl. J. Murphy.
1865 "They're coming Grandad." A tale of east Tennessee. Washington.
1869 Nora Brady's vow; and Mona, the vestal. J. B. Lippincott.
1870 Tangled paths. D. & J. Sadlier.
1887 Ada's trust. J. Murphy.
1887 Adrift. J. Murphy.
1887 Beth's promise. J. Murphy.
1887 The heiress of Carrigmona. J. Murphy.
1887 The old house of Glenaran. J. Murphy.
1887 Palms. J. Murphy.
1887 Warp and woof. J. Murphy.
1888 The fate of the Dane and other stories. J. Murphy.
1888 Zoe's daughter. J. Murphy.
1891 Two ways. J. Murphy.
1891 Tomboy. J. Murphy.
n.d. Cosina, the rose of the Algonquins. H. L. Kilner.

n.d.   The Flemings. H. L. Kilner.
n.d.   May Brooke; or, Conscience. P. J. Kenedy.
n.d.   Old gray rosary; refuge for sinners. H. L. Kilner.
n.d.   Sisters of Charity. E. Dunigan.

DWIGHT, THOMAS, 1843-1911

Birthplace: Boston, Mass. **Conversion:** 1855. **Education:** Attended school in Paris until the age of 12; Harvard Univ. (M.D., '67; A.B., '72) **General:** Dr. Dwight was an anatomy instructor at Harvard University from 1872 to 1873. He then taught at the Medical School in Maine for a time, but returned to Harvard in 1883, where he succeeded Oliver Wendell Holmes in the Parkman Professorship of Anatomy. He retained this position until his death. **Authorities:** American Catholic Who's Who. 1911; Dictionary of American Biography, v. 5; Kelly, H. A. and Burrage, W. L.: American Medical Biographies. 1920; Windle, Sir Bertram: Twelve Catholic men of Science. 1914; America, September 16, 1911; Anatomical Record, November, 1911; Guide to Catholic Literature, 1888-1940. **Bibliography:** Index Catalog of the Surgeon General's Library, Washington, D. C.

Works

1876   The anatomy of the head. H. O. Houghton.
1881   Frozen sections of a child. W. Wood.
1907   A clinical atlas. J. B. Lippincott.
1911   Thoughts of a Catholic anatomist. Longmans, Green.
1919   Human anatomy; including structure and development and practical considerations by Thomas Dwight (and others). Edited by George A. Piersol. 7th ed. J. B. Lippincott.

ELIOT, ETHEL (COOK) "Mrs. S. A. Eliot, Jr." 1890-
Birthplace: North Gage, N. Y. **Conversion:** 1925. **Former religion:** Protestant. **Education:** Pittsfield (Mass.) public schools. **General:** Mrs. Eliot began her literary career as a journalist with the Ladies' World (periodical) and contributed fairy tales and other stories to Story-Teller's Magazine. She has written eleven books for children and young people, and four novels—"Ariel Dances," "Green Doors," "Her Soul to Keep," and "Angels' Mirth." A new novel is in preparation and will be published in 1944. **Authorities:** Letter from Mrs. Eliot, November 7, 1943; American Catholic Who's Who (1942-43); Guide to Catholic Literature, 1888-1940; Who's Who Among North American Authors, v. 6; Who's Who in America (1942-43); Who's Who in the Western Hemisphere. 1943; Alexander, Calvert: Catholic Literary Revival. 1935.

Works

1918   The little house in the fairy woods. F. A. Stokes.
1923   The house on the edge of things. Beacon.
1923   The little black coal. F. A. Stokes.
1923   The wind boy. Doubleday, Doran.
1924   Buttercup days. Doubleday, Doran.
1925   Fireweed. Doubleday, Doran.
1926   Waul & Dyke, inc. Doubleday, Doran.
1927   Storey Manor. Doubleday, Doran.
1928   The dryad and the hired boy. Doubleday, Doran.
1930   The house above the trees. T. Butterworth.
1931   Ariel dances. Little, Brown.
1931   The Gay mystery. Doubleday, Doran.
1933   Green doors. Little, Brown.
1935   Her soul to keep. Macmillan.
1936   Angels' mirth. Sheed & Ward.
1939   Vanishing comrade. Sun Dial.

ELLET, ELIZABETH FRIES (LUMMIS) 1818-1877

Birthplace: Sodus Point, Lake Ontario, N. Y. **Education:** Female Sem., Aurora, N. Y. **General:** Mrs. Ellet was an historian, critic and linguist, whose writings have been credited with the rare combination of scholarship and imagination. She was deeply interested in the role of women in American history and much of her writing concerns that subject. **Authorities:** American Authors, 1600-1900; Appleton's Cyclopaedia of American Biography, v. 2; Dictionary of American Biography, v. 6; Griswold, R. W.: Female Poets of America.

Works

1834   (tr.) Euphemio of Messina, by Silvio Pellico. M. Bancroft.
1835   Teresa Contarini.
1835   Poems, original and selected. Kay & Biddle.
1839   The characters of Schiller. Otis, Broaders.
1840   Rambles about the country. Marsh, Capen, Lyon & Webb.
1840   Scenes in the life of Joanna of Sicily. Marsh, Capen, Lyon & Webb.
1848   The women of the American revolution. 3 v. C. Scribner.
1849   Evenings at Woodlawn. Baker and Scribner.
1849   Family pictures from the Bible. G. P. Putnam.
1850   Domestic history of the American revolution. Baker and Scribner.
1851   Watching spirits, with illustrations. C. Scribner.
1852   Nouvellettes of the musicians. Sheldon.
1852   Pioneer women of the West. C. Scribner.
1853   Summer rambles in the West. J. C. Riker.
1857   The practical housekeeper. Stringer and Townsend.
1859   Women artists of all ages. Harper.
1867   The queens of American society. C. Scribner.
1869   The court circles of the Republic (with sketches by Mrs. R. E. Mack). J. D. Denison.
1872   (ed.) The new cyclopedia of domestic economy. H. Bill.
n.d.   Scripture gift book. Illustrated. Putnam.

EMERY, SUSAN L., 1846-1923

Birthplace: Dorchester, Mass. **Conversion:** 1875. **Former religion:** Episcopalian. **General:** From 1871-74, Miss Emery was assistant editor of the (Prot. Epis.) Young Christian Soldier and later (1891-1925) held a similar position with the Sacred Heart Review. She also contributed to the American Catholic Quarterly, the Catholic World, Harpers, and others. **Authorities:** American Catholic Who's Who. 1911; Guide to Catholic Literature, 1888-1940; Curtis, G. P.: Some Roads to Rome in America 1902; Driscoll, A. S.: Literary Convent Women. 1928; Catholic World, December, 1936.

Works

1869　Uncle Rod's pet. Dutton.
1891　Thoughts for every day in the year from the spiritual maxims of St. John of the Cross. Flynn.
1892　Noel.
1903　Inner life of the soul. Longmans.
1906　(tr.) The petals of the Little Flower, being the translation of the French poem of a young Carmelite nun, Soeur Therèse de l'enfant Jesus. Angel Guardian press.
1910　A Catholic stronghold and its making, being a history of St. Peter's parish, Dorchester, Mass. G. H. Ellis.
n.d.　Short spiritual messages for the ecclesiastical year.

EMMET, THOMAS ADDIS, 1828-1919

Birthplace: At Univ. of Virginia (near Charlottesville). **Conversion:** 1867. **Former religion:** Protestant. **Education:** Informal early education; Univ. of Va. ('45-46); Jefferson Medical Coll., Philadelphia (grad., '50). **General:** Dr. Emmet was a grandson of the brother of the Irish patriot,

Robert Emmet, and an ardent worker for Irish Home Rule. He was a distinguished surgeon and gynaecologist, receiving many professional honors at home and abroad. In 1898 the Laetare Medal was conferred upon him, and in 1906 he was created Knight Commander of the Order of Gregory the Great, by Pius X. **Authorities:** American Catholic Who's Who. 1911; Dictionary of American Biography, v. 6; The Birthday Dinner to Thomas Addis Emmet. Bradstreet press; Emmet, T. A.: Incidents of my life. 1911; Journal of the American Irish Historical Society. 1919; Guide to Catholic Literature, 1888-1940.

Works

1868   Catalogue of the library belonging to Thomas Addis Emmet, M.D. Bradstreet.
1868   Vesico-vaginal fistula. W. Wood.
1879   The principles and practice of gynaecology. H. C. Lea.
1898   The Emmet family, with some incidents relating to Irish history. Bradstreet.
1898   A memoir of John Patten Emmet, M.D. Bradstreet.
1900   Calendar of the Emmet collection of manuscripts, etc., relating to American history; presented to the New York public library by John S. Kennedy. N. Y.
1903   Ireland under English rule. G. P. Putnam. 2 v.
1909   Battle of Harlem heights. The author.
1911   Incidents of my life. G. P. Putnam.
1915   Memoir of Thomas Addis and Robert Emmet with their ancestors an immediate family. Emmet press. 2 v.

EUSTACE, CECIL JOHN, 1903-

Birthplace: Walton-on-Thames, Surrey, England. **Came to Canada:** 1924. **Conversion:** 1929. **Former religion:** Church of England. **Education:** Marlborough House School, Hove

(1911-15); Felstead Coll., Essex, England (1915-19). **General:** After spending two years farming in England, Mr. Eustace came to Canada and became editor of Bookseller and Stationer, a publisher's trade organ. He conducted Canada's first book club, The Eaton, until its dissolution in 1929. At present he is Education Editor of J. M. Dent & Sons. The author has contributed to The English Review, Christian Science Monitor, Commonweal, and many others. His stories have been frequently selected for O'Brien's "Best Short Stories." **Authorities:** Letter from Mr. Eustace, September, 1943; Guide to Catholic Literature, 1888-1940; Eustace, C. J.: House of Bread. 1943.

Works

1927   The scarlet gentleman. A. Melrose.
1933   Romewards. Benziger (Catholic Book Club selection).
1934   Damaged lives. G. P. Putnam.
1937   Mind and the mystery. Longmans, Green.
1938   Catholicism, communism and dictatorship. Benziger.
1943   House of bread. Longmans, Green.
1944   An infinity of questions. (In preparation and may appear under another title).

FAIRBANKS, CHARLES BULLARD (Aguecheek, pseud.) 1827-1859

Birthplace: Boston, Mass. **Conversion:** 1852. **Former religion:** Unitarian; then Episcopalian. **Education:** Studied for the priesthood, Holy Cross Coll.; also in Canada, Paris and Rome; reached minor orders only, because of ill health. **General:** As "Aguecheek," Fairbanks had some fame as an essayist. He began his career as a newspaper correspondent for the Evening Gazette of Boston and later for The Transcript and The Pilot, also of that city. Although the author's book production was limited, his style is highly regarded. He died at the early age of thirty-two. **Authorities:** Guide to Catholic Literature, 1888-1940; Earls, Michael. Manuscripts and Memories. 1935; Catholic World, January, 1918.

Works

1859 Aguecheek. Shepard, Clark & Brown.
1860 Memorials of the blessed. (Contains fifty sketches of notable saints).

FAIRBANKS, HIRAM FRANCIS, father, 1845-

Birthplace: Leon, N. Y. **Conversion:** 1863. **Former religion:** Protestant. **Ordained priest:** 1868. **Education:** Lawrence Univ., Appleton, Wis.; St. Louis Univ.; St. Francis Theological Seminary, St. Francis, Wis. **General:** The author's pastoral activities were centered in Janesville and other Wisconsin cities. **Authorities:** American Catholic Who's Who. 1911.

Works

1888 A visit to Europe and the Holy Land. Catholic pub. soc.
1901 The ancestry of Henry Adams of Braintree, New England. Milwaukee, Wis. 19 p.

FARMER, FRANCIS XAVIER, father (S.J.) (Wilmoth Alexander Farmer)

Birthplace: Georgia. **Conversion:** 1915. **Former religion:**

Methodist (minister). **Education:** Emory Coll., Kentucky; Vanderbilt Univ.; Missionary Training Institute (Meth.) N. Y. **General:** As a Methodist minister the author went to China as a missionary. After the death of his wife, who is the subject of his biographical work, he returned to the same field as a Catholic priest and missionary. **Authorities:** Burton, Katherine: In No Strange Land. 1942; Far East, February, 1931; Guide to Catholic Literature, 1888-1940.

Works

1912   Ada Beeson Farmer, a missionary heroine of Kuang Si, South China, written and compiled by her husband, Rev. Wilmoth Alexander Farmer. Foote & Davies.
n.d.   My conversion. Paulist press. (Published first in Shanghai).

FIDELIS, FATHER, See Stone, James Kent, 1840-1921

FIELDS, MAURICE C., 1915-1938

Conversion: 1938. **Education:** Brooklyn Coll. (grad.); also doing advanced work in literature at time of death. **General:** An American Negro poet whose early death cut short his literary promise. **Authorities:** Guide to Catholic Literature, 1888-1940; America, October 1, 1938.

Works

1940   The collected poems . . . Exposition press.
1940   Testament of youth. Pegasus. 32 p.

FISKE, A. LONGFELLOW

Conversion: 1928. **Former religion:** Congregationalist;

then Presbyterian (minister in both denominations). **General:** Mr. Fiske is an instructor (1942) in St. Francis Xavier High School, New York City, and director of the Lecture Bureau of the National Catholic Converts League. He is an occasional contributor to Catholic periodicals. **Authorities:** Guide to Catholic Literature, 1888-1940; America, January 10, 1931.

Works

1933   The practical course in speech for Catholic high schools. W. H. Sadlier. 3 v.

FORBES, CLARENCE ALLEN, 1901-

Birthplace: Colebrook, N. H. **Conversion:** 1921. **Former religion:** Methodist. **Education:** Bates Coll. (A.B., '22); Univ. of Illinois (M.A., '24; Ph.D., '28). **General:** Professor Bates began his teaching career as instructor in Greek and Latin at the University of Cincinnati in 1925. He joined the staff of the University of Illinois in 1927 and has remained there ever since, supplementing his work with summer professorial positions at the Universities of Illinois and Oklahoma. The author contributes articles and reviews to the philological journals. **Authorities:** Letter from Mr. Forbes, December 20, 1943; America's Young Men (1938-39); American Catholic Who's Who (1942-43).

Works

1929   Greek physical education. Appleton-Century.
1933   Neoi, a contribution to the study of Greek associations. American philological ass'n.
1942   Teachers' pay in ancient Greece (University of Nebraska Studies). Lincoln, Neb.

FORD, HENRY JONES, 1851-1925

Birthplace: Baltimore, Md. **Conversion:** 1919. **Education:** Public schools; Baltimore City Coll. (grad., '68); **General:** As a journalist, Ford held his first important post as managing editor of the Baltimore American, and was later connected with the New York Sun and the Baltimore Sun. Leaving the newspaper field in 1906 he became a professor at Johns Hopkins University and from 1908 until his death he was a professor of politics at Princeton University. He contributed to the Annals of the American Academy of Political and Social Science and after his conversion was on the editorial staff of Commonweal. **Authorities:** Dictionary of American Biography, v. 6; Guide to Catholic Literature, 1888-1940; Who's Who in America (1922-23); American Political Science Review, November, 1925; Commonweal, September 9, 1925.

Works

1898   The rise and growth of American politics. Macmillan.
1901   Problems in modern democracy. Booklovers library.
1910   The cost of our national government; a study in political pathology. Columbia univ. press.
1915   The natural history of the state. Princeton univ. press.
1915   The Scotch-Irish in America. Princeton univ. press.
1916   Woodrow Wilson, the man and his work. D. Appleton.
1918   Washington and his colleagues. Yale univ. press.
1919   The Cleveland era; a chronicle of the new order in politics. Yale univ. press. (Bound with The Boss and the Machine, by S. P. Orth).
1920   Alexander Hamilton. C. Scribner.
1924   Representative government. H. Holt.

FORD, (JULIA) LAUREN, 1891-

General: Miss Ford contributes occasionally (illustrations, etc.) to Liturgical Arts and America. Her first book is a collection of Bible stories, lithographed in color. The later book is composed of antiphons in Latin, with music (plain chant). **Authorities:** Library of Congress Catalog of Printed Cards. 1943; Reviews of "The Ageless Story" in Ave Maria, April, 13, 1940; Columbia, January, 1940; Liturgical Arts, April, 1940.

Works

1934 Little book about God. Doubleday, Doran.
1939 The ageless story, with its antiphons, pictured by Lauren Ford. Dodd, Mead.

FRASER, MARY (CRAWFORD) "Mrs. Hugh Fraser"
1851-

Birthplace: Rome Italy, of American parents. **Education:** In Rome and on the Isle of Wight. **General:** Mrs. Fraser was a daughter of the sculptor, Thomas Crawford and sister of the author F. Marion Crawford (q.v.). In 1873 she became the wife of Hugh Fraser, British Minister to Japan. **Authorities:** American Catholic Who's Who. 1911; Guide to Catholic Literature, 1888-1940.

Works

1895 The brown ambassador; the story of the three days moon (with J. I. Stahlman). Macmillan.
1896 Palladia. Macmillan.
1898 Looms of time. D. Appleton.
1899 The custom of the country: tales of new Japan. Macmillan.
1899 Diplomatist's wife in Japan. Hutchinson. 2 v.
1899 Letters from Japan. Macmillan. 2 v.
1899 The splendid Porsenna. J. B. Lippincott.

1901	A little grey sheep. J. B. Lippincott.
1901	Marna's mutiny. Dodd, Mead.
1904	The stolen emperor. G. Long.
1905	A maid of Japan. H. Holt.
1906	In the shadow of the Lord: a romance of the Washingtons. H. Holt.
1908	The heart of a geisha. G. P. Putnam.
1909	Giannella. B. Herder.
1909	Warriors of old Japan. Houghton, Mifflin.
1910	A diplomatist's wife in many lands. Dodd, Mead. 2 v.
1912	Further reminiscenses of a diplomatist's wife. Hutchinson.
1912	Golden rose (with J. I. Stahlman). Dodd, Mead.
1912	Reminiscenses of a diplomatist's wife. Hutchinson.
1913	The honour of the house. (with J. I. Stahlmann). Dodd, Mead.
1913	Italian yesterdays. Dodd, Mead. 2 v.
1914	Seven years on the Pacific slope (with Hugh C. Fraser). Dodd.
1915	More Italian yesterdays. Hutchinson.
1915	(tr.) The Patrizi memoirs. Hutchinson.
1915	Storied Italy. Dodd, Mead.

GALLAGHER, SISTER MARY ANTONIO (Richard W. Alexander, pseud.) 1846-1916

Birthplace: Philadelphia, Pa. **Conversion:** Before 1864. **Former religion:** Protestant (father maintained tradition of Hogan schism). **Education:** St. Joseph's Acad., Emmittsburg, Md.; St. Xavier's Acad., until 1864. **General:** The author wrote originally under the pen name "Mercedes" and later as "Richard Alexander;" the latter to compliment both Bishop Richard Phelan of Pittsburgh and the Rev. Alexander Doyle, C.S.P. of New York. She contributed poetry and sketches to periodicals and wrote more than twenty plays for girls. **Authorities:** Letter from Mother M. Irenaeus, St. Mary's Convent, Pittsburgh, August 4, 1943;

American Catholic Who's Who. 1911. Guide to Catholic Literature, 1888-1940; Memoirs of the Pittsburgh Sisters of Mercy, 1843-1917. 1918.

Works

1885   Wild flowers from "the mountainsides," poems and dramas. J. B. Lippincott.
1897   Mosaics. Beatty, Pa.
1903   (comp.) The Mercy manual, containing the Little Office of the B.V.M., and for the dead. St. Xavier's convent print.
1908   A missionary's notebook. Catholic standard and times.
1911   Heart songs. St. Xavier's convent print.
1914   The hand of mercy. P. J. Kenedy.

GALLITZIN, DEMETRIUS AUGUSTINE, father, 1770-1841

Birthplace: The Hague. **Came to U. S.** 1792. **Conversion:** 1787. **Former religion:** Greek Orthodox. **Education:** Trained under excellent tutors. **Ordained priest:** 1795. **General:** Prince Gallitzin came to the United States incognito as Augustine Smith and used that name long afterwards. He was a finished linguist and his zeal as a controversialist and missionary made him one of the outstanding figures of his day. Father Gallitzin was the first priest to receive a full theological training in the United States. **Authorities:** Catholic Encyclopedia, v. 6; Dictionary of American Biography, v. 7; Guide to Catholic Literature, 1888-1940; Brownson, S. J.: Life of Prince Gallitzin, Prince and Priest. 1873; Heyden, Thomas: Memoir of the Life and Character of the Rev. Prince Gallitzin. 1869; Hugel, P.: Royal Son and Mother. 1902; Lemke, P. H.: Life and Work of Prince D. A. Gallitzin. 1940.

1816 Defense of Catholic principles in a letter to a Protestant minister. S. Engles.
1817 An appeal to the Protestant public.
1820 Letters to a Protestant friend on the Holy Scriptures. T. Foley.
1834 Six letters of advice to the gentlemen Presbyterian parsons.
1940 Gallitzen's letters, a collection of the polemical works . . . (1770-1840). Angelmodde press.

GAMBLE, ANNA DILL, 1887-

Birthplace: Paris, France. **Conversion:** 1917. **Former religion:** Episcopalian. **Education:** Private schools; York (Pa.) Collegiate Institute (grad., '93). **General:** Miss Gamble has been occupied since 1938 with the writing of a history of the old Jesuit mission called Conowago, near York, Penna. This mission site held the oldest Catholic church in the thirteen Colonies, outside Maryland, and was established when Catholicism was driven out of Maryland. **Authorities:** Letter from Miss Gamble, November 13, 1943; Guide to Catholic Literature, 1888-1940.

Works

1920 My road to Rome. P. Reilly. pa.
1936 Introduction to Mexico (with others). Catholic assoc. for international peace. pa.

GARLAND, AUGUSTUS HILL, 1832-1899

Birthplace: Tipton County, Tenn. **Education:** Private school in Washington, D. C.; St. Mary's Coll., Lebanon Ky.; St. Joseph's Coll., Bardstown, Ky. (grad., '49). **Gen-**

eral: Garland taught school for a time in Arkansas before studying law with his stepfather. He then practiced that profession for eleven years and was elected Representative to the First Confederate Congress holding office from 1861 to 1864. The next year, and twice thereafter, he was sent to the U. S. Senate. In 1874 Garland was inaugurated as Governor of Arkansas and resigned that post a year later to become Attorney General of the United States. **Authorities:** Catholic Builders of the Nation, v. 3, p. 352; Biographical Directory of the American Congress, 1774-1927; Dictionary of American Biography, v. 7; Newberry, Farrar: A Life of Mr. Garland of Arkansas. 1908; Shinn, Josiah: Pioneers and Makers of Arkansas. 1908.

Works

1898   Experience in the Supreme court of the United States, with some reflections and suggestions as to that tribunal. J. Byrne.

1898   A treatise on the constitution and jurisdiction of the United States courts, on pleading, practice and procedure (with others). T. & J. W. Johnson. 2 v.

GOLDSTEIN, DAVID, 1870-

Birthplace: "Home city," Boston, Mass. **Conversion:** 1905. **Former religion:** Judaism, then Marxism. **General:** Mr. Goldstein is a Catholic outdoor lay apologist who resigned from the Socialist movement in 1903. He organized the "Catholic Truth Guild" with Martha Moore Avery in 1906—the organization to be called later, "Catholic Campaigners for Christ." In 1917 he was national lecturer of the Knights of Columbus. Niagara University conferred an honorary degree upon him in 1939. **Authorities:** American Catholic Who's Who (1942-43); Book of Catholic Authors, 1st series; Guide to Catholic Literature, 1888-1940; Slayton, J. W.: Attack of the Roman Catholic Church on Socialism through David Goldstein. 191– (Slayton takes exception to Mr. Goldstein's position).

Works

1919   Bolshevism, its cure (with Martha Moore Avery). Boston school of political economy.

1924   Campaigning for Christ (with Martha Moore Avery). Pilot.

1931   Campaigners for Christ handbook. T. J. Flynn.

1936   Autobiography of a Campaigner for Christ. Catholic campaigners for Christ.

1940   Jewish panorama. Catholic campaigners for Christ.

1943   Letters of Hebrew-Catholic to Mr. Isaacs. Radio replies press.

GOODYEAR, WILLIAM HENRY, 1846-1923

Birthplace: New Haven, Conn. **Conversion:** 1880. **Education:** After attending private schools in England he went to Russell's School in New Haven, Conn.; Yale Univ. (A.B. '67). **General:** Goodyear was the son of Charles Goodyear, founder of the rubber industry. His prime activity was in Roman and medieval antiquities and his investigations of architectural refinements took him on several visits to the sites of ancient civilizations. In 1882 he became curator of the Metropolitan Museum in New York, holding that position for eight years. Later he went to the Brooklyn Institute of Arts and Sciences. From 1895-1914 he was occupied with a survey of architectural monuments of Europe; while contributing regularly to the Architectural Record and other journals. **Authorities:** American Catholic Who's Who. 1911; Dictionary of American Biography, v. 7; Brooklyn Museum Quarterly, July, 1923; Journal of the Royal Institute of British Architects, June, 1906; November, 1907; Sturgis, Russell: Dictionary of Architecture and Building, 1902, v. 3.

Works

1883 Ancient and modern history. W. H. Sadlier.
1888 A history of art. A. S. Barnes.
1891 A grammar of the lotus. Sampson, Low, Marston.
1893 Roman and medieval art. Flood and Vincent.
1894 Renaissance and modern art. Flood and Vincent.
1902 Architectural refinements of St. Mark's at Venice. Macmillan.
1904 Vertical curves and other architectural refinements. Macmillan.
1905 Illustrated catalogue of photographs and surveys of architectural refinements in medieval buildings. Morrison and Gibbs.
1909 The desirable projection of art museums as suggested by the desirable classification of art libraries. Pittsburgh (?).
1912 Greek refinements. v. 1 (The author died before this work was completed).

GRANT, DOROTHY (FREMONT) 1900-

Birthplace: New York City. **Conversion:** 1934. **Former religion:** Episcopalian. **Education:** Grammar and high schools in New York City, supplemented by extensive reading, chiefly historical. **General:** While a Yeomanette in the first World War, Mrs. Grant was assistant to the editor of the Naval Medical Bulletin. Later she was founder and publisher of The Patter, of Manhasset, L. I., and is at present associate editor of the Long Island Forum. The author is a voluminous writer, contributing to the Catholic World, Ave Maria and other national magazines. She is the wife of Douglas Malcolm Grant, the painter, and niece of John Moody (q.v.). **Authorities:** Letter from Mrs. Grant, September 22, 1943; American Catholic Who's Who (1942-43); Bruce Publishing Co.: Between the Lines, Summer, 1943; Grant, D. F.: What Other Answer? 1943.

Works

1943 What other answer? Bruce.

GREENE, EDWARD LEE, 1843-1915

Birthplace: Hopkinson, R. I. **Conversion:** 1885. **Former religion:** Baptist, later Episcopalian (minister, 1871-84). **Education:** Public high school; Albion Coll., Wis. (Ph.B., '66); Jarvis Coll. (Ph.D.) **General:** Professor Greene taught botany at the University of California from 1885-95 and then at Catholic University of America until 1904. He made important contributions to the science of botany and was awarded the degree (LL.D.) by Notre Dame University in 1894. His valuable herbarium and botanical library is housed at Notre Dame. **Authorities:** American Authors, 1600-1900; American Catholic Who's Who. 1911; Dictionary of American Biography, v. 7; Guide to Catholic Literature, 1888-1940; Catholic World (port.) July, 1898.

Works

1887-05 Pittonia, a series of papers relating to botany and botanists. Berkeley, Calif. 5 v.

1889-90	Illustrations of west American oaks. Bosqui.
1891-97	Flora franciscana, an attempt to classify and describe the plants of middle California. Cubery. 4 pts.
1894	Manual of the botany of the region of San Francisco Bay. Cubery.
1901	Plantae Bakerianae (with others). Washington. 3 v.
1903-12	Leaflets of botanical observation and history. 2 v.
1909	Landmarks of botanical history . . . Part I, prior to 1562 A.D. Smithsonian institution.
1912	Carolus Linnaeus. C. Sower.
1914	Cybele Columbiana, a series of studies in botany, chiefly North American. Preston & Rounds, v. 1, no. 1.

GREIN, LUDWIG, 1896-

Birthplace: Kirtorf, Germany; **Came to U. S.:** 1925. **Conversion:** 1926. **Former religion:** Lutheran. **Education:** Public schools (1902-10); Technical school (1910-14); Navy school (1914-15). **General:** Mr. Grein was a wireless operator with the German navy (zeppelins) from 1915 to 1918, when he was sent to a hospital with injuries. Recovering in 1920, he entered the service of the Reichspost as postal clerk, telegrapher, and cashier, leaving in 1924 to come to the United States. Mr. Grein credits the example of his Catholic wife in leading him into the Church. A second book, "Americans and Other People," is in preparation, and like "Peace and Bread," also is "somewhat autobiographical, and shows the conversion and spiritual struggles of a convert." **Authorities:** Letter from Mr. Grein, November 1, 1943.

Works

1942 Peace and bread. Dorrance.

GRIERSON, FRANCIS, 1848-1927

Birthplace: Birkenhead, Cheshire, England. **Came to U. S.** 1848. **Conversion:** 1917. **Education:** Musical education (two years); his schooling was evidently received piecemeal as it is unrecorded. **General:** After leaving the Illinois prairie and the Middle West where his youth was spent, Grierson passed many years in Europe as a concert pianist; later exhibiting his versatile genius as composer, essayist and novelist. As a musician he gained international fame, but changed his name from Benjamin Henry Jesse Francis Shepard, in order to prove to himself that he could succeed as a literary artist without the aid of his musical reputation. **Authorities:** Dictionary of American Biography, v. 7; Guide to Catholic Literature, 1888-1940; Twentieth Century Authors; Tonner, W.: The genius of Francis Grierson. 1927. Also see Reader's Guide to Periodical Literature for numerous articles on Grierson's work.

Works

1899 Modern mysticism, and other essays. G. Allen.
1899 La revolte idealiste. Paris.
1901 The valley of shadows: recollections of the Lincoln country, 1858-1863. H. O. Houghton.
1910 Portraits.
1911 The humour of the underman, and other essays. Swift.
1911 La vie et les hommes.
1913 The Celtic temperament, and other essays. 4th ed. J. Lane.
1914 Parisian portraits. J. Lane.
1918 Abraham Lincoln, the practical mystic. J. Lane.
1918 Illusions and realities of the war. J. Lane.
1921 Psycho-phonic messages, recorded by Francis Grierson. Austin pub. co.

GURIAN, WALDEMAR, 1902-

Birthplace: St. Petersburg, Russia. **Former religion:** Judaism. **Education:** Attended universities of Bonn, Cologne, Munich and Breslau, receiving the degree, Ph.D. from the latter institution. **General:** Living in Europe during the chaotic period of Russia and Germany's political experiments, Professor Gurian has found ample background for his books in his own experiences. Since 1937 he has been associate professor of political science at the University of Notre Dame, and in 1939 he became editor of the Review of Politics, published at the University. **Authorities:** American Catholic Who's Who (1942-43); Guide to Catholic Literature, 1888-1940.

Works

1929   Social and political ideas of French Catholicism, 1789-1915. Volksverein Munchen, Gladbach.
1932   Bolshevism: theory and practice, translated by E. I. Watkin. Macmillan.
1932   Um des reiches zukunft. Freibourg, B. Herder.
1936   Hitler and the Christians. Sheed and Ward.
1938   The rise and decline of Marxism, translated by E. F. Peeler. Burns, Oates & Washbourne.

HAAS, ROSAMOND, 1908-

Birthplace: Kalamazoo, Mich. **Conversion:** 1933. **Former religion:** Methodist Episcopal. **Education:** Western State Teachers Coll. (A.B., '29); Univ. of Michigan (M.A., '34) **General:** Miss Haas is a new poet whose first work in book form is listed below. She contributes to the Commonweal and other periodicals. **Authorities:** Letter from Miss Haas, October, 1943.

Works

1944   Delay is the song. Dutton.

HALDEMAN, SAMUEL STEHMAN (Felix Ago, pseud.) 1812-1880

Birthplace: Locust Grove, Pa. **Conversion:** 1846. **Education:** Tutored in Dr. Keagy's classical school; Dickenson Coll., Carlyle, Pa. (2 years). **General:** Professor Haldeman spent much of his life teaching the two subjects, zoology and philology, and was outstanding in both. He was a professor of zoology at Delaware College for a time, and later at Franklin Institute, Philadelphia. From 1851 to 1855 and 1868 to 1880 he taught at the University of Pennsylvania, and as an authority on the dialects of the American Indian and Chinese languages, he was preeminent. **Authorities:** Dictionary of American Biography, v. 8; Hart, C. H.: Memoir of S. S. Haldeman. 1881; Livingston, John: Portraits of Americans Now Living. 1854, v. 4; American Catholic Historical Society. Records, September, 1898.

Works

1842	Monograph of the freshwater univalve mollusca of the United States. Acad. of natural science.
1842-43	Zoological contributions. Issued by the author.
1849	Some points in linguistic ethnology.
1850	Zoology of invertebrate animals.
1851	Elements of Latin pronunciation. J. B. Lippincott.
1855	(ed.) Statistics of coal, by R. C. Taylor. 2d ed. rev. J. W. Moore.
1856	Relations of the English and Chinese languages.
1860	Analytic orthography. J. B. Lippincott.
1864	Tours of a chess knight. E. H. Butler.
1865	Affixes in their origin and application. E. H. Butler.
1868	Rhymes of the poets, by Felix Ago. E. H. Butler.
1872	Pennsylvania Dutch. Reformed church pub. board.
1877	Outlines of etymology. J. B. Lippincott.
1879	Reports upon archaeological and ethnological collections from the vicinity of Santa Barbara, California (with others). Gov't print. off.

1881   Word building. J. B. Lippincott.
1898   The Clarendon dictionary (with W. H. Browne). University pub. co.
       (Haldeman published many other monographs and papers besides the works listed here)

HARD, WILLIAM, 1878-

Birthplace: Painted Post, N. Y. **Conversion:** 1934. **Former religion:** Methodist; later Episcopalian. **Education:** Philander Smith Inst., Mussoorie, India; University Coll., London; Northwestern Univ., Evanston, Ill. (A.B., 1900; L.H.D.; fellow in history, 1900-01) **General:** While occupied with newspaper work from 1901 to 1906, and editing The Neighbor, the author headed the Northwestern University Settlement for two years. For a time he was a radio commentator, and is at present (1943) devoting his whole time as "Roving Editor" for the Reader's Digest magazine. **Authorities:** Letter from Mr. Hard, August 8, 1943; American Catholic Who's Who (1942-43); Who's Who in America (1942-43).

Works

1910   Injured in the course of duty (with others). Ridgway.
1911   The women of tomorrow. Baker & Taylor.
1917   How the English take the war. Hodder & Stoughton. 32 p. (Also translated into the Danish).
1919   Raymond Robin's story of Bolshevist Russia (with others).
1920   Raymond Robin's own story; with many illustrations from photographs. Harper.
1928   Who's Hoover? Dodd, Mead.
1937   Managerial and political aspects of labor (with J. A. Voss). American management ass'n.

HARDIN, MARTIN D., 1837-1923

Birthplace: Jacksonville, Ill. **Conversion:** 1864. **Education:** West Point Military Academy (grad. '59) **General:** Martin D. Hardin fought through the Civil War and was mustered out in 1866 as Brigadier-General. Later he read law in Chicago in the office of Scammon, McCogg & Fuller and was admitted to the bar in 1871. He practiced law in that city for many years and was associated with the Chicago Literary Club. **Authorities:** American Catholic Who's Who. 1911; Dictionary of American Biography, v. 8.

Works

1890 History of the Twelfth Regiment, Pennsylvania Reserve volunteer corps . . . N. Y., The author.

HARLAND, HENRY (Sidney Luska, pseud.) 1861-1905

Birthplace: New York City. **Conversion:** 1898. **Education:** Public schools in N. Y. C.; Adelphi Acad., Brooklyn (1871-72); Harvard Divinity School (short period); Coll. of the City of N. Y. (1877-80); Univ. of Paris. **General:** Harland spent considerable time in European travel, returning to a desk in the New York Surrogate's office during 1886. The next year he again went to Europe and founded, with Aubrey Beardsley, the Yellow Book Magazine, which he conducted from 1892-97. **Authorities:** American Authors, 1600-1900; Dictionary of American Biography, v. 8; Guide to Catholic Literature 1888-1940. The Irish Monthly, April, 1911.

Works

1885 As it was written: a Jewish musician's story. Cassell.

1886 Mrs. Peixada. Cassell.
1887 A land of love.
1887 The yoke of the Thorah. Cassell.
1888 My uncle Florimond.
1889 Grandison Mather. Cassell.
1889 A Latin-quarter courtship and other stories. Cassell.
1890 Two voices.
1890 Two women or one.
1891 Mea culpa; a woman's last word. Street.
1893 Mademoiselle Miss; to which is added The light sovereign, a farcical comedy (with Hubert Crackenthorpe). F. F. Lovell.
1895 Grey roses. W. F. Roberts.
1898 Comedies and errors. J. Lane.
1900 The cardinal's snuff-box. J. Lane.
1902 The Lady Paramount. J. Lane.
1902 My friend Prospero. McClure, Phillips.
1909 The royal end (completed by his wife). Dodd, Mead.

HARNEY, JOHN MILTON, father (O.P.) 1789-1825

Birthplace: Sussex County, Del. **Conversion:** Ca. 1820. **Education:** Studied medicine. **General:** Father Harney was a brother of General William Selby Harney, Indian fighter and Union Army officer. He was widely travelled and edited a newspaper for a time in Savannah, Ga. The greater part of the author's poetry appeared only after his death, and then was published in magazines. **Authorities:** Appleton's Cyclopaedia of American Biography, v. 3; Griswold, R. W.: Poets and poetry of America. 16th ed., 1855.

Works

1816 Crystalina; a fairy tale in six cantos. G. F. Hopkins.

HARRIS, JOEL CHANDLER, 1848-1908

Birthplace: Near Eatonton, Ga. **Conversion:** 1908. **Edu-**

cation: Miss Davidson's school and the local academy in Eatonton for short periods. **General:** From youth to old age, Harris held a pen in his hand; first as apprentice to the editor of The Countryman, and later as editor of the Atlanta (Ga.) Constitution. He retained the latter position for twenty-five years. The Uncle Remus magazine, which he founded in 1907, was the author's final editorial effort, and when it was consolidated with the Home Magazine in 1908 he continued to write essays and stories for the combined publication until his death. **Authorities:** American Authors, 1600-1900; Dictionary of American Biography, v. 8; Guide to Catholic Literature, 1888-1940; Harlow, A. F.: Joel Chandler Harris, plantation story teller. 1941; Harris, J. C.: The Life and Letters of J. C. Harris. 1918; Toulmin, H. A.: Social historians. 1911; Wiggins, R. L.: The Life of Joel Chandler Harris. 1918.

Works

1881   Uncle Remus; his songs and his sayings. D. Appleton.
1883   Nights with Uncle Remus. H. O. Houghton.
1884   Mingo and other sketches in black and white. H. O. Houghton.
1887   Free Joe, and other Georgian sketches. C. Scribner.
1889   Daddy Jake, the runaway, and short stories told after dark. Century.
1890   Life of Henry W. Grady, including his writings and speeches. Cassell.
1891   Balsam and his master and other sketches and stories. H. O. Houghton.
1892   On the plantation. D. Appleton.
1892   Uncle Remus and his friends. H. O. Houghton.
1894   Little Mr. Thimblefinger and his queer country. H. O. Houghton.
1895   Mr. Rabbit at home. H. O. Houghton.
1896   Georgia from the invasion of De Sota to recent times. D. Appleton. (Also published as Stories of Georgia).

1896 Story of Aaron (so named) the son of Ben Ali. H. O. Houghton.
1898 Tales of the home folks in peace and war. H. O. Houghton.
1899 Chronicles of Aunt Minervy Ann. C. Scribner.
1899 Plantation pageants. H. O. Houghton.
1900 On the wing of occasion. Doubleday.
1901 A little Union scout. Duckworth.
1902 Gabriel Tolliver, a story of Reconstruction. McClure, Phillips.
1902 The making of a statesman and other stories. McClure, Phillips.
1903 Uncle Remus returns. McClure, Phillips.
1903 Wally Wanderoon and his story-telling machine. McClure, Phillips.
1905 Told by Uncle Remus. McClure, Phillips.
1907 Uncle Remus and Bre'r Rabbit. F. A. Stokes.
1909 Bishop and the boogerman. Doubleday.
1909 Shadow between his shoulder-blades. Small, Maynard.
1910 Little Mr. Thimblefinger stories. Houghton, Mifflin.
1910 Uncle Remus and the little boy. Small, Maynard.
1931 Joel Chandler Harris, editor and essayist; miscellaneous, literary, political and social writings. Univ. of North Carolina press.

HARRIS, MIRIAM (COLES) 1834-1925

Birthplace: On the island of Dosoris, near Long Island, N. Y. **Former religion:** Attended the "Little Church Around the Corner" (P.E.) New York City. **Education:** St. Mary's Hall, Burlington, N. J.; Madame Canda's School, N. Y. C. **General:** Mrs. Harris began contributing to periodicals at an early age and published her first novel "Rutledge" when she was twenty-six. Much of her time was spent abroad after the death of her husband, Sidney S. Harris, and it was during this time that she produced her book of Spanish travels. **Authorities:** American Authors, 1600-1900; American Catholic Who's Who. 1911;

Dictionary of American Biography, v. 8; Guide to Catholic Literature, 1888-1940; Who's Who in America (1920-21).

Works

1860   Louie's last term at St. Mary's. C. Scribner.
1860   Rutledge. Derby & Jackson.
1862   The Sutherlands. (11th ed.) C. Scribner.
1863   Frank Warrington. C. Scribner.
1865   St. Philip's. C. Scribner.
1867   A rosary for Lent; or, Devotional readings, original and compiled. G. W. Carleton.
1867   Roundhearts, and other stories. C. Scribner.
1870   Miss. G. W. Carleton.
1871   Richard Vandermarck. C. Scribner.
1874   (ed.) Dear feast of Lent, a series of devotional readings. Dutton.
1875   (ed.) Marguerite's journal, a story for girls (by Victorine Monniot, and translated by Lucy W. Baxter). G. W. Carleton.
1875   Perfect Adonis. G. W. Carleton.
1881   Happy-go-lucky. G. W. Carleton.
1884   Phoebe, a novel.
1891   An utter failure. D. Appleton.
1892   A chit of sixteen and other stories. G. W. Dillingham.
1898   A corner of Spain. H. O. Houghton.
1907   The tents of wickedness. D. Appleton.

HARTE, GEOFFREY BRET, See Bret Harte, Geoffrey

HASSARD, JOHN ROSE GREEN, 1836-1888

Birthplace: New York City. **Conversion:** 1851. **Former religion:** Episcopalian. **Education:** St. John's Coll., N. Y. (grad., '55). **General:** Hassard was the first editor of the Catholic World but his principal work was done on the

New York Tribune. He was both historian and music critic, and in the latter capacity an authority on Richard Wagner, the composer. **Authorities:** Catholic Encyclopedia, v. 7; Dictionary of American Biography, v. 8; Guide to Catholic Literature, 1888-1940; Bishop, J. B.: Notes and anecdotes of many years. 1925; Catholic World, June, 1888.

Works

1864   (ed.) The wreath of beauty. D. Appleton.
1865   (ed.) Reflections and meditations . . . from Fenelon.
1866   The life, correspondence, and writings of the Most Reverend John Hughes, D.D. D. Appleton.
1875   A life of Pope Pius IX.
1877   Richard Wagner at Bayreuth.
1878   (comp.) A history of the United States of America. Catholic pub. soc.
1881   A Pickwickian pilgrimage. J. R. Osgood.
1887   The New York Tribune's history of the United States. Rand McNally.

HAWKS, EDWARD WILLIAM, monsignor, 1878-
    Birthplace: Crickhowel, Wales. **Conversion:** 1908. **Former religion:** Anglican (minister, 1905-08). **Ordained priest:** 1911. **Education:** Private schools; Univ. of London; Bishop's Coll., Quebec; Anglican Sem. (Wis.); St. Charles Sem. (Cath.) Philadelphia. **General:** Monsignor Hawks was one of the youngest of twenty Protestant clergymen to enter the Church with William McGarvey (q.v.) on the issue of Modernism. The author has been a columnist, and a contributor to periodicals and the daily press. He was made Domestic Prelate in 1936. **Authorities:** Letters from Monsignor Hawks, August 7, 27, 1943; American Catholic

Who's Who (1942-43); Book of Catholic Authors, 2d ser.; Guide to Catholic Literature, 1888-1940; Curtis, G. P.: Beyond the Road to Rome. 1914.

Works

1930 Conversions of 1908.
1935 William McGarvey and his open pulpit. 1870-1908. Dolphin.
1936 Difficulties of Myron Digby.
1936 A pedigree of Protestantism. P. Reilly.
1937 History of the parish of St. Joan of Arc, Harrowgate, Philadelphia. P. Reilly.
1939 Difficulties of Father Callaghan.
1940 How it looks now.

HAWTHORNE, ROSE, See Lathrop, Mother Mary Alphonsa (Hawthorne) 1851-1926

HAYES, ALICE JEANNETTE, 1855-1920

General: For nearly thirty years, Miss Hayes was matron in the women's reformatory at Sherborn, Massachusetts. **Authorities:** Driscoll, A. S.: Literary Convert Women. 1928.

Works

1911 A convert's reason why. Riverside press.

HAYES, CARLTON JOSEPH HUNTLEY, 1882-

Birthplace: Afton, N. Y. **Conversion:** 1904. **Former re-**

ligion: Baptist. **Education:** Columbia Univ. (A.B., M.A., Ph.D., 1904-09). **General:** Professor Hayes spent the greater part of his teaching career as a teacher of history at Columbia University, New York City, where he was Seth Low Professor of History and executive officer of the department of history from 1938 to 1942, when he was appointed United States Ambassador to Spain. He was a captain on the staff of Military Intelligence from 1918-19 and major in the Officers' Reserve Corps from 1928-34. Mr. Hayes is on the Editorial Council of Commonweal. **Authorities:** American Catholic Who's Who (1942-43); Guide to Catholic Literature, 1888-1940; Who's Who Among North American Authors (1933-35); Who's Who in America (1942-43).

Works

1909   An introduction to the sources relating to the Germanic invasions. Columbia univ. press.
1912   A syllabus of modern history (with R. L. Schuyler). Columbia univ. press.
1913   British social politics (with others). Ginn.
1916   A political and social history of modern Europe. Macmillan. 2 v.
1919   The League of Nations, principles and practice.
1920   A brief history of the great war. Macmillan.
1921   History of diplomacy and international relations (with P. T. Moon). Macmillan.
1923   Modern history (with P. T. Moon). Macmillan.
1923   Teachers manual to accompany Modern history (with P. T. Moon). Macmillan.
1924   Modern recent political theory. (co-author).
1924   These eventful years. (co-author).
1926   Essays on nationalism. Macmillan.
1929   Ancient and medieval history (with P. T. Moon). Macmillan.
1929-33 (ed.) Social and economic studies of post-war France.

1930	France; a nation of patriots. Columbia univ. press.
1931	Historical evolution of modern nationalism. R. R. Smith.
1931	A quarter-century of learning.
1932	World history (with others). Macmillan.
1932-36	A political and cultural history of modern Europe. Macmillan. 2 v.
1936	(ed.) The American way; a study of human relations among Protestants, Catholics and Jews (with others). Willett, Clark.
1941	A generation of materialism, 1871-1900. Harper.
1942	This inevitable conflict. Columbia univ. press.

HAYWORD, WILLIAM LEETE LONGINUS, father, 1870-

Birthplace: Morley, N. Y. **Conversion:** 1908. **Former religion:** Protestant Episcopal, minister, 1894-1908). **Education:** Public schools and Howe Grammar School, Lima, Indiana; Nashotah (Wisc.) Protestant Episcopal Sem. **General:** Father Hayword is a descendant of William Leete, first governor of the New Haven Colony. He taught at Racine College Grammar School one year and then became assistant pastor at St. Elizabeth's (Epis.) Church in Philadelphia, where he remained until 1908. Father Hayword is now Rector of St. Alice's Church, Upper Darby, Pa. **Authorities:** American Catholic Who's Who. 1911.

Works

1907	Obsequiale. Longmans, Green.
1940	The C.S.S.S.; the quest and goal of the founder, William McGarvey. Jefferies and Manz.
1940	Pro-Roman movement in the United States (the life of William McGarvey). Jefferies and Manz.

HECKER, ISAAC THOMAS, father, 1819-1888

Birthplace: New York (state). **Conversion:** 1844. **Former religion:** Parents, Methodist; Hecker considered the Episcopal church, among others, but eventually rejected it. **Ordained priest:** 1849. **Education:** Self-taught through wide reading and cultured associations; studied philosophy and theology at Brook Farm (2 years). **General:** As a youth Father Hecker helped his brothers in the family-owned bakery but his idealism led him from this prosaic pursuit to a friendship with Orestes Brownson (q.v.) with whom he was to eventually help found and edit the Catholic World. After leaving the Redemptorists Father Hecker founded, with others, the Paulists, in 1859 and became the first Superior General of that Congregation. **Authorities:** Dictionary of American Biography, v. 8; Guide to Catholic Literature, 1888-1940; Burton, Katherine: Celestial Homespun. 1943; Burton, Katherine: In No Strange Land. 1942; Elliott, W.: Life of Father Hecker. 1891; Holden, V. F.: Early Years of Isaac Thomas Hecker, 1819-1844. 1939; Maignen, Chas.: Etudes sur l'americanisme. Le pere Hecker, est-il un saint? 1899; Sedgwick, H. D.: Father Hecker. 1900.

Works

1855 Questions of the soul. D. Appleton.
1857 Aspirations of nature. J. B. Kirker.
1861 (ed.) The young converts; or, Memoirs of the three sisters, Debbie, Helen and Anna Barlow. Compiled by a lady. Edited by the Rev. I. T. Hecker. P. O'Shea.
1875 The church and the age. Catholic book exchange.
1879 Catholicity in the United States.
1881 Catholics and Protestants agreeing on the school question.

HEDGES, SAMUEL COLAHAN BERNARD, father, 1854-1916.

Birthplace: Circleville, O. **Conversion:** 1870. **Former religion:** Protestant. **Education:** Everts High School, Circleville; Seton Hall Coll., South Orange, N. Y. (M.A.) **General:** After his conversion Father Hedges was professor of English at Seton Hall College and later, pastor of St. Stephen's Church, Arlington, N. J. He contributed to various Catholic magazines. **Authorities:** American Catholic Who's Who, 1911; Guide to Catholic Literature, 1888-1940.

Works

1892 Statistics concerning education in the Philippines. 30 p.
1893 Father Marquette; Jesuit missionary and explorer.

HEGGIE, CORA M. A., 1861-

Birthplace: Springfield, Ill. **Conversion:** ca. 1879. **Former religion:** Parents, Protestant but she "believed in no particular creed." **Authorities:** Consult her work below.

Works

1880 The life and trials of a young lady convert. Palmer & Bacon.

HEMENWAY, ABBY MARIA (Marie Josephine, pseud.) 1828-1890

Birthplace: Ludlow, Vt. **General:** Much of Miss Hemenway's work concerns the history of Vermont, which she published, edited and wrote. Assisted in the work by her sister Mrs. Carrie H. Payne, she edited and published The Vermont Historical Gazetteer: A Magazine Embracing a History of Each Town, Civil, Ecclesiastical, Biographical and Military, in five volumes. The author resided in Vermont until 1885 when she moved to Chicago, Ill., where she died in 1890. **Authorities:** Cyclopaedia of American Biographies, v. 3; Young, Alfred: Catholic and Protestant Countries Compared. 1903 (Reference, only).

Works

1858	(ed.) Poets and poetry of Vermont. G. A. Tuttle.
1863	Songs of the war. J. Munsell.
1865	The mystical rose; or, Mary of Nazareth. D. Appleton.
1867	Rosa Immaculata, or, The tower of ivory. P. O'Shea.
1873	The house of gold and the Saint of Nazareth, by Marie Josephine. Kelly, Piet.
1878	The Clark papers. Mrs. Meech and her family. A. M. Hemenway.
1878	Fanny Allen, the first American nun. (Drama.)
1886-89	Notes by the path of the Gazeteer. 2 v. A. M. Hemenway.

HENDERSON, ISAAC AUSTIN, 1850-1909

Birthplace: Brooklyn, N. Y. **Conversion:** 1896. **Former religion:** Protestant. **Education:** Private schools and under tutors; Williams Coll. (M.A., J.D.) **General:** Henderson became connected with the New York Evening Post in 1872 and eventually publisher of that paper. In 1881 he resigned and went to live in London and Rome where he devoted his time to writing and social work. The author was appointed private chamberlain to Pope Pius X in 1903. **Authorities.** Catholic Encyclopedia, v. 7; Guide to Catholic Literature, 1888-1940.

1886 The prelate, a novel. Ticknor.
1888 Agatha Page. Ticknor. (Later dramatized as "The Silent Battle")
1901 The mummy and the humming bird. (Drama)
1909 Out yonder; a play in four acts.

HEWETSON, GEORGE BENSON. d. 1939

Birthplace: England. **Conversion:** 1914. **Former religion:** Anglican (minister, 1891-1913). **General:** Mr. Hewetson contributed occasionally to periodical literature, particularly the Catholic World, and at one time was an assistant professor of English at DePaul University, Chicago. **Authorities:** Guide to Catholic Literature, 1888-1940.

Works

1918 The desired of all nations; a drama in three acts. The author.
n.d. The call of the Rockies (poems).

HEWIT, AUGUSTINE FRANCIS, father (C.S.P.) (Nathaniel Augustus Hewit) 1820-1897

Birthplace: Fairfield, Conn. **Conversion:** 1846. **Former religion:** Congregationalist (minister, 1842); later Episcopalian (minister, 1843-46). **Ordained priest:** 1847. **Education:** Phillips Andover Acad.; Amherst Coll. (grad., '39). **General:** Father Hewit was the son of a prominent Congregationalist minister. After his ordination to the priesthood he became a teacher in a collegiate institute in Charleston, S. C. While engaged in this activity he assisted in compiling Bishop England's works for publication. Shortly thereafter he entered the Congregation of the Holy Redeemer (1849) but with Father Hecker (q.v.) and others, left to found the Paulists. He became one of the foremost apologists of his day and a voluminous writer, particularly for the Catholic World and the American Catholic Quarterly Review. He was elected the second Superior General of the Congregation of St. Paul. **Authorities:** Catholic Encyclopedia, v. 7; Dictionary of American Biography, v. 8; Guide to Catholic Literature, 1888-1940; American Catholic Quarterly Review, July, 1903; Catholic World, August, 1897.

Works

1846   Reasons for submitting to the Catholic church. Charleston, S. C.
1850   (ed.) Complete works of Bishop England. Baltimore, Md.
1856   Life of Guendaline, Princess Borghese. P. O'Shea.
1857   Life of Dumoulin-Borie. (Later edition published by P. O'Shea).
1865   The life of Reverend Francis A. Baker.
1865   The little angel of the Copts.
1868   Problems of the age; with studies in St. Augustine on kindred topics. Columbus press.
1870   Light in darkness. Christian press.
1870   Treatise on the obscure night of the soul.
1874   King's highway; or, The Catholic church the way of salvation. Catholic pub. soc.
1895   Teaching of St. John the Apostle. Catholic book exchange.
n.d.   (ed.) Highways of life. Paulist press.
n.d.   Life of Bishop Borie, martyred in China. P. O'Shea.
n.d.   Life of the Egyptian Aloysius. P. O'Shea.

HEWIT, NATHANIEL AUGUSTUS, See Hewit, Augustine Francis, father, 1820-1897

HILL, JAMES JEROME, 1838-1916

Birthplace: Rockwood, Ontario. **Conversion:** 1916. **Former religion:** Mother, Methodist; father, Baptist. **Education:** District school, then Rockwood Acad. **General:** Hill left his father's farm to enter business in St. Paul about 1856. He rose rapidly, eventually becoming president of the St. Paul, Minneapolis & Manatoba Railway Company, and held that position from 1882 to 1890. In 1888 he became interested in building the Great Northern Railway, and was president of the entire Great Northern system from 1889 to 1907. Hill's life-long love for books led him to erect the famous Hill Reference Library in St. Paul, and at his wife's request (he was received into the Church on his deathbed), endowed the St. Paul Theological (Cath.) Seminary with a gift of $500,000. **Authorities:** Dictionary of American Biography, v. 9; Who's Who in America (1916-17); Catholic Builders of the Nation. 1923; Pyle, J. G.: Life of James J. Hill. 1917. 2 v.

Works

1908 Future of rail and water transportation. St. Paul, The author.
1908 Natural wealth of the land and its conservations. St. Paul, The author.
1910 Highways of progress. Doubleday, Page.

HILGARD, EUGENE WOLDEMAR, 1833-1916

Birthplace: Zweibrücken (Bavaria). **Came to U. S.:** 1836. **Conversion:** ca. 1855. **Education:** Early schooling at home from his father; Homeopathic Medical Coll., and Franklin

Institute in Philadelphia; Univ. of Heidelberg (Ph.D., '53); Univ. of Zurich. **General:** After finishing his university work Hilgard spent two years (1854-55) doing geological research in Spain. He then became a chemist with the Smithsonian Institution, and also an assistant on the State Geological Survey of Mississippi. He remained with the Survey, of which he was later to become its chief, until 1860. Hilgard resigned as State Geologist in 1866 to become a professor of chemistry in the state university, but resumed the work in 1870 as Director. In 1873 he was called to the University of Michigan as professor of geology and natural history. The author's last post was that of professor of agriculture and director of the Agricultural Experiment Station at Berkeley, California. He was fluent in French and Spanish, and knew Greek, Latin, Italian and Portuguese. **Authorities:** Catholic Encyclopedia, v. 17 (Suppl. I); Dictionary of American Biography, v. 9; Hilgardia, published by the Agricultural Experimental Station at Berkeley, May, 1925; Merrill, G. P.: Contributions to a History of State Geology and Natural History Surveys. 1920; Geographical Society of America. Bulletin, v. 28, 1917; University of California Chronicle, April, 1916.

Works

1860   Geology and agriculture in the state of Mississippi. (Printed in 1860 but not issued, because of the War, until 1866).
1870   Geology of the Mississippi Delta.
1906   Soils, their formation, properties, and relations to climate and plant growth in the humid and arid regions. Macmillan.
1910   Agriculture for schools of the Pacific slope (with Winthrop J. Van L. Osterhout). Macmillan.

HILLIARD, MARION PHARO, 1871-

Conversion: 1913 (?) **Authorities:** Guide to Catholic Literature, 1888-1940.

Works

1936 Gracious years; a true story of discovery and fulfillment. St. Anthony's guild.

HOARE, SISTER MARY REGIS (S.C.)

Works

1942 Virgin soil; Mother Seton from a different point of view. Christopher.

HOBBES, JOHN OLIVER, pseud., See Craigie, Pearl Mary Teresa (Richards) 1867-1906

HOFFMAN, ROSS JOHN SWARTZ, 1902-

Birthplace: Harrisburg, Pa. **Conversion:** 1931. **Former religion:** Agnostic. **Education:** Lafayette Coll. (A.B., '23); Univ. of Pa. (M.A., '26; Ph.D., '32) **General:** Dr. Hoffman has been an associate professor of history at Fordham University since 1938. He has received honorary degrees from Villanova and Marquette Universities, and is a frequent contributor to the national reviews. **Authorities:** Letter from Dr. Hoffman, November 21, 1943; American Catholic Who's Who (1942-43); Book of Catholic Authors, 3d ser.; Guide to Catholic Literature, 1888-1940; Sheed, F. J.: Sidelights on the Catholic Revival. 1940.

1933 Great Britain and the German trade rivalry, 1875-1914. Univ. of Pennsylvania press.
1933 Visual outline of medieval history. Longmans, Green.
1934 Restoration. Sheed & Ward.
1935 The will to freedom. Sheed & Ward.
1938 Tradition and progress, and other historical essays in culture, religion and politics. Bruce.
1939 The organic state; an historical view of contemporary politics. Sheed and Ward.
1942 The great republic; a historical view of the international community and the organization of peace. Sheed & Ward.
1943 The origins and background of the second world war (with C. Grove Haines). Oxford univ. press.

HOLSAPPLE, LLOYD BURDWIN, 1884-

Birthplace: Hudson, N. Y. **Conversion:** 1931. **Former religion:** Protestant Episcopal (minister, 1910-29). **Education:** Yale Univ. (A.B. '05); Oxford Univ. (A.B. '10; A.M. '14). **General:** In 1906, Mr. Holsapple became Master of St. Paul's School, Concord, New Hampshire, and a year later Head Master of the Kent School in Connecticut. He later served various Protestant Episcopal churches and was a chaplain during the first World War. After his conversion, the author was instructor, and later associate professor of Latin and Greek in Manhattanville College. He contributes to various journals, including the Classical Bulletin. **Authorities:** American Catholic Who's Who (1942-43); Guide to Catholic Literature, 1888-1940.

1936   (ed.) Latin for use; an anthology of Latin through the ages. F. S. Crofts.
1942   Constantine the Great. Sheed & Ward.

HOTSPUR, pseud., **See** Walworth, Mansfield Tracy, 1830-1873

HOWARTH, ELLEN CLEMENTINE (DORAN) 1827-1899

Birthplace: Cooperstown, N. Y. **General:** Little is known of the author's early background except that she left school at the age of seven to work in a factory. She married Joseph Howarth in 1846. **Authorities:** Appleton's Cyclopaedia of American Biography, v. 6; Young, Alfred: Catholic and Protestant Countries Compared. 1903 (Reference only).

Works

1864   The wind-harp and other poems. W. P. Hazard.
1868   Poems, with introduction by Richard W. Gilder. M. R. Dennis.
1872   The guerrilla chief. A drama in five acts. Murphy and Bechtel.

HULL, ROBERT REUEL, 1892-

Conversion: 1922. **Former religion:** Disciples' church (minister). **General:** Mr. Hull contributes both prose and verse to periodicals and is associate editor of Our Sunday Visitor. **Authorities:** Guide to Catholic Literature, 1888-1940.

1926 The syllabus of errors of Pope Pius IX; the scourge of liberalism. Our Sunday Visitor.

1931 The perfect love, and other poems. Three worlds press.

HUNT, DUANE GARRISON, bp., 1884-

Birthplace: Reynolds, Nebr. **Conversion:** Before 1916. **Ordained priest:** 1920. **Consecrated bishop:** 1937. **Education:** Cornell Coll., Mt. Vernon, Ia. (A.B. '07); Univ. of Chicago (1912-13); Univ. of Ia. (1911-12); St. Patrick's Sem. (1916-20). The author has been bishop of Salt Lake since 1937. The degree, LL.D., was conferred upon him by the University of Portland in 1935. **Authorities:** American Catholic Who's Who (1942-43); Guide to Catholic Literature, 1888-1940; Who's Who in America (1942-43).

Works

1936 The people, the clergy and the church; an answer to accusations against the Catholic church. Paulist press.

1940 Radio addresses. Intermountain Catholic truth soc.

HUNT, GAILLARD, 1862-1926

Birthplace: New Orleans. **Conversion:** 1902. **Education:** Emerson Institute, Washington, D. C. (Litt. D.) **General:** Mr. Hunt held various important government posts and as Chief of the Division of Manuscripts of the Library of Congress he had ready access to the source materials which comprise the foundation for his historical works. He was a lecturer at both Johns Hopkins and George Washington

114

Universities. **Authorities:** American Catholic Who's Who. 1911; Dictionary of American Biography, v. 9; Guide to Catholic Literature, 1888-1940; Who's Who Among North American Authors (1921).

Works

1888	The American passport. Gov't print. off.
1892	Fragments of revolutionary history. Historical print. club.
1900-10	(ed.) The writings of James Madison. G. P. Putnam. 9 v.
1901	Calendar of applications and recommendations for office during the presidency of George Washington. Gov't print. off.
1902	The life of James Madison. Doubleday, Page.
1905	(ed.) Disunion sentiment in Congress in 1794, by John Taylor of Caroline . . . W. H. Lawdermilk.
1906	(ed.) The first forty years of Washington society, by Mrs. St. Harrison Smith. C. Scribners.
1908	John C. Calhoun. G. W. Jacobs.
1908	(ed.) The journal of the debates in the convention which framed the Constitution of the United States. G. P. Putnam. 2 v.
1909	The history of the seal of the United States. Washington, Dept. of State.
1910-22	The journals of the Continental Congress. v. 16 and 25.
1914	The Department of State of the United States. Yale univ. press.
1914	Life in America one hundred years ago. Harper.
1920	(ed.) The debates in the Federal Convention of 1787 (with Brown Scott). Oxford univ. press.

HUNTINGTON, JEBIDIAH VINCENT (John Vincent, pseud.) 1815-1862

Birthplace: New York City. **Conversion:** 1849. **Former religion:** Congregationalist; then Protestant Episcopal (minister, 1841-46). **Education:** Univ. of New York (grad., '35); Univ. of Pa. (M.D., '38). **General:** Huntington was descended from an old and wealthy New England family who figured prominently in early American history. He taught philosophy at St. Paul's School, Flushing, L. I., while studying theology to prepare himself for the Episcopalian ministry. A few years after his ordination he became interested in the Oxford Movement in England, and this caused him to become dissatisfied with Protestantism. He went to Rome after resigning his rectorship in 1846, and returned to the United States a Catholic. Huntington edited the shortlived Metropolitan magazine from 1853 to 1854, and later the St. Louis Leader. **Authorities:** American Authors, 1600-1900; Catholic Encyclopedia, v. 7; Dictionary of American Biography, v. 9; Guide to Catholic Literature, 1888-1940; Huntington, J. V.: Alban. 1851. (Autobiographical novel); American Catholic Historical Society. Records, September, December, 1905.

Works

1843   The northern dawn, and other poems.
1843   Poems. Wiley and Putnam.
1849   Lady Alice; or, The new Una. D. Appleton.
1851   Alban; or, The history of a young Puritan. Colburn. 3 v.
1852   The pretty plate. J. S. Redfield.
1852   St. Vincent de Paul and the fruits of his life.
1853   America discovered: a poem. E. Dunigan. 32 p.
1853   The forest; a sequel to Alban. J. S. Redfield.
1854   (tr.) Narrative of a voyage to the Northwest Coast in the years 1811, 12, 13, 14, by Gabriel Franciere. J. S. Redfield.
1854   (tr.) Short and familiar answers to objections against religion, by Segur.
1859   Blond and brunette.
1860   Rosemary; or, Life and death. D. & J. Sadlier.

n.d.   Gropings after truth: a life journey from new England Congregationalism to the one Catholic apostolic church. Catholic pub. co.

IRONSIDE, GEORGE ED., d. ca. 1827.

Conversion: 1817. **Former religion:** Protestant (minister). **General:** Dr. Ironside became a Catholic with other distinguished converts, including Mother Seton (q.v.) and the Reverend Virgil Barber. He taught for a time at Georgetown College. **Authorities:** Catholic Encyclopedia, vols. 11, 15. (short references); Parsons, Wilfred: Early Catholic Americana. 1939.

Works

1816   (ed.) Institutio graecae grammatices compendiaria. Ed. 2. G. Long.

1817   (ed.) The Alexandria controversy: or, A series of letters between M. B. and Quaero on the tenets of Christianity. W. Duffy.

1820   (ed.) A grammar of the Greek language: originally composed for the college school at Gloucester: in which it has been the editor's design to reject what, in the most improved editions of Cowden, is redundant. Fourth American ed., carefully revised and edited. Evart Duyckinck and G. Long.

1826   (ed.) Homeri Ilias, graece et latine . . . E. Duyckinck and G. Long.

IVES, LEVI SILLIMAN, 1797-1867

Birthplace: Meriden, Conn. **Conversion:** 1852. **Former religion:** Presbyterian; then Protestant Episcopal (minister, 1822-31; bishop, 1831-52). **Education:** Hamilton Coll.;

Chelsea Sem. (Epis). **General:** Levi Silliman Ives became the first Protestant Episcopal Bishop of North Carolina in 1831, but a study of the Protestant revolt in England eventually led him to resign his bishopric, amid a storm of controversy, to become a Catholic layman. Since Ives had a wife and children he had little to gain but the "peace of a good conscience," for his heroic decision cost him position, funds, prospects and many old friends. Upon becoming a Catholic he taught in St. John's College, Fordham, N. Y., and lectured in various Catholic Colleges. He founded the Catholic Male Protectory in New York City; was active in the work of the House of the Holy Angels, and for some time was president of the New York conference of the St. Vincent de Paul Society. **Authorities:** Catholic Encyclopedia, v. 8; Dictionary of American Biography, v. 9; Guide to Catholic Literature, 1888-1940; Burton, Katherine: In No Strange Land. 1942; Hannon, B.: Memoir of a Great Convert; Mason, R. S.: A letter to the Bishop of N. C. on the Subject of His Late Pastoral on the Salisbury Convention. 1850; O'Grady, J.: Levi Silliman Ives. 1933.

Works

1840 New manual of devotions; humility a ministerial qualification. Stanford & Swords.
1844 The apostle's doctrine and fellowship. D. Appleton.
1849 The obedience of faith. Stanford & Swords.
1853 Trials of a mind in its progress toward Catholicism: a letter to his old friends. M. T. Richardson.
n.d. Catechism for oral teaching. Stanford & Swords.

JOHNSTON, RICHARD MALCOLM (Philemon Perch, pseud.) 1822-1898

Birthplace: Near Powellton, Ga. **Conversion:** 1875. **Former religion:** Baptist (father a preacher). **Education:** Country school; Mercer Univ. (A.B., '41); studied law and admitted to bar in 1843. **General:** Johnston taught school and practiced law from 1844 to 1857, and in that year was offered the presidency of his alma mater, Mercer University. At the same time he was also offered a judgeship, and the chair of rhetoric and belle-lettres at the University of Georgia. He accepted the latter position, and remained there until 1861. The following year he opened the Pen Lucy School in Baltimore, with Sidney Lanier as one of his staff, and continued it for several years. His *apologia* appeared after his death in, "Truth." **Authorities:** American Authors, 1600-1900; Catholic Literature, 1888-1940; Brinson, L. B.: A study of the Life and Works of R. M. Johnston. 1937; Johnston, R. M.: Autobiography. 1900; Johnston, R. M.: Truth. 1898; Stedman, E. C. and Weeks, S. B.: Literary Estimate and Bibliography of R. M. Johnston. 1898; Catholic World, November, 1898; August, 1937.

Works

1860	The English classics: a historical sketch. J. B. Lippincott.
1864	Georgia sketches.
1871	Dukesborough tales. Turnbull.
1873	English literature: a historical sketch (with W. H. Browne). Univ. pub. co.
1878	Life of Alexander H. Stephens (with W. H. Browne). J. B. Lippincott.
1881	Essays.
1884	Old Mark Langston; a tale of Duke's creek. Harper.
1885	Two gray tourists. Baltimore pub. co.
1888	Ogeechee cross-firings; a novel. Harper.
1890	Widow Guthrie. D. Appleton.
1891	The Primes and their neighbors. D. Appleton.

1891-92	Studies, literary and social (1st and 2d series). Bowen-Merrill. 2 v.
1892	Mr. Fortner's marital claims and other stories. D. Appleton.
1894	Little Ike Templin, and other stories. Lothrop.
1897	Old times in middle Georgia. Macmillan.
1898	Pearce Amerson's will. Way and Williams.
1898	Truth. Raleigh, N. C.
1900	Autobiography. W. Neale.
n.d.	Chronicles of Mr. Bill Williams. D. Appleton.

JOHNSTON, SISTER MARY FRANCIS (O.S.U.), (Stephen Morris Johnston, pseud.) **originally** Sue Mildred Lee Johnston, 1900-

Birthplace: Paris, Texas. **Conversion:** Before 1932. **Former religion:** Protestant. **Education:** Christian Coll., Columbia, Mo.; Univ. of Dallas; Catholic Univ. of America (A.B.). **General:** Sister Mary Francis has contributed a large number of short stories and some poetry to the Magnificat, Scribners, Outlook, Yale Review, and others. Before becoming a Religious the author wrote feature stories for the Dallas (Tex.) News and various ranch and farm periodicals. **Authorities:** Letter in Library of Congress. Catalog Division (clarifies author's name and pseudonym); Who's Who Among North American Authors (1933-35).

Works

1932	Ellen of the plains country: a novel of Catholic life in the great Southwest. Benziger.
1933	God's candles. (radio play)
1933	Overlord. C. Scribner.
1933	Sonny. Benziger.
1935	Girl of the Riverland. Benziger.
1937	Light shining: the life and letters of Mother Mary Joseph Dallmer, Ursuline of the Roman union. Benziger.

JOHNSTON, STEPHEN MORRIS, pseud., See Johnston, Sister Mary Francis, 1900-

JOHNSTON, SUE MILDRED LEE, See Johnston, Sister Mary Francis, 1900-

JULIANA, SISTER MARY, See Bedier, Julie, 1896-

KEASBEY, LINDLEY MILLER, 1867-

Birthplace: Newark, N. J. Conversion: ca. 1925. Former religion: Anglican, later Agnostic, etc. Education: Harvard Univ. (A.B., '88); Columbia Univ. (A.M., '89; Ph.D., '90); Kaiser Wilhelm Univ., Strassburg, Germany (R.P.D., summa cum laude, '92). General: Dr. Keasbey was professor of political science in the University of Colorado from 1892 to 1895 and at Bryn Mawr College until 1905. In that year he became professor and head of the department of political science at the University of Texas. The author retired in 1938 to Tucson, Arizona, but continues his writing for periodicals and has several books in preparation, including, "Confessio Viatoris: An Intellectual Autobiography," and Dollars and Democracy." Authorities: Letters from Dr. Keasbey, July 27, 29, 1943; American Catholic Who's Who (1942-43); American Men of Mark (1916); American Men of Science (1906); Who's Who in America (1916-17).

Works

1890 The early diplomatic history of the Nicaragua canal. Holbrook.

1896 The Nicaragua canal and the Monroe doctrine; a political history of isthmus transit. G. P. Putnam.

1899 (tr.) The economic foundations of society, by Achille Loria.

1900 The institution of society.

KENT, MICHAEL, pseud., **See** Brown, Beatrice Bradshaw

KERNAN, WILLIAM FERGUS, 1892-

Birthplace: New Orleans, La. **Conversion:** 1931. **Former religion:** Methodist. **Education:** Tulane Univ. (B.A., '12); Harvard Univ. (M.A., '16); **General:** William Kernan was teaching medieval philosophy at Harvard when the United States entered the war in 1914. He enlisted and was commissioned a second lieutenant. Rising to the rank of captain during the war he entered the Organized Reserves in 1929 and was promoted to the rank of major. From 1939-40 he taught military science and tactics at Ball High School, Galveston, Texas. In August, 1940, he was promoted to lieutenant colonel. Colonel Kernan's two latest books on the world struggle achieved a wide popularity. **Authorities:** Letter from Colonel Kernan, October 3, 1943; American Catholic Who's Who (1944-45); Current Biography (1942).

Works

1927 (tr.) The conduct of war, by Marshal Foch (published serially in The Journal of the Royal Artillery, Woolwich, Eng.).

1936 History of the 103d Field Artillery, A.E.F. State of Rhode
        Island.
1942 Defense will not win the war. Little, Brown.
1943 We can win this war. Little, Brown.

KEYES, EDWARD LAWRENCE, 1843-1924.

Birthplace: Charleston, S. C. **Conversion:** "Early in career." **Education:** Private tutoring; Yale Univ. (grad., '63); New York Univ. (M.D., '66); Studied medicine in Paris, France. **General:** Dr. Keyes, one of the best known physicians of his day and a pioneer in the treatment of social diseases, was made a Knight of St. Gregory by Pius X for his contributions to medical science. He began his career as a captain in the Federal army as a member of his father's staff. After the war and upon completion of his studies, he became an associate of Dr. William H. Van Buren in New York City. His classes in Bellevue Hospital included that of demonstrator of anatomy, and in 1870, the author delivered the first course of lectures on dermatology ever to be given on that subject in the United States. Because of the similarity in the names, he is sometimes confused with Dr. Edward Loughborough Keyes, his son. **Authorities:** American Catholic Who's Who. 1911; Dictionary of American Biography, v. 10.

Works

1874 A practical treatise on the surgical diseases of the genitourinary organs (with W. H. Van Buren). D. Appleton.
1877 The tonic treatment of syphilis. D. Appleton.
1880 The venereal diseases. W. Wood.
1890 Some fallacies concerning syphilis. G. S. Davis.
1908 Syphilis; a treatise for practitioners (with E. Loughborough Keyes). D. Appleton.

1910 The fear of death. The author.
1910 Diseases of the genito-urinary organs (with E. Loughborough Keyes). D. Appleton.
1917 Urology.

KEYES, FRANCES PARKINSON (WHEELER) 1885-

Birthplace: Univ. of Virginia (Charlottesville). **Conversion:** 1939. **Former religion:** Episcopalian. **Education:** Private schools in Boston, Geneva, and Berlin. **General:** Mrs. Keyes' professional travels have taken her to most parts of the world. From 1925 to 1926 she traveled on assignment for Good Housekeeping Magazine, and repeated the assignment from 1937 to 1939. The author edited the D. A. R. magazine for two years but left that position when she differed with the organization's policy. In 1937 she edited the National Historical Magazine, and since 1941 has been on the teaching staff of Our Lady of the Lake College, San Antonio, Texas. **Authorities:** American Catholic Who's Who (1942-43); Guide to Catholic Literature, 1888-1940; Twentieth Century Authors; Who's Who in America (1942-43); Catholic Bookman, September, 1939; Magnificat, July, 1941.

Works

1919 The old Gray homestead. Houghton, Mifflin.
1921 Career of David Noble. F. A. Stokes.
1924 Letters from a senator's wife. D. Appleton.
1930 Queen Anne's lace. H. Liveright.
1931 Lady Blanche farm. H. Liveright.
1931 Silver seas and golden cities. H. Liveright.
1933 Senator Marlowe's daughter. J. Messner.
1934 The safe bridge. J. Messner.
1935 The happy wanderer. J. Messner.

1936   Honor bright. J. Messner.
1937   Capital kaleidoscope. Harper.
1937   Pioneering people of New England. Judd & Detweiler. 47 p.
1937   Written in heaven. J. Messner.
1938   Parts unknown. J. Messner. (Ambassadress: alternate title).
1939   The great tradition. J. Messner.
1940   Along a little way. P. J. Kenedy.
1940   Bernadette, maid of Lourdes. J. Messner. (Sublime Shepherdess: alternate title).
1940   Fielding's Folly. J. Messner.
1941   All that glitters. J. Messner.
1941   Grace of Guadalupe. J. Messner.
1942   Crescent carnival. J. Messner.
1943   If ever I cease to love. London, Eyre & Spotteswood.
1944   Also the hills. J. Messner.

KILMER (ALFRED) JOYCE, 1886-1918

Birthplace: New Brunswick, N. Y. **Conversion:** 1913. **Former religion:** Episcopalian. **Education:** Rutgers (grad., '04); Columbia Univ. **General:** Joyce Kilmer condensed a varied career into a short life. He was at various times a book salesman, lexicographer, school teacher (instructor in Latin, Morristown, N. J., High School), poet, critic, book reviewer, literary editor (The Churchman), poetry editor (Literary Digest), and finally, soldier. The author, who is credited with making a considerable contribution to the Catholic literary revival in America, died on the battlefields of France at the age of thirty-two. **Authorities:** Dictionary of American Biography, v. 10; Guide to Catholic Literature, 1888-1940; Twentieth Century Authors; Alexander, C.: Catholic Literary Revival; Bregy, Katherine: Poets and Pilgrims. 1925; Campion Coll. of the Sacred Heart: Kilmer and Campion. 1937; Kilmer, A. J.: Leaves

From My Life. 1925; Kilmer, Annie: Memories of My Son, Sergeant Joyce Kilmer. 1920.

Works

1911 Summer of love. Baker & Taylor.
1914 Trees, and other poems. G. H. Doran.
1916 The circus; and other essays. L. J. Gomme.
1917 (ed.) Dreams and images; an anthology of Catholic poets. Boni and Liveright.
1917 Main street, and other poems. G. H. Doran.
1917 (comp.) Literature in the making, by some of its makers. Harper.
1918 Joyce Kilmer; edited with a memoir by Robert Cortes Holliday. G. H. Doran. 2 v.
1925 Leaves from my life. Frye.
n.d. Contemporary drama (with J. J. Daly).

KILMER, ALINE (MURRAY) 1888-1941

Birthplace: Norfolk, Va. **Conversion:** 1913. **Education:** Rutgers Prep. School, New Brunswick, N. Y.; Vail-Deane School, Elizabeth, N. J. **General:** The author was the wife of Joyce Kilmer (q.v.). After his death in 1918 she lectured for many years on poetry and literature and contributed occasionally to periodical literature. **Authorities:** American Catholic Who's Who (1940-41); Current Biography (1941); Who's Who in America (1940-41); Catholic World, July, 1924; Guide to Catholic Literature, 1888-1940.

Works

1919 Candles that burn. G. H. Doran.
1921 Vigils. G. H. Doran.
1923 Hunting a hairshirt, and other spiritual adventures. G. H. Doran.

1925 The poor king's daughter, and other poems. G. H. Doran.
1927 Emmy, Nicky and Greg. G. H. Doran.
1929 Buttonwood summer. Doubleday, Doran.
1929 Selected poems. Doubleday, Doran.

KINSMAN, FREDERICK JOSEPH, 1868-

Birthplace: Warren, O. **Conversion:** 1919. **Former religion:** Protestant Episcopal (minister, 1896-1908; bishop, 1908-1919) **Education:** St. Paul's school, Concord, N. H.; Oxford Univ. (grad., '87); Keble Coll., Oxford, Eng., (grad., '94); Oxford Univ. (B.A., '94; M.A., '99; D.D., '11); Berkeley Divinity School, Conn. (S.T.D., '09); Washington Coll. (LL.D., '12). **General:** Dr. Kinsman was Master of St. Paul's school from 1895-97 and in that year became rector of St. Martin's church, New Bedford, Mass. where he remained until 1900. He then spent eight years in teaching church history, first at Berkeley Divinity School and later at General Theological Seminary. He became Bishop of Delaware in 1908 and resigned in 1919 to enter the Catholic Church. **Authorities:** American Catholic Who's Who (1942-43); Guide to Catholic Literature, 1888-1940; Who's Who in America (1932-33); America, September 6, 1919.

Works

1910 Principles of Anglicanism. Longmans, Green.
1913 Catholic and Protestant. Longmans, Green.
1915 Prayers for the dead. Young churchman. 31 p.
1920 Salve mater. Longmans, Green.
1921 Trent; four lectures on practical aspects of the Council of Trent. Longmans, Green.
1924 Americanism and Catholicism. Longmans, Green.
1936 Reveries of a hermit. Longmans, Green.

KITE, ELIZABETH SARAH, 1864-

Birthplace: Philadelphia, Pa. **Conversion:** 1906. **Former religion:** Quaker. **Education:** In Paris, London and Germany. **General:** After teaching in California and Massachusetts schools, Miss Kite was a field investigator in the study of mental degeneracy from 1909 to 1918. Since 1921 she has been engaged in historical research in the Library of Congress Manuscript Division. In 1932 she became Archivist of the American Catholic Historical Society. Her work in Franco-American history was applauded by the French in 1908 when she was awarded the *Secour Aux Blesses*. Later (1933) Miss Kite was made a *Chevalier de le Legion d'Honneur*. **Authorities:** American Catholic Who's Who (1942-43); Guide to Catholic Literature, 1888-1940.

Works

1916 (tr.) The development of intelligence in children, by Alfred Binet and Th. Simon. Williams and Wilkins.

1916 (tr.) The intelligence of the feebleminded, by Alfred Binet and Th. Simon. Williams and Wilkins.

1918 Beaumarchais and the war of American independence. R. G. Badger. 2 v.

1929 L'Enfant and Washington, 1791-1792. Johns Hopkins press.

1931 Correspondence of General Washington and Comte de Grasse.

1933 Brigadier General Louis Lebegue Duportail, commandant of engineers in the Continental army, 1777-1883. Johns Hopkins press.

1934 Lafayette and his companions on the "Victoire." American Catholic Historical society. (Reprint in parts)

1936 Catholic part in the making of America, Part I, 1565-1850. Dolphin.

KOBBE, CAROLYN THERESE (WHEELER) 1862-

Conversion: 1932. **General:** Mrs Kobbe was attached to no particular creed, but studied Spiritism, Christian Science, Theosophy, and the tenets of Calvin and Luther before embracing Catholicism. She spent considerable time in European travel. **Authorities:** Letter from Mrs. Kobbe, September, 1943; Kobbe, C. T.: My Spiritual Pilgrimage. 1935.

Works

1935 My spiritual pilgrimage; an attempt to help those who want to find peace and happiness in this changing world. Devin-Adair.

LANDRETH, HELEN

Conversion: 1939. **General:** Miss Landreth is an American residing in Ireland. **Consult:** Guide to Catholic Literature, 1888-1940.

Works

1936 Dear dark head; an intimate story of Ireland. McGraw-Hill.

LANE, JAMES WARREN, 1898-

Birthplace: Bay Ridge, Brooklyn, N. Y. **Conversion:** 1931. **Former religion:** Protestant Episcopal. **Education:** Yale Univ. (A.B., '21); Harvard Univ. (M.A., '26). **General:** As a student Mr. Lane edited the Yale Literary Magazine and has continued ever since as a journalist and free lance writer. Since 1927 he has been editor of the Author's League Bulletin, and in 1934 was art critic on Parnassus. **Authorities:** American Catholic Who's Who (1942-43).

1937 Masters in modern art. Chapman and Grimes.
1937 The work of Georgia O'Keefe, a portfolio of twelve paintings with an introduction by James W. Lane and an appreciation by Leo Katz. Knight & Millet.
1942 Whistler. Crown publishers.

LARSSON, RAYMOND ELLSWORTH, 1901-

Birthplace: Green Bay, Wis. **Former religion:** Lutheran. **Education:** East High School, Green Bay. **General:** Mr. Larsson began his career as a journalist on midwestern and eastern newspapers. After two years of travel and study in Europe he founded and edited the literary magazines, Tempo, of Danvers, Mass. (1921) and Prairie, of Chicago. He is the founder of the Society of St. Jude in Jesus Christ. **Authorities:** American Catholic Who's Who (1942-43); Guide to Catholic Literature, 1888-1940.

Works

1929 O city, cities! Payson & Clarke.
1932 Wherefore. Peace.
1933 Sheaf. Modern editions press.
1937 (comp.) Poetry out of Wisconsin (with others). H. Harrison.
1940 Weep and prepare; selected poems, 1926-1939. Coward-McCann.
1941 Perfect vessel.
1942 (ed.) Saints at prayer. Coward-McCann.

LATHROP, GEORGE PARSONS, 1851-1898

Birthplace: Near Honolulu, of American parents. **Conversion:** 1891. **Former religion:** Unitarian. **Education:** Private schools in New York City; Dresden, Germany (1867-70); Columbia Law School (1870). **General:** Besides writing numerous books, Lathrop was assistant editor of the Atlantic Monthly from 1875 to 1877 and later (1877-79) editor of the Boston Courier. He was one of the founders of the American Copyright League. After his death Mrs. Lathrop became Mother Alphonsa (q.v.) famous for her work with cancer patients. **Authorities:** American Authors, 1600-1900; Catholic Encyclopedia, v. 16; Dictionary of American Biography, v. 11; Guide to Catholic Literature, 1888-1940; Theatre, December 12, 1887.

Works

1875	Rose and roof-tree. J. R. Osgood.
1876	A study of Hawthorne. J. R. Osgood.
1877	Afterglow. W. F. Roberts.
1878	A masque of poets, including Guy Vernon, a novelette in verse. W. F. Roberts.
1878	Somebody else. W. F. Roberts.
1881	Spanish vistas. Harper.
1882	An echo of passion. H. O. Houghton.
1882	In the distance. J. R. Osgood.
1884	History of the Union League of Philadelphia. J. B. Lippincott.
1884	Newport. C. Scribner.
1884	True, and other stories. Funk & Wagnall.
1886	"Behind time." Cassell.
1887	Elaine, by Alfred Tennyson, dramatized (with Henry Edwards).
1887-88	(ed.) The complete works of Nathaniel Hawthorne. Houghton Mifflin. 12 v.
1888	Along the shore. Ticknor.
1888	Gettysburg: a battle ode. C. Scribner. 18 p.
1889	Two sides of a story, and other stories. Cassell.
1890	Would you kill him? Harper.
1892	Dreams and days, poems. C. Scribner.

1894 A story of courage; annals of the Georgetown convent of the Visitation of the B. V. M. (with Mrs. Lathrop). Riverside press.

1896 The scarlet letter; a dramatic composition . . . music by Walter Damrosch. Transatlantic pub. co.

LATHROP, MOTHER MARY ALPHONSA (HAWTHORNE) 1851-1926

Birthplace: Lenox, Mass. **Conversion:** 1891. **Former religion:** Her husband, G. P. Lathrop (q.v.) was a Unitarian. **Education:** No formal education but private schools in a cultured background. **General:** The author was the last surviving daughter of Nathaniel Hawthorne. She traveled widely in Europe and after her marriage became interested in the welfare of the victims of incurable cancer. Her literary work ceased when it was crowded out by her newfound mission of mercy. After Lathrop's death she devoted herself, as Mother Alphonsa, exclusively to the work, being aided by the Third Order of St. Dominic, which was formed to assist her. **Authorities:** Dictionary of American Biography, v. 1; Guide to Catholic Literature, 1888-1940; Burton, Katherine: Sorrow Built a Bridge. 1937; Driscoll, A. S.: Literary Convert Women. 1928; Walsh, J. J.: Mother Alphonsa. 1930

Works

1888 Along the shore. Ticknor.

1888 Poems.

1895 A story of courage; annals of the Georgetown convent of the Visitation of the B. V. M. (with G. P. Lathrop). Riverside press.

1897 Memories of Hawthorne. Houghton, Mifflin.

LATHROP, ROSE (HAWTHORNE) "Mrs George Parsons" **See** Lathrop, Mother Mary Alphonsa (Hawthorne) 1851-1926

LAWRENCE, RAYMOND P., father, 1886-
Birthplace: Skaneateles, N. Y. **Conversion:** 1912. **Former religion:** Presbyterian; later Episcopalian. **Ordained priest:** 1917. **Education:** Columbia Univ. (grad., '10); St. Bernard's (Cath.) Sem., Rochester, N. Y. **General:** Father Lawrence is pastor of St. Mary's Church, Clinton, N. Y. He is also spiritual director of Catholic students at Hamilton Coll., and auxiliary chaplain to the military personnel on the Hamilton campus. **Authorities:** Letter from Father Lawrence, October 30, 1943; Guide to Catholic Literature, 1888-1940.

Works

1920   Journey home. Ave Maria press.

LEARNED, ELLIN CRAVEN, "Mrs. Frank Learned," 1850-1940
Birthplace: New Jersey. **Conversion:** 1927. **Education:** Private schools in New York City. **General:** Mrs. Learned was deeply interested in the problems of young women and maintained contact with them by correspondence conducted through such periodicals as the Delineator, Ladies World, etc. From 1904-05 she was editor of the Girls Friendly Magazine and previously (1890-94; 1896-99) was on the staff of the Churchman. The author sponsored the

133

third ship (U.S.S. Craven) to be named in honor of her father, Captain Tunis A. M. Craven, U.S.N., who went down with his vessel in the battle of Mobile Bay, August 5, 1864. **Authorities:** Letter from Mother M. Teresa, Parish Visitors of Mary Immaculate, July 31, 1943; Guide to Catholic Literature, 1888-1940; Who Was Who (1897-1942); Who's Who Among North American Authors (1933-35); Learned, E. C.: Finding the Way. 1940; The Catholic News, February 13, 1937.

Works

1905 Ideals for girls; talks on character, life and culture, by Mrs. Frank Learned (Pricilla Wakefield).
1906 The etiquette of New York today. F. A. Stokes.
1923 Everybody's complete etiquette. F. A. Stokes.
1940 Finding the way. Parish visitors of Mary Immaculate press.

LEE, ELIZABETH LAURA, pseud., See Battle, Jesse Mercer

LEMKE (PETER) HENRY, 1796-1882
Birthplace: Rhena, Mecklenburg. **Came to U. S.:** 1834 **Conversion:** 1824. **Former religion:** Protestant (minister) **Ordained priest:** 1826. **General:** Father Lemke came to the United States as a missionary in 1834 and shortly thereafter was sent as an assistant to the aging Father Gallitzin (q.v.) at Loretto, Pa. He laid out a town nearby and called it Carrolltown after the first U. S. Catholic bishop. Later he brought the Benedictines to the United States and joined that community. He died at Carrolltown. **Authorities:** Cath-

olic Encyclopedia, v. 9; Guide to Catholic Literature, 1888-1940; Ave Maria (in six parts) 1883, v. 19.

Works

1861 Leben und Wirken des Prinzen Demetrius Augustin von Gallitzen. Münster. (A translation of this work, by Joseph C. Plumpe and published by Longmans, Green, appeared in 1940)

LEVY, ROSALIE MARIE, 1889-

Birthplace: Delhi, La. **Conversion:** 1912. **Former religion:** Judaism. **Education:** Gonzaga Coll. (1918-19); Fordham Univ. (1935) **General:** From 1909-23 Miss Levy held a secretarial position, later becoming an illustrator and lecturer. **Authorities:** American Catholic Who's Who (1942-43); Guide to Catholic Literature, 1888-1940; Driscoll, A. S.: Literary Convert Women. 1928; Levy, R. M.: Thirty years with Christ. 1943.

Works

1919 The heavenly road. Baltimore City ptg. & bdg. co.
1924 (ed.) Why Jews become Catholics; authentic narratives. The editor.
1926-35 (comp.) Heart talks with Jesus. (Five series). The compiler.
1927 Judaism and Catholicism. The author.
1930 (comp.) Heart talks with Mary. N. Y. The compiler.
1940 (ed.) Stepping stones to sanctity. N. Y. The editor.
1943 Thirty years with Christ. The author.

LOGAN, JOHN DANIEL, 1869-1929

Birthplace: Canada. **Came to U. S.:** ca. 1926. **Conver-**

sion: 1918. **Education:** Harvard Graduate School. **General:** Mr. Logan was on the faculty of Marquette University at the time of his death. **Authorities:** Guide to Catholic Literature, 1888-1940.

Works

1900   The structural principles of style applied. A manual of English prose composition. Wiley & Danforth.

1923?   (ed.) Thomas Chandler Haliburton, by John Daniel Logan. Ryerson.

1924   Highways of Canadian literature; a synoptic introduction to the literary history of Canada (English) from 1760-1924 (with D. G. French) McClelland & Stewart.

1926   A literary chameleon; a new estimate of Mr. H. L. Mencken. Milwaukee, Privately printed. 22 p.

n.d.   Mater coronata.

LOOMIS, JAMES, pseud., **See** Small, James Loomis, 1878-

LORD, ROBERT HOWARD, father, 1885-

Birthplace: Plano, Illinois. **Conversion:** 1926. **Former religion:** Protestant Episcopal. **Ordained priest:** 1929. **Education:** Northwestern Univ.; Harvard Univ. (A.B., '06; A.M., '07; Ph.D., '10); Studied at Universities of Vienna, Berlin and Moscow; St. John's Sem., Brighton, Mass. (1926-29) **General:** Father Lord began his teaching career at Harvard in 1910 as instructor in history, and advanced to full professor in 1924. Since 1930 he has been professor of church history at St. John's Seminary. **Authorities:** American Catholic Who's Who (1942-43); Guide to Catholic Literature, 1888-1940; Who's Who in America (1926-27).

1915 The second partition of Poland; a study in diplomatic history. Harvard univ. press.

1920 Some problems of the Peace Conference (with Charles Homer Haskins). Harvard univ. press.

1924 Origins of the war of 1870, new documents from the German archives. Harvard univ. press.

1932 Archibald Cary Coolidge, life and letters (with Harold Jefferson Coolidge). Houghton, Mifflin.

LUSKA, SIDNEY, pseud., **See Harland, Henry, 1861-1905**

LYNN, JEANNETTE (MURPHY) 1905-

Birthplace: Boulder, Mont. **Former religion:** Congregationalist. **Education:** Tabor College, Iowa (B.A., '26); Univ. of Wisconsin (Cert. in Library Science); Univ. of Chicago (M.A., '35) **General:** Mrs. Lynn has made a career of the library profession since 1926. She contributes occasionally to professional reviews and since 1939 has been special cataloger in the Joint University Libraries, Nashville, Tenn. **Authorities:** American Catholic Who's Who (1942-43); Guide to Catholic Literature, 1888-1940; Who's Who in Library Service. 1933.

1937 (comp.) An alternative classification for Catholic books; a scheme for Catholic theology, canon law and church history, to be used with the Dewey decimal, Classification decimal, or Library of Congress classifications . . . Bruce; American Library ass'n.

McGARVEY, WILLIAM, father, 1861-1924

Birthplace: Philadelphia, Pa. **Conversion:** 1908. **Former religion:** Protestant Episcopal (minister, 1886-1908). **Ordained priest:** 1911. **Education:** General Theological Sem., N. Y. C. (B.D., '87); Nashotah (Epis.) Sem. (D.D., '99); St. Charles (Cath.) Sem., Overbrook, Pa. (1908-09). **General:** William McGarvey, as the leader of the Anglo-Catholic (Anglican) party and "master" of a religious community of fifty clergymen, created a ferment in the whole P. E. church in his efforts to keep "heretics" out of Episcopalian pulpits. Twenty of the ministers under his jurisdiction and influence entered the Church and sixteen became priests. At the time of his conversion Father McGarvey was compared with Newman because he came in on an issue—the issue of Modernism. He ranks with Ives, Brownson and Hecker among the great converts to the Church in America. **Authorities:** Letters from Monsignor Edward Hawks, August 7, 27, 1943; Guide to Catholic Literature, 1888-1940; Who's Who in America (1920-21); Hawks, Edward: William McGarvey and the Open Pulpit. 1935; Hayward, W. L.: The C.S.S.S.; the Quest and Goal of the Founder. 1940; Hayward, W. L.: Pro-Roman Movement in the United States (The Life of William McGarvey). 1940.

Works

1891 The ceremonies of low celebration.
1893 Catechetical instruction.
1894 The Council of Nicaea.
1895 Liturgica Americanae. E. S. Gorham.
1900 The doctrine of the Church of England on the Real Presence.
1905 Ceremonies of the Mass (with C. P. A. Burnett). Longmans, Green.

MacGILL, CAROLINE ELIZABETH

Birthplace: Resident of Cambridge, Mass. General: An occasional contributor of short stories to periodicals. Authorities: Guide to Catholic Literature, 1888-1940.

Works

1917 History of transportation in the United States before 1860, ed. by B. H. Meyer and prepared by Caroline E. MacGill and a staff of collaborators. Carnegie institution.
1925 This country of mine; a book for young Americans. Loyola univ. press.

MACKIN, SARAH MARIA ALOISA (BRITTON) SPOTTISWOOD, 1850-1923

Birthplace: Troy, Mo. Conversion: 1894. Education: Nazareth Acad., Bardstown, Ky. (grad., '67); Mrs. McCauley's school (N. Y.). General: Mrs. Mackin's great-grandfather commanded the man-of-war Tempest in the American Revolution and her father was James H. Britton, sometime mayor of St. Louis. Her many charities caused Pope Leo XIII to create her a Papal Countess. Authorities: American Catholic Who's Who. 1911; Guide to Catholic Literature, 1888-1940.

Works

1896 A society woman on two continents. Transatlantic pub. co.
n.d. From Rome to Lourdes. Colliers.

MACKINTOSH, HUGH FRASER, 1862-

Birthplace: Hamilton, Ontario. Conversion: 1883. Education: In the local schools of Guelph, Ontario. General:

Mr. Mackintosh, one of the founders and sometime editor of the Catholic Weekly Review, Toronto, was also on the editorial staff of the Catholic Record of London, Ontario, He has contributed to Walsh's Magazine, Toronto, Century, and the Records of the American Catholic Historical Society. **Authorities:** American Catholic Who's Who. 1911.

Works

1888 Life of Father Louis della Vagna, Capuchin. Toronto.
1892 Life of Bishop Power, first bishop of Toronto (in memorial volume, archdiocese of Toronto).
n.d. Life of Bishop Macdonnell, first bishop of Kingston.

MacLEAN, WILLIAM MICHAEL STANLEY MOORE, 1909-

Birthplace: Detroit. **Conversion:** 1933. **Former religion:** Presbyterian. **Education:** Coll. of the City of Detroit (A.B., '31); Wayne Univ. (A.M., '34). **General:** Mr. MacLean has been a clinical psychiatrist in the Detroit public schools since 1934. **Authorities:** American Catholic Who's Who (1942-43); Guide to Catholic Literature, 1888-1940.

Works

1938 (comp.) Notable personages of Polish ancestry. Unique press.
1943 Language and its relation to the individual. (in preparation)

MacLEOD, XAVIER DONALD, father, 1821-1865

Birthplace: New York City. **Conversion:** 1853? **Former**

religion: Protestant Episcopal (minister, 1845-) **Ordained priest:** 1861. **Education:** Columbia Coll. (Univ.) N. Y. C. **General:** After his ordination Father MacLeod was a professor at Mt. St. Mary's Seminary, and contributed to periodicals, including the Knickerbocker magazine. He was killed by a train while en route to the bedside of a dying person. **Authorities:** Appleton's Cyclopaedia of American Biography, v. 4; Shea, J. G.: History of the Catholic Church in the U. S., v. 4. (Short reference); Guide to Catholic Literature, 1888-1940.

Works

1841 Plasmion, a poem, delivered before the Philomathean and Eucleian societies of the University of the city of New York, July 13, 1841. Press of Piercy & Reed. 20 p.

1852 The life of Sir Walter Scott. C. Scribner.

1852 Pynnshurst; his wanderings and ways of thinking. C. Scribner.

1853 The bloodstone. C. Scribner.

1856 Biography of Hon. Fernando Wood, mayor of the city of New-York. O. F. Parsons.

1857 The life of Mary, queen of Scots. Sadlier.

1861 Our Lady of Litanies. J. P. Walsh.

1866 Devotion to the Blessed Virgin Mary in North America. Virtue & Yorston. (Appeared earlier (1861) in Orsini, Mathieu. Life of the Blessed Virgin Mary).

MacNUTT, FRANCIS AUGUSTUS, 1863-1927

Birthplace: Richmond, Ind. **Conversion:** 1883. **Education:** Exeter; Harvard Univ. **General:** MacNutt was in the diplomatic service during the Harrison administration, serving as Secretary to the U. S. legations at Constantinople and Madrid. He spent many years in Rome where his personal chronicle, "Papal Chamberlain," was written. The work was intended originally for private circulation only. **Authorities:** Guide to Catholic Literature, 1888-1940; MacNutt, F. A.: Papal chamberlain. 1936.

Works

1908   The letters (of) Hernando Cortez (translated and edited by F. A. MacNutt). G. P. Putnam. 2 v.

1912   De orbe novo (by) Martyr d' Anghiera (translated by F. A. MacNutt). A. H. Clarke.

1919   Bartholomew de las Casas: his life, his apostolate and his writings. G. P. Putnam.

1936   Papal chamberlain; ed. by J. J. Donovan. Longmans, Green.

(The author also wrote the following plays: Balboa; Easter; Macedonia; Only Fanny; The smiling cavalier; The victorious duchess; Xilona)

MAGARET, HELENE, 1906-

Birthplace: Omaha, Nebr. **Conversion:** 1942. **Former religion:** Protestant; attached to no denomination; held attitude of "suspended judgment." **Education:** Barnard Coll. (A.B., '32); State Univ. of Iowa (M.A., '38; Ph.D., '40). **General:** Miss Magaret held positions as a Spanish translator with various commercial firms in Omaha before beginning her college education. In 1932 she was awarded the Mariana Griswold Van Rensselaer Poetry Prize from Columbia University and later (1938) received an A.A.U.W. Fellowship of $1500 to write the life of Father De Smet. Besides contributing to poetry anthologies, the author has written for various periodicals, including Poetry World, New Masses and Commonweal. She is now (1943) working on a novel to be brought out by Bruce, publishers, while continuing as professor of English at the College of Saint Teresa, Winona, Minn. **Authorities:** Letter from Miss Magaret, July 31, 1943; Book of Catholic Authors. 1st ser.; Who's Who in America (1942-43); American Catholic Who's Who (1944-45).

Works

1934 The trumpeting crane. Farrar & Rinehart.
1937 The great horse; a narrative poem. Farrar & Rinehart.
1940 Father De Smet; pioneer priest of the Rockies. Farrar & Rinehart.
1941 Change of season. Farrar & Rinehart.

MAHAN, BRUCE ELLIS, 1890-

Birthplace: Bedford, Ia. **Conversion:** 1913. **Former religion:** Baptist. **Education:** State Univ. of Iowa (A.B., '14; Ph.D., '27). **General:** Since 1929 Mr. Mahan has been Director of the Extension Division of the State Univ. of Iowa. Besides writing historical reviews, he collaborated in the "Dictionary of American Biography." **Authorities:** Letter from Mr. Mahan, July, 1943; American Catholic Who's Who (1942-43); Guide to Catholic Literature, 1888-1940; Who's Who in America (1942-43).

Works

1924 State and local history in the high school. State historical society of Ia.
1926 Old Fort Crawford and the frontier. State historical society of Ia.
1927 The pioneers; a pageant of early Iowa. State historical society of Ia.

1928　The story of the Indian, a pageant of early Iowa. State historical society of Ia.

1929　Stories of Iowa for boys and girls (with R. A. Gallagher). Macmillan.

MAIRE, FREDERICK

Birthplace: Altkirk, Alsace. **Conversion:** 1887. **Education:** Government schools and colleges of France. **General:** As an instructor in the decorative art, Mr. Maire was an expert in color factories. Besides his numerous manuals he contributed to Painting and Decorating; the Modern Painter; and other professional journals. From 1887-88 he edited House Painting and Decorating; a Journal Devoted to the House Painter and the Decorator. **Authorities:** American Catholic Who's Who. 1911.

Works

1901　The modern wood finisher; a practical treatise on wood finishing in all its branches. Press of the western painter.

1908　Modern pigments and their vehicles. J. Wiley.

1910　Colors, what they are and what to expect of them. F. J. Drake.

1910　Exterior painting; a series of practical treatises on materials, tools and appliances used. F. J. Drake.

1910　Modern painter's cyclopedia. F. J. Drake.

1911　Carriage painting; a series of practical treatises on the painting of carriages and wagons. F. J. Drake.

1911　Wood finisher; a series of practical treatises on hardwood finishing. F. J. Drake.

MARIE, JOSEPHINE, pseud., See Hemenway, Abby Maria, 1828-1890

144

MARTIN, ELIZABETH GILBERT (DAVIS) (Lewis Dorsay, pseud.)

Birthplace: Albany, N. Y. **Conversion:** 1870. **Education:** Albany Female Acad. and Normal School. **General:** As the wife of Homer Martin, the painter, the author spent several years writing and assisting her husband in France and England. Besides being a frequent contributor to The Nation, Mrs. Martin translated fifteen of the books of Imbert de Saint-Amand, two of which are listed below. These translations, mainly French history and biography, were published by Charles Scribner between the years 1891 and 1915. **Authorities:** American Catholic Who's Who. 1911; Guide to Catholic Literature, 1888-1940.

Works

1886 Whom God hath joined. A novel. H. Holt.
1890 John Van Alstyne's factory.
1891 (tr.) Marie Antoinette and the downfall of royalty, by Imbert de Saint-Amand. C. Scribner.
1904 Homer Martin: a reminiscence, October 28, 1836—February 12, 1897. W. Macbeth.
1905 (tr.) The dollar hunt. From the French. Benziger.
1915 (tr.) The youth of the Duchess of Angouleme, by Imbert de Saint-Amand. C. Scribner.

MASON, EMILY VIRGINIA, 1815-1909

Birthplace: Lexington, Ky. **Education:** Troy (N. Y.) Female Acad. **General:** Miss Mason will be chiefly remembered for her work in Confederate hospitals during the Civil War. She wrote her "Southern Poems of the War" for the purpose of obtaining money to educate the orphan daughters of Confederate soldiers. After achieving success in this endeavor she spent fifteen years in France as assistant principal of an American school for young women. **Authorities:** Appleton's Cyclopaedia of American Biography, v. 4; Young, Alfred: Catholic and Protestant Countries Compared. 1903 (Reference only).

Works

1867   The Southern poems of the war. J. Murphy.
1871   (ed.) Journal of a young lady of Virginia in 1782. J. Murphy.
1872   Life of Gen. Robert Edward Lee. J. Murphy.

MAYNARD, THEODORE, 1890-

Birthplace: Madras, India. **Came to U. S.:** 1920. **Conversion:** 1913. **Former religion:** Congregationalist. **Education:** Studied for the ministry; Fordham Univ. (A.B.); Georgetown (M.A.); Catholic Univ. of America (Ph.D.) **General:** Before his conversion, Theodore Maynard was a minister for a short period, holding a pulpit during a visit to the United States in 1910. After his conversion he considered becoming a Religious but a seven months trial caused him to reconsider in favor of a writing career. After establishing residence in the United States, Mr. Maynard reversed the usual procedure by becoming a college professor before he secured his academic degrees. The author's thorough Catholicism and Americanism is abundantly evident in his "Story of American Catholicism." **Authorities:** American Catholic Who's Who (1942-43); Book of Catholic Authors, 1st ser.; Guide to Catholic Literature, 1888-1940; Maynard, Theodore: The World I Saw. 1938.

1915 Laughs and whiffs of song.
1917 Drums of defeat, and other poems. E. MacDonald.
1918 Folly.
1919 Carven from the laurel tree; essays. McBride.
1919 Poems. Frederick A. Stokes.
1919 A tankard of ale, an anthology of drinking songs. E. Mac-
  Donald.
1921 The divine adventure; a novel. F. A. Stokes.
1921 The last knight, and other poems. F. A. Stokes.
1922 Our best poets, English and American. H. Holt.
1926 (comp.) The book of modern Catholic verse. H. Holt.
1928 (comp.) The book of modern Catholic prose. H. Holt.
1928 Exile, and other poems. Dial press.
1930 De Soto and the conquistadores. Longmans, Green.
1933 Preface to poetry. Century.
1934 The connection between the ballade, Chaucer's modifica-
  tion of it, rime royal, and the Spenserian stanza. Catholic
  univ. of America.
1936 Man and beast. Longmans, Green.
1936 The odyssey of Francis Xavier. Longmans, Green.
1938 The world I saw. Bruce.
1939 Apostle of charity; the life of St. Vincent de Paul. Dial
  press.
1940 Queen Elizabeth. Bruce.
1941 Not even death; a book of poems. St. Anthony guild.
1941 The story of American Catholicism. Macmillan.
1942 The reed and the rock, portrait of Simon Bruté. Longmans,
  Green.
1943 Orestes Brownson. Macmillan.

MERCEDES, pseud., See Gallagher, Sister Mary Antonio,
1846-1916

MERRILL, WILLIAM STETSON, 1866-1942
Birthplace: Newton, Mass. **Conversion:** 1892. **Former**

religion: Swedenborgian; later, "rationalist." **Education:** Harvard (A.B.) **General:** Mr. Merrill was assistant librarian of the Harvard University Library from 1884 to 1888, leaving that position to join the staff of the Newberry Library of Chicago, where he remained until 1930. He edited, with T. E. Judge, the short-lived Catholic Review of Reviews, in 1904. From 1913 to 1931 he edited the "American Library Association Periodical Index." Besides contributing to the professional journals, the author collaborated in the "Catholic Builders of the Nation." **Authorities:** American Catholic Who's Who (1911; 1942-43); Curtis, G. P.: Beyond the Road to Rome. 1914; Curtis, G. P.: Some Roads to Rome in America. 1909; Who's Who in Library Service. 1933; Guide to Catholic Literature, 1888-1940.

Works

1891 (comp.) Index to publications. 1879-1889. (Compiled for the Archaeological institute of America). J. Wilson.
1928 Code for classifiers, principles governing the consistent placing of books in a system of classification. American library association. (This is a revision of the original work published in 1914).

MILES, GEORGE HENRY, 1824-1871

Birthplace: Baltimore, Md. **Conversion:** ca. 1840 **Former religion:** His maternal grandmother, Jewish; father, English. **Education:** Mt. St. Mary's Coll., Md. (A.B., '43) **General:** Miles began his career with the practice of law but in 1851 accepted a position as professor of English in Mt. St. Mary's College. He taught there continuously (except for the years, 1863-65) devoting his leisure time to the writing craft until his death. His success as a dramatist was

148

achieved early when "Mohammed, the Arabian Prophet" won a $1,000 award offered by the actor, Edwin Forest for the best original play in five acts. All of Miles' literary work is permeated by a deep religious spirit. **Authorities:** American Authors, 1600-1900; Catholic Encyclopedia, v. 10; Dictionary of American Biography, v. 12; Guide to Catholic Literature, 1888-1940; Boyle, E.: Biographical Sketches of Distinguished Marylanders; Quinn, A. H.: History of the American Drama from the Beginning to the Civil War. 1912.

Works

1844   Michael di Lando: Gonfalconier of Florence.
1847   Discourse in commemoration of the landing of the Pilgrims of Maryland. Emmetsburg, Printed at the "Star office." 39 p.
1850   Loretto; or, The choice. (10th ed. published by Kelly, Hedian and Piet. 1859).
1850   Mohammed, the Arabian prophet. Phillips, Sampson.
1851   The governess; or, The effects of good example. Hedian & O'Brien.
1852   Hernando de Soto.
1857   Mary's birthday; or, The cynic. W. V. Spencer. 36 p.
1859   Señor Valiente; a comedy. H. Taylor.
1860   Seven sisters.
1866   Christine, a troubadour's song, and other poems. L. Kehoe.
1868   Abou Hassan, the Wag; or, The sleeper awakened; an extravaganze. J. T. Ford.
1870   A review of Hamlet. Kelly, Piet. 43 p.
1871   The truce of God . . . a tale of the eleventh century. J. Murphy.
1907   Said the rose, and other lyrics. Longmans, Green.

MILLAR, MOORHOUSE FRANCIS XAVIER, father (S.J.) 1886-
Birthplace: Mobile, Ala. **Conversion:** 1897. Ordained

priest: 1919. **Education:** In Europe and later at Loyola Coll., Baltimore. **General:** Father Millar has taught in various American Jesuit colleges on the Atlantic seaboard. At present (1943) he is on the Editorial Advisory Board (philosophy, sociology and government) of Thought, Fordham University Quarterly. **Authorities:** Guide to Catholic Literature, 1888-1940.

Works

1922 The state and the church (with John A. Ryan). Macmillan.
1928 Unpopular essays in the philosophy of history. Fordham univ. press.

MILLS, PHILO LAOS, father, 1870-

Birthplace: Hartford, Conn. **Conversion:** 1890. **Former religion:** Protestant Episcopal. **Education:** Early study in schools of Naples and Rome; also in Stuttgart; Royal Gymnasia, Hanover (Germany); Magdalen Coll., Oxford (grad.); theological studies completed at Catholic Univ. of America; holds the degrees, S.T.D., M.A.O.S., and is an Honorary Lecturer of the Royal Asiatic Soc. of Bombay. **General:** Father Mills is the son of an Anglican minister and Oriental scholar. After his conversion in Ghent, Belgium, he was employed in a locomotive works in England until his return to the United States in 1900. The author then began his studies for the priesthood, and was ordained by Cardinal Gibbons. It was while engaged in parish duties in Washington (1912-21) that he wrote his monumental work, "Prehistoric Religion," for which he received a Papal Doctorate and permission to live as a hermit, in order to further his work as a Bible scholar under ideal conditions. He built the hermitage, "Mausoleum of the Magi," near Catholic University, and gave numerous lectures, drawing upon data gathered on a two-year trip to India for his work, "Asiatic Arcadia." Father Mills has been engaged for several years on a new work, "Athanasia, Life Eternal." **Authorities:** Letter from Mr. John J. Cavanogh, Jr., Washington, D. C., November 26, 1943; Guide to Catholic Literature, 1888-1940.

Works

1919   Prehistoric religion: a study in pre-Christian antiquity. Capital publishing co.
1923   Psychology of the superconscious. The author.
1931   Asiatic Arcadia; or, Lost paradise. Bengalese press.
1933   Adamanta. Bengalese press.

MITCHELL, JOHN, 1870-1919

Birthplace: Braidwood, Ill. **Conversion:** 1907. **Former religion:** Presbyterian. **Education:** A few weeks a season in the district school; studied law for one year. **General:** Orphaned at six and working in the coal mines three years later, John Mitchell rose to become president of the American Mine Workers and next to Samuel Gompers in power in the American Federation of Labor. His coolness in controversy caused Theodore Roosevelt to say of him on one occasion, "There was only one man in the room that behaved like a gentleman and that man was not I." **Authorities:** American Catholic Who's Who. 1911; Dictionary of American Biography, v. 13; Encyclopedia of Social Sciences, v. 10; Who's Who in America (1918-19); Gluck, E.: John Mitchell, Miner—Labor's Bargain With the Gilded

Age. 1929 (Contains complete bibliography); Independent, December 25, 1902; Outlook, March 24, 1906.

Works

1903 Organized labor; its problems, purposes and ideals and the present and future of American wage earners. American book and Bible house.
1913 The wage earner and his problems. P. S. Ridsdale.

MONROE, N(ELLIE) ELIZABETH, 1896-

Birthplace: Chanceford, Pa. **Conversion:** 1933. **Former religion:** Presbyterian. **Education:** Oberlin Coll., four year scholarship (1915-19); Univ. of Pa., Six years scholarship and fellowship (M.A., '23; Ph.D., '29); Columbia Univ., Grad. School of Journalism (1929-30). **General:** Miss Monroe has taught in various schools and colleges since 1919, beginning her teaching career at Shippenburg (Pa.) High School in that year. From 1923 to 1929 she was an instructor at Temple University, leaving to join the staff of Hunter College, N. Y. Since 1935 the author has been a professor in the English Department, Graduate Division, of Brooklyn College. Besides writing for the periodicals, College English, Education Forum, and other publications, she is a regular contributor of book reviews to the Catholic World. A novel by Miss Monroe is to be released in 1944. **Authorities:** Letter from Miss Monroe, December 13, 1943; American Catholic Who's Who (1944-45).

Works

1929 Nicholas Breton, pamphleteer. Philadelphia.
1941 The novel and society. Univ. of North Carolina press.

MOODY, JOHN, 1868-

Birthplace: Jersey City, N. J. **Conversion:** 1931. **Former religion:** Episcopalian. **Education:** Attended high school and later through systematic self-study and wide reading achieved a complete collegiate education. **General:** Mr. Moody began literary production at an early age. At sixteen he was writing salable short stories and editing and publishing his own magazine. At nineteen he edited a professional local newspaper, The Bayonnette, in Bayonne, N. J., but finding this unprofitable entered Wall Street while still a young man. He spent ten years (1890-1900) mastering the technique of the financial district and then conceived the need for an authoritative service to investors. From this was evolved the Moody's Investors Service (statistical data on securities of governments, utilities, banks, railroads and industrial enterprises) of which he is still President. **Authorities:** Letter from Mr. Moody, July, 1943; American Catholic Who's Who (1942-43); Book of Catholic Authors, 2d ser.; Guide to Catholic Literature, 1888-1940; Who's Who in America (1942-43); Moody, John: Fast by the Road. 1942; Moody, John: The Long Road Home; an autobiography. 1933.

Works

1900-43	Moody's manual of investments, American and foreign. (Annual)
1904	The truth about the trusts; a description and analysis of the American trust movement.
1906	The art of Wall street investing.
1907	The investor's primer.
1912	How to analyze railroad reports.
1912	How to invest money wisely.
1919	The masters of capital; a chronicle of Wall street. Yale univ. press.

1919   The railroad builders; a chronicle of the welding of the states. Yale univ. press.

1925   Profitable investing; fundamentals of the science of investing. Forbes pub. co.

1933   The long road home; an autobiography. Macmillan.

1942   Fast by the road. Macmillan.

MOON, PARKER THOMAS, 1892-1936

Birthplace: New York City. **Conversion:** 1914. **Former religion:** Methodist Episcopal. **Education:** Columbia Univ. (B.D., Ph.D.) **General:** Dr. Moon was a professor of history in Columbia University from 1913-36, joining the staff as a Fellow. From 1921-31 he was Managing Editor of the Political Science Quarterly. During the World War the author was on the Col. House Commission of Inquiry and Secretary of the Commission on Territorial problems at the Paris Peace Conference. In 1926 Moon was elected president of the American Catholic Historical Association. **Authorities:** American Authors (1933-35); American Catholic Who's Who (1934-35); Who's Who Among North American Authors (1933-35); Guide to Catholic Literature, 1888-1940; Catholic World, July, 1936.

Works

1921   The labor problem and the social Catholic movement in France; a study in the history of social politics. Macmillan.

1923   Modern history (with Carlton J. H. Hayes). Macmillan.

1923   Teacher's manual to accompany *Modern history* (with Carlton J. H. Hayes). Macmillan.

1925   Syllabus on international relations. Macmillan.

1926   Imperialism and world politics. Macmillan.

1927   Raw materials and their effect upon international relations (with George Otis Smith and others).

1929 Ancient and medieval history (with Carlton J. H. Hayes). Macmillan.
1929 Ancient history (with Carlton J. Hayes). Macmillan.
1929 The United States and the Caribbean (with others). Univ. of Chicago press.
1932 World history (with others). Macmillan.

MOSBY, THOMAS SPEED, 1874-

Birthplace: Linn, Mo. **Conversion:** 1899. **Education:** After finishing elementary and high school he studied law. **General:** The author held many political and civic positions, including State Pardon Attorney of Missouri from 1905 to 1909. At one time he edited the Jefferson City Daily and Weekly Democrat, and was later editor and owner of the Missouri Dairyman. Mr. Mosby is interested in juvenile delinquency and made a statistical study of juvenile idleness as a source of crime. **Authorities:** American Catholic Who's Who. 1911.

Works

1903 Ben Blunt, his life and story, an historical romance. Press of Commercial print. co.
1913 Causes and cures of crime. C. V. Mosby.
1921 Little journeys to Parnassus. Message.
n.d. Supreme Court practice manual. Hugh Stephens.

MURFEY, ETTA JOSEPHEAN, 1892-

Birthplace: New York City. **Conversion:** 1935. **Education:** New York Normal College; Columbia Univ. **General:** The author is an occasional contributor to periodicals and editor of Poetry Caravan magazine. **Authorities:** American Catholic Who's Who (1942-43).

1937 Petals of song (poems), illustrated by Leander Leitner. The author.

1942 (comp.) Tempo rubato; an anthology of poems on music. Lakeland, Fla., The compiler.

MUSSER, BENJAMIN FRANCIS, 1889-

Birthplace: Lancaster, Pa. **Conversion:** 1908. **Former religion:** Protestant Episcopal. **Education:** Nashota Sem. (Epis.) Wisconsin; St. Joseph's Coll., N. Y. **General:** Mr. Musser is the Poet Laureate of New Jersey. From 1926 to 1929 he was editor, with Lucia Trent and Ralph Cheney, of Contemporary Verse. Besides his many books, the author has contributed to numerous anthologies and compiled about ten collections of verse. **Authorities:** American Catholic Who's Who (1942-43); Guide to Catholic Literature, 1888-1940; Who's Who Among North American Authors (1927-28); America, January 9, 1937; Saturday Review of Literature, January 27, 1934.

Works

1912 Angels of the sanctuary.
1914 Outside the walls, tributes to the principles and practice of Roman Catholicism. B. Herder.
1924 Chiaroscuro. Four seas.
1924 Pierrot.
1926 Son of Momus.
1927 Gallimaufry (essays).
1927 Rushlights: LXX sonnets and a few others.
1927 Straws on the wind. (essays)
1927 Untamed. H. Harrison.
1929 Dipped in aloes; a book of unpleasant poems. Bozart.

1929 (ed.) The first Japm anthology, selected by readers from the first and second volumes of Japm: The Poetry Weekly. Bozart.

1930 Bucolics and caviar. Bozart.

1930 Selected poems. Caxton.

1931 Bensbook. Oglethorpe univ. press.

1932 De re franciscana. Franciscan press.

1932 Diary of a twelve-year-old, transcribed from the early hieroglyphic of Benjamin Musser. Caxton.

1932 One-man show; end papers and marginalia. Oglethorpe univ. press.

1932 (comp.) Seeds of laurel. Parnassus.

1933 Franciscan poets. Macmillan.

1933 Poems, 1930-1933. Caxton.

1934 A chaplet of sanctuaries. Magnificat.

1934 Star-gazer. Driftwind.

1936 End of singing; musical settings by Charles Howard March (and others). Magnificat.

1937 What is your name? The Catholic church and nomenclature. Magnificat.

1937 Marvelous boy. Driftwind.

1938 Bird below the waves. Magnificat.

1943 The Beloved Mendicant. Magnificat.

NEALIS, JEAN ELIZABETH URSULA (WILKINSON) 1840?-1910

Birthplace: Fredericton, New Brunswick. **Conversion:** 1861. **Former religion:** Her uncle and teacher was pastor of the Church of the Advent, Boston. **Education:** Private schools and private tutoring in Fredericton and Boston. **General:** The poet was a close friend of Eliza Allen Star (q.v.) whom she met on the campus of the University of Notre Dame. Mrs. Nealis is said to have entered the Church through reading books opposed to Catholicity. **Authorities:** American Catholic Who's Who. 1911.

1885 Drift. Preface by Mrs. J. Sadlier. Pustet.

NEWCOMB, COVELLE, "Mrs. Addison Burbank," 1908-

Birthplace: San Antonio, Texas. **Conversion:** 1925. **Former religion:** Anglican. **Education:** Incarnate Word Coll., San Antonio; Washington Univ., St. Louis, Mo.; Hunter Coll., N. Y. C.; Columbia Univ. (M.A.). **General:** Miss Newcomb is the wife of the artist-author, Addison Burbank (q.v.) and daughter of James Pearson, historian of Texas. She has traveled widely, and teaches university classes during the summer. **Authorities:** American Catholic Who's Who (1942-43); Book of Catholic Authors, 1st ser.; Guide to Catholic Literature, 1888-1940.

Works

1940 Black fire, a story of Henri Christophe. Longmans, Green.
1941 The red hat; a story of John Henry Cardinal Newman. Longmans, Green.
1942 Vagabond in velvet, the story of Miguel de Cervantes. Longmans, Green.
1943 Silver saddles; illustrated by Addison Burbank. Longmans, Green.

NICHOLLS, CHARLES WILBUR de LYON (Shelton Chauncey, pseud.) 1854-1924

Birthplace: Nicholls, Conn. **Conversion:** 1899. **Former religion:** Protestant Episcopal (minister, 1888-99). **Education:** De Graff's Military Institute; Wilson's Grammar

School, Rochester, N. Y.; Williston Sem., East Hampton, Mass. (grad., '74); after short period at Yale Univ., attended Bristol's Conservatory of Music ('74-76); Johns Hopkins Univ. ('77-80); philosophy, Concord Summer School of Philosophy ('82-84); Seabury Divinity School ('82-84); General Theological Sem. (grad. '87); Gregorian Univ., Rome, Italy ('99-'00). **General:** After serving as pastor in various Protestant Episcopal churches in the U. S., Dr. Nicholls traveled extensively in Europe. He was the founder of the Scions of Colonial Cavaliers, and in 1900 originated the Sunday Schools Association for Underprivileged Children. **Authorities:** American Catholic Who's Who. 1911; Who's Who in America (1922-23)

Works

1894 The Greek Madonna. G. W. Dillingham.
1899 The decadents. J. S. Ogilvie.
1903 The Sunday kindergarten art history catechism.
1904 The ultra-fashionable peerage of America. G. Harjes.
1907 The Sunday kindergarten primer of American philosophy.
1910 Annals of a remarkable salon.
1911 The art-history primer.
1912 The 469 ultra-fashionables of America, a social guide book a register to date. Broadway pub. co.

NICHOLS, ANNE, 1890?-

Birthplace: The South (U. S.) **Conversion:** 1928. **Former religion:** Father, Russian; mother, Irish. **General:** As a playwright, Miss Nichols will live longest in "Abie's Irish Rose;" that phenomenal play that holds the record as having the world's longest run (2532 performances) and whose popularity still continues. Hitler mentions it in "Mein

Kampf"—its most successful European run was in Berlin. The play has been shown in China as well as in a half-dozen countries of Europe. Miss Nichols began her career as an actress, playing vaudeville in New York City. **Authorities:** Guide to Catholic Literature, 1888-1940; Parker, John: Who's Who in the Theatre. 1939; Portland Oregonian, September 26, 1943.

Works

1919 Down Limerick way.
1919 Heart's desire (with Adelaide Matthews).
1919 Seven miles to Arden.
1919 Linger longer Letty.
1920 The gilded cage.
1921 The happy cavalier.
1921 Just married (with Adelaide Matthews).
1921 Love's dreams.
1922 Abie's Irish Rose. (Published as a novel by Harper in 1927).
1922 The land of romance.

NIXON-ROULET, MARY F., See Roulet, Mary F.
Nixon-   d. 1930

NUTTING, WILLIS DWIGHT, 1900-

Birthplace: Iowa City, Iowa. **Conversion:** 1930. **Former religion:** Brought up as Presbyterian; later became Anglican (minister 1923-30). **Education:** State Univ. of Iowa (A.B., '21); Univ. of Oxford (B.A., '23; B.Litt., '24); State Univ. of Iowa (Ph.D., '33). **General:** Professor Nutting is at present an associate professor of history at the University of Notre Dame. He is married and has three children. **Authorities:** Letter from Mr. Nutting, October 6, 1943; Guide to Catholic Literature, 1888-1940.

Works

1932   How firm a foundation? Sheed & Ward.

OLF, LILLIAN (BROWNE) 1880-

Birthplace: Bradford, Mass. **Conversion:** 1938. **Former religion:** Congregationalist. **Education:** The Bradford grammar and high school; Bradford Academy (grad.); Wellesley Coll.; Columbia Univ., N. Y. (Extension Division). **General:** Mrs. Browne-Olf began her literary career at Bradford Academy by taking all the literary prizes offered. Besides writing her books she is a lecturer, and has contributed to several anthologies of poetry. She says, "Four extended periods in Rome and the Continent gave me a broad outlook on the culture and civilization of Europe which I discovered were the fruits of the Church. I re-evaluated my former historical studies on the spot (and) achieved final emancipation from the bigotry against Catholicism." "Pius XI" was written while the author was still a non-Catholic. **Authorities:** Letter from Mrs. Browne-Olf, August 2, 1943; American Catholic Who's Who (1942-43).

Works

1919   (comp.) The grail of life; an anthology on heroic death and immortal life (with John H. Holmes).
1938   Pius XI; Apostle of peace. Macmillan.

161

1941 Their name is Pius: portraits of five great modern popes. Bruce.
1943 The sword of Saint Michael. Bruce.

O'MALLEY, SALLIE MARGARET (HILL) 1861-

Birthplace: Centreville, Indiana. **Conversion:** 1886. **Former religion:** Her husband was a Catholic. **Education:** Calhoun (Mo.) Female Sem.; Univ. of Mo. (grad.) **General:** The wife of Charles J. O'Malley, poet and editor, Mrs. O'Malley illustrated many of her husband's poems and composed the music for a number of songs. She published more than four hundred short stories and contributed to many national magazines, including Harper's Bazaar and Catholic World. **Authorities:** American Catholic Who's Who. 1911; Guide to Catholic Literature, 1888-1940.

Works

1888 The boys of the prairie. Lothrop.
1897 An heir of dreams. Benziger.
1897 Tales of Bonne Femme.
1900 The brown princess.
1904 On quiet byways.
1909 The white flame.

PALMER, BENJAMIN WHIPPLE, 1889-

Birthplace: Fairbault, Minn. **Conversion:** 1913. **Former religion:** Episcopalian. **Education:** Univ. of Minn. (A.B., '11; LL.B., '13; M.A., '14) **General:** Except for a brief period (1914-15) as instructor in political science at the University of Minnesota, Mr. Palmer has continued in the practice of law in St. Paul and Minneapolis. He is an occasional contributor to Catholic periodicals. **Authorities:** American Catholic Who's Who (1942-43); Guide to Catholic Literature, 1888-1940.

Works

1914 Swamp land drainage, with special reference to Minnesota. Univ. of Minn. press.
1929 Manual of Minnesota law. West pub. co.
1939 Marshall and Taney; statesmen of the law. Univ. of Minn. press.
1942 Business law: with social and personal applications (with Robert O. Skar). McGraw-Hill.

PARKER, WILLIAM THORNTON, 1849-

Birthplace: Boston, Mass. **Education:** St. Paul's School, Concord, N. H.; Univ. of Vienna; Univ. of Munich (1873). **General:** Dr. Parker began his medical career as a surgeon in the U. S. Army. Later he was professor of medical jurisprudence in the College of Physicians and Surgeons, Chicago. Besides his prose writings he is the author of several devotional hymns. **Authorities:** American Catholic Who's Who. 1911; Guide to Catholic Literature, 1888-1940; List of books by Dr. W. Thornton Parker. Northampton, Mass. 1919. 2 p.

Works

1894 Gleanings from Parker records, A.D. 1271 to 1893. G. Chase.
1913 Personal experiences among our North American Indians from 1867 to 1885. The author (?)
1915 Gleanings from colonial and American records of Parker and Morse families, A.D. 1585-1915. The author.
1916 Annals of old Fort Cummings, New Mexico, 1867-8. The author.

1918   Personal experiences among our North American Indians.
          Suppl. The author.

PECK, THEODORA AGNES, 1882-

Birthplace: Burlington, Vt. **Conversion:** 1920. **Education:**
Burlington High School (grad., '00); Univ. of Vermont
(1904). **General:** The author is an active member of the
D. A. R., U. S. Daughters of 1812, League of the Sacred
Heart, and other organizations. She entered the Church
because of its stand on divorce. **Authorities:** American
Catholic Who's Who (1942-43); Guide to Catholic Litera-
ture, 1888-1940.

Works

1905   Hester of the Grants; romance of Old Bennington. Duf-
          field (?).
1908   The sword of Dundee; tale of "bonnie Prince Charlie."
          Duffield.
1914   White dawn; a legend of Ticonderoga. Revell.

PEGIS, ANTON CHARLES, 1905-

Birthplace: Milwaukee, Wis. **Conversion:** 1930. **Former
religion:** Greek Orthodox. **Education:** Marquette Univ.
(A.B., '28; M.A., '29); Univ. of Toronto (Ph.D. '31). **General:** Professor Pegis was instructor and later assistant professor of philosophy at Marquette University from 1931 to
1937. Since then he has been at Fordham University Graduate School in the same capacity and engaged at the same
time as assistant editor of New Scholasticism, and associate
editor of Thought. **Authorities:** American Catholic Who's
Who (1942-43); Guide to Catholic Literature, 1888-1940.

1934 St. Thomas and the problem of the soul in the thirteenth
      century. St. Michael's college.
1939 Saint Thomas and the Greeks. Marquette univ. press.

PEGIS, JESSIE (CORRIGAN) 1907-

Birthplace: Milwaukee, Wis. **Former religion:** Protestantism. **Education:** Univ. of Wisconsin ('23-'25); Marquette Univ. (A.B., '27; M.A., '29). **General:** Jessie Corrigan is the wife of Anton Pegis (q.v.). She is an occasional contributor to periodical literature. **Authorities:** American Catholic Who's Who (1942-43).

Works

1928 Chrysalis songs, by Jessie Donalson Corrigan; with an introduction by George N. Schuster. Marquette univ. press.

PERCH, PHILEMON, pseud., See Johnston, Richard Malcolm, 1822-1898

PITTAR, MRS. FANNY MARIA

Authorities: Autobiographical work below.

Works

1847 A Protestant converted to Catholicity by her Bible and
      prayer book. H. McGrath.

POPE, SIR JOSEPH, 1854-1926

Birthplace: Charlottetown, Prince Edward I. **Conversion:**

1875. **General:** The author began his career in the civil service of Canada in 1878. From 1882 to 1892 he was private secretary to Sir John Macdonald and later Under-Secretary of State for External Affairs. **Authorities:** American Catholic Who's Who. 1911; Guide to Catholic Literature, 1888-1940.

Works

1890   Jacques Cartier, his life and voyages. A. S. Woodburn.

1894   Anglican claims in the light of history. Catholic truth soc. Canada.

1894   Memoirs of Sir John Alexander Macdonald, first prime minister of the Dominion of Canada. E. Arnold. 2 v.

1895   (ed.) Confederation; begin a series of hitherto unpublished documents bearing on the British North America act. Carswell.

1903   The tour of Their Royal Highnesses the Duke and Duchess of Cornwall and York through the Dominion of Canada in the year 1901.

1915   The day of Sir John Macdonald; a chronicle of the first prime minister of the Dominion. Brook.

1921   (ed.) Correspondence of Sir John Macdonald; selections from the correspondence . . . made by his literary executor, Sir Joseph Pope. Doubleday, Page.

PORTUONDO, JOSEPHINE B. (THOMAS) 1867-1940

Birthplace: Belleville, Ill. **Conversion:** 1885. **Education:** Ursuline Convent, Springfield, Ill.; Loretto Acad., Nerinx, Ky. **General:** Mrs. Portuondo was the granddaughter of William H. Bissell, first Republican governor of Illinois. She contributed occasionally to Benziger's magazine and the Catholic Standard and Times. **Authorities:** American

Catholic Who's Who (1911; 1942-43); Guide to Catholic Literature, 1888-1940.

Works

1907 True historical stories for Catholic children. H. L. Kilner.

PRESTON, THOMAS SCOTT, monsignor, 1824-1891

Birthplace: Hartford, Conn. **Conversion:** 1849. **Former religion:** Episcopalian (minister, 1846-49) **Ordained priest:** 1850. **Education:** Washington (now Trinity) Coll. (grad., '43); General Theological Sem., N. Y. (grad., '46). **General:** Before his conversion, Monsignor Preston served as a minister in various New York Episcopal churches. He was ordained a priest the same year that he resigned his last Episcopal charge. The author founded the Sisters of the Divine Compassion, and in 1881 was made Prothonotary Apostolic by Leo XIII. **Authorities:** Catholic Encyclopedia, v. 12; Dictionary of American Biography, v. 15; Guide to Catholic Literature, 1888-1940; Brann, H. A.: Rt. Rev. Thomas Preston, V.G.

Works

1860 Ark of the covenant. P. J. Kenedy.
1860 The Purgatorian manual; or, selections of prayers and devotions with appropriate reflections; for the use of the members of the Purgatorian society in the diocese of New York. P. O'Shea.
1863 Life of St. Mary Magdalene. P. O'Shea.
1866 Life of St. Vincent de Paul.
1867 Sermons for the principal seasons of the sacred year (2d ed.) D. & J. Sadlier.
1868 Reason and revelation. Catholic pub. house.

1869   The triumph of the faith.

1870   The Catholic view of the public school question. R. Coddington. 44 p.

1870   Christ and the church.

1871   The vicar of Christ; or, Lectures upon the office and prerogatives of our Holy Father the Pope. R. Coddington.

1874   Lectures upon the devotions to the most Sacred Heart of Jesus Christ. R. Coddington.

1878   The Divine sanctuary.

1878   The Protestant reformation.

1878   Ritualism.

1879   The Divine Paraclete. A short series of sermons upon the person and office of the Holy Ghost. R. Coddington.

1882   Protestantism and the Church.

1884   God and reason; lectures upon the primary truths of natural religion. R. Coddington.

1885   The sacred year.

1885   The watch on Calvary. Meditations on the seven last words of our dying Redeemer. R. Coddington.

1887   Gethsemani. Meditations on the last day on earth of Our Blessed Redeemer. R. Coddington.

QUIRK, CHARLES JOAQUIN, father, 1889-

Birthplace: New Orleans, La. **Conversion:** 1905. **Former religion:** Attended Methodist church, then Episcopalian but not affiliated; Mother attracted toward Catholicism toward end of life. **Education:** Finished high school and college as Jesuit; Woodstock Coll. (A.B. '14); four years study in Europe; St. Louis Univ. (M.A. '38). **General:** Father Quirk began writing books before he engaged in teaching and now combines the two activities. He headed the department of English at Spring Hill College, Mobile, from 1925 to 1939, and since then has been professor of English at Loyola University, New Orleans. His poetry has appeared in many American magazines and anthologies

168

and also in English, Irish, Australian and Indian publications. **Authorities:** Letter from Father Quirk, August 8, 1943; American Catholic Who's Who (1942-43); Book of Catholic Authors, 1st series; Guide to Catholic Literature, 1888-1940; Fortnightly Review, November, 1931.

Works

1926   Sails on the horizon. Stratford.
1929   Interlude; a group of poems. J. E. Duval.
1931   Candles in the wind. Dial press.
1934   Gesture before farewell. Dial press.
1936   Full circle. J. E. Duval.
1937   Catholic mysticism of Alice Meynell. St. Louis univ.
1943   Midsummer singing; a book of original verses (in preparation).
1944   The realms of gold; an anthology of great American and English sonnets (in preparation).

REEVE, ARTHUR BENJAMIN, 1880-1936

Birthplace: Patchogue, N. Y. **Conversion:** 1926. **Education:** Princeton Univ. (grad., '03); law studies at N. Y. Law School. **General:** The creator of Craig Kennedy studied law but never practiced. In 1906 he was assistant editor of Public Opinion and in the same year became editor of Our Own Times; holding the latter post until 1910. Craig Kennedy made his first appearance in the Cosmopolitan Magazine in 1910 and its success led the author to continue writing stories and novels in the same vein. **Authorities:** American Catholic Who's Who (1934-35); Guide to Catholic Literature, 1888-1940; Twentieth Century Authors; Who's Who Among North American Authors (1933-35); Haycraft, H.: Murder for pleasure, the Life and Times of the Detective Story. 1941.

1911　The poisoned pen, the further adventures of Craig Kennedy.

1912　The black hand.

1912　The silent bullet; the adventures of Craig Kennedy. Dodd, Mead.

1914　The dream doctor. Hearst's international library.

1915　The exploits of Elaine.

1915　The gold of the gods; the mystery of the Incas solved by Craig Kennedy. Hearst's international library.

1915　The war terror; further adventures of Craig Kennedy. Hearst's international library.

1916　Constance Dunlap, woman detective. Hearst's international library.

1916　The romance of Elaine. Hearst's international library.

1916　The social gangster. Hearst's international library.

1917　The adventures; a Craig Kennedy detective story. Harper.

1917　Treasure train. Harper.

1918　The Panama plot. Harper.

1919　The master mystery. Grosset & Dunlap.

1919　The soul scar; a Craig Kennedy scientific mystery novel.

1921　The film mystery. Harper.

1921　The mystery mind. Grosset and Dunlap.

1923　Craig Kennedy listens in. Harper.

1924　Atavar; a Craig Kennedy novel. Harper.

1925　The boy scout's Craig Kennedy. Harper.

1925　Craig Kennedy on the farm. Harper.

1925　The fourteen points, tales of Craig Kennedy.

1926　Pandora. Harper.

1926　The radio detective. Grosset & Dunlap.

1931　Golden age of crime. Mohawk.

1932　The kidnap club. Macaulay.

1934　The clutching hand; a Craig Kennedy novel. Reilly & Lee.

1935　Enter Craig Kennedy. Macaulay.

1936　The stars scream murder; a Craig Kennedy novel. D. Appleton-Century.

n.d.　The return of the riddle rider.

REID, CHRISTIAN, pseud., See Tiernan, Frances Christine (Fisher), 1846-1920

RICHARDS, HENRY LIVINGSTON, 1814-1903

Birthplace: Granville, O. **Conversion:** 1852. **Former religion:** Protestant Episcopal (minister, 1842—). **Education:** Kenyon Coll. (grad., '38). **General:** Dr. Richards was a descendant of New England Puritans. After his conversion and removal to Boston, he was a frequent contributor to the Catholic Review and the Sacred Heart Review. The author was a zealous advocate of religious education and for twenty-three years was connected with the Boston Board of Charities. **Authorities:** Guide to Catholic Literature, 1888-1940; Richards, J. H.: Loyal Life. 1913; America, November 22, 1913.

Works

1902 Fifty years in the Church. (Contains an extended sketch of the Oxford Movement in the U. S.)

RICHARDS, JARRETT THOMAS

Birthplace: Chambersburg, Pa. **Conversion:** 1886. **Education:** Switzerland, Germany, and Columbia Univ. Law School (1864). **General:** Richards was a descendant of early settlers of Maryland. He went to California in 1868 and practiced law in that state until his death, having been elected mayor of Santa Barbara in 1875. The work listed below is a semi-autobiographical novel. **Authorities:** American Catholic Who's Who, 1911. (Entry under Richards, Garrett T.); Guide to Catholic Literature, 1888-1940.

Works

1914 Romance on El camino real. B. Herder.

RICHARDS, WILLIAM, 1819-1899

Birthplace: Granville, O. (?) **Conversion:** 1853. **Former religion:** Episcopalian. **Education:** Attended Kenyon Coll., during same period as his brother Henry Livingston Richards (q.v.) who graduated in 1838. **Authorities:** Autobiographical work listed below.

Works

✗ 1895   On the road to Rome, and how two brothers got there. Benziger.

ROBINS, JULIA GORHAM, 1846-

Birthplace: Boston. **Conversion:** 1899. **Education:** Private schools of Boston. **General:** The author was an occasional contributor to the Sacred Heart Review and to America. **Authorities:** American Catholic Who's Who. 1911; Driscoll, A. S.: Literary Convert Women. 1928.

Works

n.d.   Lectures on Greek sculpture and archaeology.
n.d.   New England conversion. Paulist press. pa.

ROCKNE, KNUTE KENNETH, 1888-1931

Birthplace: Voss, Norway. **Came to U. S.:** 1893. **Conversion:** 1925. **Former religion:** Lutheran. **Education:** Chicago public schools; Notre Dame Univ. (B.S., '14). **General:** The noted football coach of Notre Dame University began his career in 1915 as a chemistry teacher. In 1918, Rockne became head football coach upon the resignation of Jessie

Harper, and held that position until his death. He conducted summer schools for coaches, toured Europe, and was a sales promotion manager for the Studebaker Corporation while holding his unchallenged position as dean of American football. **Authorities:** Dictionary of American Biography, v. 16; Guide to Catholic Literature, 1888-1940; Brown, Warren: Rockne. 1931; Harrow, Robert: Rockne, Idol of American Football. 1931; Hurt, H. W.: Goals, the Life of Knute Rockne. 1931; Huston, McCready: Salesman from the Sidelines, Being the Business Career of K. K. Rockne. 1932; Knute Rockne's Career. Minneapolis, Modern Magazines, Inc., 1931; Lovelace, D. W.: Rockne of Notre Dame. 1931; Rockne, K. K.: The Autobiography. 1930; Stuhldreher, H. A.: Knute Rockne, Man Builder. 1931.

Works

1925 Coaching. Devin-Adair.
1925 The four winners—the head, the hands, the foot, the ball. Devin-Adair.
1926 Rockne's football problems. Menomonie, Wis. 41 leaves.
1931 The autobiography of Knute Rockne. Bobbs-Merrill.
1931 Training, conditioning, and the care of injuries (with Walter E. Meanwell). Madison, Wis.

ROULET, MARY F. NIXON- d. 1930

Birthplace: Indianapolis. **Conversion:** 1894. **Education:** Philadelphia Conservatory of Music. **General:** Mrs. Nixon-Roulet was the daughter, niece, and granddaughter of non-Catholic clergymen. Besides writing more than twenty volumes, she contributed to most of the principal Catholic magazines in the United States during her lifetime. **Au-**

thorities: Guide to Catholic Literature, 1888-1940; Ave Maria, September 13, 1930.

Works

1897	With a pessimist in Spain. A. C. McClurg.
1898	Lasca, and other stories. B. Herder.
1899	Blue lady's knight. B. Herder.
1899	A harp of many chords. B. Herder.
1899	Indian folk tales. American book co.
1900	God, the king, my brother. L. C. Page.
1901	St. Anthony in art, and other sketches. Marlier.
1906	The trail of the dragon, and other stories (with others). Benziger.
1906-09	Little cousin series. L. C. Page. (6 v.).
1908	Japanese folk stories and fairy tales. American book co.
1909	Seven little Marshalls. Benziger.
1910	A bit of old ivory, and other stories (with others). Benziger.
1910	The Spaniard at home. A. C. McClurg.
1912	The waif of Rainbow court. B. Herder.
1914	Little Marshalls at the lake. Benziger.
1915	The mirror. B. Herder.

RUSSELL, IRWIN, 1853-1879

Birthplace: Port Gibson, Miss. **Conversion:** 1870 (?) **Education:** Early education at home; St. Louis Univ. (grad., '69); studied law in Port Gibson. **General:** As a child, Russell was extremely precocious, reading Milton intelligently at the age of six. At nineteen he was admitted to the bar but soon left this calling to follow a literary career. He contributed poetry to Puck, Appleton's Journal, St. Nicholas, Scribners, and others—much of his poetry being in the Negro dialect. He is credited with influencing Joel Chandler Harris (q.v.) on the use of this form. The poet died

174

while giving aid in a yellow fever epidemic. **Authorities:** American Authors, 1600-1900; Dictionary of American Biography, v. 16; Guide to Catholic Literature, 1888-1940; Baskerville, W. M.: Southern Writers. 1897; Russell, Irwin: Christmas Night in the Quarters, and an Historical Sketch by M. G. Fulton. 1917; The Critic, October 27, and November 3, 1888.

Works

1888   Poems. Century.
1913   Christmas night in the quarters; pen drawings by the late
       David B. Page. W. O. Graham.

SARGENT, DANIEL, 1890-

Birthplace: Boston. **Conversion:** 1909. **Former religion:** Unitarian. **Education:** Groton School; Harvard Univ. (A.B., '13; M.A., '14). **General:** Mr. Sargent began his career in 1914 on the teaching staff of Harvard University, leaving in 1916 to join the French army. Later he transferred to the United States armed forces. In 1922 he returned to the faculty of Literature and History at Harvard where he remained until 1936. The author has spent considerable time in France and Italy in travel and study, and since 1936 has devoted his time exclusively to writing. **Authorities:** American Catholic Who's Who (1942-43); Book of Catholic Authors. 1st series; Guide to Catholic Literature, 1888-1940.

Works

1915   Our gleaming days. R. G. Badger.
1921   The door, and other poems. R. G. Badger.
1924   The road to Welles-Perrennes; a story in verse. Four seas.
       46 p.

1930 My account of the flood, by Noah's brother-in-law; with authentic illustrations as lately discovered. B. Humphries.
1932 The song of the three children. B. Humphries.
1933 Thomas More. Sheed and Ward.
1935 Four independents. Sheed and Ward.
1935 God's ambuscade; a book of poems. Longmans, Green.
1936 Catherine Tekakwitha. Longmans, Green.
1939 Our land and Our Lady. Longmans, Green.
1941 All the day long; James Anthony Walsh, co-founder of Maryknoll. Longmans, Green.
1941 Christopher Columbus. Bruce.

SARGENT, HENRY LEONARD, father (O.S.B.), 1857-

Birthplace: Boston, Mass. **Conversion:** 1909. **Former religion:** Anglican (minister, 1885-1909). **Education:** Harvard (B.A., '79); General Theological Sem. (B.D., '86). **Ordained priest:** 1911. **General:** Father Sargent was a member of the Anglican Order of Holy Cross from 1891 to 1909, and after becoming a Catholic he joined the Benedictine Order in 1914. He is the founder of the Portsmouth (R. I.) priory and contributes occasionally to periodical literature. **Authorities:** American Catholic Who's Who (1942-43); Guide to Catholic Literature, 1888-1940; Curtis, G. P.: Beyond the Road to Rome. 1914; Sargent, H. L.: Pictures and Persons. 1931.

Works

1931 Pictures and persons. Washington, St. Anselm's priory.

SAVAGE, COURTENAY, 1890-

Birthplace: New York City. **Conversion:** 1937. **Former religion:** Episcopalian. **Education:** Under private tutors and

176

at Columbia Univ. (1911-12). **General:** While Mr. Savage is probably best known as a playwright, he has written a great deal in other fields as well. He has contributed short stories and articles to most of the English and American publications, with a number of his stories translated into foreign tongues. Likewise, a number of his plays have been purchased by motion picture producers. From 1935 to 1936 the author was Director of Drama and Continuity with the Columbia Broadcasting System and later wrote "day and night-time" radio programs. In 1941 he supervised the Bishop's Relief programs and after Pearl Harbor took over publicizing the National Catholic Community Service. **Authorities:** Letters from Mr. Savage, August 2, 11, 1943; American Catholic Who's Who (1942-43); Book of Catholic Authors. 2d series; Guide to Catholic Literature, 1888-1940; Who's Who in America (1942-43).

Works

1925 Don't bother with Mother (with E. B. Dewing).
1926 They all want something; a comedy in a prologue and three acts. S. French.
1928 The buzzard.
1929 I'm wise. (Produced in England).
1929 The queen of Kingdom Corners; a comedy in three acts (with Wallace Pack). W. H. Baker.
1930 The queen at home (with V. Cosby and S. Ward).
1930 Virtue's bed.
1932 The flying vagabond; a play in three acts. W. H. Baker.
1933 Nellie was a lady. W. H. Baker.
1933 The little dog laughed (from Merrick's, The Elevation of Lulu).
1935 Loose moments; a comedy in three acts (with Bertram Hobbs). S. French.
1937 Forever and forever.
1939 Safe crossing.

SCHULTZ, CHARLES HENRY, 1856-1932

Birthplace: Philadelphia, Pa. **Conversion:** 1904. **Former religion:** Episcopalian (minister, 1887). **Education:** Racine Coll., Wis.; General Theological Sem., N. Y. C.; Marquette Univ. (M.A.) **General:** From 1906 to 1908 Schultz was Master of the Newman School and then left to found and direct the Carlton Academy (N. Y.). He remained with this school until 1918. The author was associated with St. John's Atonement College from 1908 to 1923 and later with St. Francis College. **Authorities:** American Catholic Who's Who. 1911.

Works

1926 Sacred eloquence; a guide book for seminarians. Murphy.

SEARLE, GEORGE MARY, father (C.S.P.), 1839-1918

Birthplace: London, Eng., of American parents. **Came to U. S.:** 1840. **Conversion:** 1862. **Former religion:** Episcopalian, then Unitarian. **Ordained priest:** 1871. **Education:** Brookline (Mass.) high school; Harvard Univ. (grad., '57). **General:** Before his ordination as a Paulist, Father Searle was an assistant professor at the United States Naval Academy. From 1889 to 1897 he was a professor of astronomy and mathematics at Catholic University of America. In 1898, in recognition of his abilities as an astronomer, Father Searle was appointed Director of the Vatican Observatory. He was Superior General of the Congregation of St. Paul from 1904 to 1910. **Authorities:** American Catholic Who's Who. 1911; Appleton's Cyclopaedia of American Biography, v. 5; Guide to Catholic Literature, 1888-1940; Curtis, G. P.: Some Roads to Rome in America. 1909; America,

178

July 27, 1918; Catholic World, February, 1898; August, 1904.

Works

1877 Elements of geometry. J. Wiley.
1895 Plain facts for fair minds; an appeal for candor and common sense. Catholic book exchange.
1905 How to become a Catholic. Catholic book exchange.
1910 "Sumner's method" for finding a ship's position. Condensed and improved. D. Van Nostrand.
1916 The truth about Christian Science. Paulist press.

SEAWELL, MOLLY ELLIOT (Foxcroft Davis, pseud.), 1860-1916

Birthplace: Gloucester County, Va. **Conversion:** 1878. **Former religion:** Protestant Episcopal. **Education:** At home, attending formal school only occasionally. **General:** Miss Seawell successfully assumed the support of her family upon the death of her father by entering the writing field. She became a political correspondent in Washington, D. C., for New York journals, and in 1895 won a $3,000 prize offered by the New York Herald for her "Sprightly Romance of Marsac." Besides her books, the author contributed to many of the leading periodicals. **Authorities:** American Catholic Who's Who. 1911; Dictionary of American Biography, v. 16; Guide to Catholic Literature, 1888-1940; Twentieth Century Authors; Curtis, G. P.: Beyond the Road to Rome. 1914; Curtis, G. P.: Some Roads to Rome in America. 1909; Library of Southern Literature, v. 11.

Works

1888 The Berkeleys and their neighbors. American news co.
1890 Little Jarvis. D. Appleton.

1890	Throckmorton. D. Appleton.

1890   Throckmorton. D. Appleton.

1891   Maid Marion and other stories. D. Appleton.

1891   Midshipman Paulding. D. Appleton.

1893   Children of destiny. D. Appleton.

1893   Paul Jones. D. Appleton.

1893   Through thick and thin, and The midshipman's mess. D. Lothrop.

1894   Decatur and Somers. D. Appleton.

1894   Maid Marion (play).

1895   Quarterdeck and foksle. W. A. Wilde.

1896   The sprightly romance of Marsac. C. Scribner.

1896   A strange, sad comedy. Century.

1897   The history of the Lady Betty Stair. C. Scribner.

1897   Twelve naval captains. C. Scribner.

1897   A Virginia cavalier. Harper.

1898   The loves of the lady Arabella. Macmillan.

1898   The Rock of the Lion. Harper.

1899   The lively adventures of Gavin Hamilton. Harper.

1900   The house of Egremont. C. Scribner.

1901   Laurie Vane, and other stories. W. A. Wilde.

1901   Papa Bouchard. C. Scribner.

1902   Francezka. Bowen-Merrill.

1903   Despotism and democracy; a study of Washington society and politics. McClure, Phillips.

1903   The fortunes of Fifi. Bobbs-Merrill.

1903   The great scoop. Illustrated by W. F. Stecher. L. C. Page.

1905   Mrs. Darrell. Macmillan.

1906   The chateau of Montplaisir. D. Appleton.

1906   The victory. D. Appleton.

1907   The secret of Toni. D. Appleton.

1908   The imprisoned midshipmen. D. Appleton.

1908   The last duchess of Belgarde. D. Appleton.

1909   Boys on the railroad (with others). Harper.

1909   The whirl; a romance of Washington society. Dodd, Mead.

1910   The marriage of Theodora. Dodd, Mead.

1911   The jugglers; a story. Macmillan.

1912   The son of Columbus. Harper.

1914   Betty's Virginia Christmas. J. B. Lippincott.

1915   The diary of a beauty. J. B. Lippincott.

1916   Betty at Fort Blizzard. J. B. Lippincott.

SENER, SAMUEL MILLER, 1855-1911

Birthplace: Lancaster, Pa. **Conversion:** 1874. **Education:** Public schools of Lancaster; studied law, and was admitted to the bar in 1877. **General:** Mr. Sener did not devote himself exclusively to the practice of law; at various times he was engaged as a journalist on local newspapers, including the New Era. The author was prominent in local historical circles and for several years was librarian of the Lancaster County Historical Society. He contributed to the United States Catholic Historical Researches, and other publications. **Authorities:** Letter from the Lancaster Free Public Library, Lancaster, Pa., December 17, 1943; American Catholic Who's Who. 1911; Lancaster County Historical Society Papers. 1912.

Works

1894 The Catholic church at Lancaster Country. (From the Records of the American Catholic Historical Society. 1894).

1895 Lancaster barracks, where the British and Hessian prisoners were detained during the Revolution. S. M. Sener.

1895 (comp.) Old-time heroes of the War of the Revolution and of 1812-'14. Harrisburg pub. co.

1896 The Sehner ancestry. Compiled from authentic records and illustrated with wappen, or coats of arms, and stammhaus in Schwaigern, Würtemberg. Dedicated to John Fick Sehner, by Samuel Miller Sener. Lancaster, Pa.

SETON, ELIZABETH ANN, MOTHER, 1774-1821

Birthplace: New York City. **Conversion:** 1805. **Former religion:** Episcopalian. **Education:** Chiefly at home by her father, supplemented by wide reading. **General:** The saintly woman who is called the founder of the parochial school system in the United States, opened a school for poor girls in Baltimore after the death of her husband in 1803. She and her fellow teachers adopted the habit and rule of the Sisters of Charity of St. Vincent de Paul. Mother Seton was three times named Superior of the Community, which in 1911 was to number more than 6,000 members originating from the Baltimore foundation. **Authorities:** Catholic Encyclopedia, v. 13; Dictionary of American Biography, v. 16; Guide to Catholic Literature, 1888-1940; Feeney, Leonard: Elizabeth Seton, An American Woman. 1938; Hoare, S. M. R.: Virgin Soil, Mother Seton from a Different Point of View. 1942; Malloy, L.: Life Story of Mother Seton. 1924; O'Neil, M. C.: Mother E. A. Seton (from work of De Barberey); Ponet, M.: Une Fille Americaine de Monsieur Vincent. 1938; Thirteen Volumes of Letters, Diaries and Documents in the Archives of the Motherhouse at Emmitsburg, Md.

Works

1817 Memoirs of Mrs. S*** written by herself. A fragment of real history. Isaac A. Kollock.

1929 A daily thought from the writings of Mother Seton, selected by the Reverend Joseph B. Code. Emmitsburg, Sisters of Charity of St. Vincent de Paul.

1936 The soul of Elizabeth Seton; a spiritual autobiography culled from Mother Seton's writings and memoirs by a Daughter of charity of St. Vincent de Paul. Benziger.

SHEPPERSON, SISTER MARY FIDES, 1867-

Birthplace: Danville, Pa. **Conversion:** 1886. **Former religion:** Methodist Episcopal. **Education:** Duquesne Univ.

(A.B., M.A.); Univ. of Pittsburgh (Ph.D., '23). **General:** Sister Mary Fides' teaching career began when she entered the convent of the Sisters of Mercy in 1888. She is the founder of the Society of St. Francis, and at present is professor and head of the department of history at Mount Mercy College, Pittsburgh. **Authorities:** Letter from Sister M. Fides, August 18, 1943; American Catholic Who's Who (1911; 1942-43); Guide to Catholic Literature, 1888-1940.

Works

1897 Harp of Milan. J. H. Yewdale.
1911 Cloister chords: an educator's year book. Ainsworth.
1914 Battles of destiny. Mt. Mercy College.
1915 Selections from the Scriptures; gleanings from the Old Testament. Ainsworth.
1923 A comparative study of St. Thomas Aquinas and Herbert Spencer. Univ. of Pittsburgh.
1933 Seventeen crises in world history. Whittet & Shepperson. (Published earlier as Battles of Destiny)
1939 Life of St. Francis of Assisi in silhouettes. Albany, N. Y., American humane ass'n.

SHIPMAN, ANDREW JACKSON, 1857-1915

Birthplace: Springvale (Fairfax County), Va. **Conversion:** ca. 1876. **Education:** Taught by his learned grandfather; Georgetown Acad., D. C. (grad., '74); Georgetown Coll. (1878). **General:** After a year as editor of the Vienna Times in Fairfax County, Shipman became superintendent of a coal mine employing many immigrants of Slavic origin. His zeal for the temporal and spiritual welfare of this group eventually led him to master many of the languages of southeastern Europe. His particular interest was in the Catholics of the Greek and Ruthenian rites, whose faith he believed endangered by the strangeness with which they

183

were regarded by Catholics of the Roman rite. After becoming a prominent lawyer he spent many of his vacations in Slavic countries. Shipman contributed articles to the Catholic Encyclopedia, Century, McClures, Pravoslavny Viestnik, and other periodicals. **Authorities:** American Catholic Who's Who. 1911; Dictionary of American Biography, v. 17; The Catholic Encyclopedia and Its Makers. 1917. Pallen, C. B.: Memorial of Andrew J. Shipman, his Life and Writings. 1916; Records of the American Catholic Historical Society, December, 1917; Guide to Catholic Literature, 1888-1940.

Works

1911 (tr.) The Holy Mass according to the Greek rite. (Translated into English for the first time). 48 p.
1916 A memorial of Andrew J. Shipman, his life and writings, edited by Conde B. Pallen. Encyclopedia press.

SHOLL, ANNA McCLURE (Geoffrey Corson, pseud.)

Birthplace: Philadelphia. **Conversion:** 1916. **Education:** Ogontz (Pa.) Sem. (grad.); Cornell (1892-94). **General:** Miss Sholl began her career as an editorial writer for the New York Commercial Advertiser in 1896, and the next year collaborated in Warner's "Library of the World's Best Literature." She was art editor of the Success Library Club in 1901. **Authorities:** Letter from Miss Sholl, July 30, 1943; American Catholic Who's Who (1942-43); Sholl, Anna: The Ancient Journey. 1917.

Works

1903 The law of life. (novel) D. Appleton.
1905 The port of storms. D. Appleton.

1908	The greater love. Outing pub. co.
1915	Blue blood and red. H. Holt.
1915	This way out. Hearst's international library.
1917	The ancient journey. Longmans.
1918	Faery tales of Weir. E. P. Dutton.
1921	The unclaimed letter. Dorrance.
n.d.	The four wax figures. (Published in England)
n.d.	The disappearance of the Dale family. (Published in England)

SKINNER, HENRIETTA CHANNING (DANA) "Mrs. Henry Whipple Skinner," 1857-1928.

Birthplace: Boston, Mass. **Conversion:** 1878. **Former religion:** Episcopalian. **Education:** Radcliff (1886-87); also in France and Germany; studied music in France. **General:** Mrs. Skinner was the daughter of Richard H. Dana, author of "Two Years Before the Mast," and granddaughter of R. H. Dana, Senior, founder of the North American Review. The author lived about eight years in Europe, chiefly in France, Italy and Germany. She was a member of many patriotic and historical societies, and for six years president of the Order of Descendants of Colonial Governors. **Authorities:** American Catholic Who's Who. 1911; Guide to Catholic Literature, 1888-1940; Who's Who Among North American Authors (1929-30); Curtis, G. P.: Some Roads to Rome in America. 1909.

Works

1899	Espiritu Santo; a novel. Harper.
1901	Heart and soul; a novel. Harper.
1912	Faith Brandon; a novel. D. Appleton.
1913	Their choice; a novel. Benziger.

1928   Echo from Parnassus; being girlhood memories of Long-
        fellow and his friends. H. H. Sears.
n.d.   Unbidden guest. Benziger.

SLOAN, WILLIAM HILL, 1843-

Birthplace: Fort Washita, Indiana Territory (Oklahoma). **Conversion:** 1908. **Former religion:** Baptist (minister, '73-1908). **Education:** By the Christian Brothers, Santa
Fe, N. M.; Commercial Coll., Leavenworth, Kan.; Univ. of
Rochester, Rochester, N. Y. (A.B.; M.A.); Baptist Theological Sem., Rochester (1870-73). **General:** After serving
as a Union soldier in the Civil War, Sloan studied for the
ministry and was ordained in 1873. Shortly thereafter he
was sent as a missionary to Rangoon, Burma, where he remained three years. Much of his later career was spent as
a Baptist missionary to Mexico where he taught, wrote,
and operated his own printing press. Most of his writings
appeared in Spanish, including his "Concordance." He became a Catholic while in Mexico. **Authorities:** American
Catholic Who's Who. 1911.

Works

n.d.   A practical method with the Burmese language. Rangoon,
        American Mission press.
n.d.   Concordance to the Holy Scriptures. (In Spanish and
        printed by the author on his own press.)

SMALL, JAMES LOUIS (James Loomis, pseud.) 1878-1938

Authorities: Guide to Catholic Literature, 1888-1940.

186

1914 (ed.) Within my parish; notes from the daybook of a deceased parish priest, edited by James Loomis, M.D. Dolphin press.
1920 Home—then what? The mind of the doughboy, A. E. F., by the doughboy himself. G. H. Doran.
1931 Heroes of the trail. Bruce.

SMITH, SARA TRAINER, d. 1899

General: None of this author's work appeared during her lifetime and little is recorded of her personal history. **Authorities:** Guide to Catholic Literature, 1888-1940.

Works

1900 Fred's little daughter. Benziger.
1900 Old Charlmont's seed-bed. Benziger.
1900 The room of the rose, and other stories. J. J. McVey.
1901 Milly Aveling. Benziger.
1905 (tr.) The violin maker, from the original by Otto von Schaching, pseud.

SPALDING, JAMES FIELD, 1839-1921

Birthplace: Cambridge, Mass. **Conversion:** 1892. **Former religion:** Protestant Episcopal (minister, 1869-91) **Education:** Williston Sem., Easthampton, Mass.; Williams Coll. (grad., '62; A.M., '65; S.T.D., '87). **General:** While engaged in the ministry, Dr. Spalding spent the years 1865 to 1870 as principal of the Round Hill School in Northampton. From 1899 to 1903 he was a professor of English at Boston College and later lectured at several Catholic colleges. He contributed to the leading literary periodicals.

Authorities: American Catholic Who's Who. 1911; Guide to Catholic Literature, 1888-1940; Curtis, G. P.: Some Roads to Rome in America. 1909.

Works

1886 The teaching and influence of St. Augustine. J. Pott.
1898 The world's unrest and its remedy. Longmans, Green.

SPEARMAN, FRANK HAMILTON, 1859-1937

Birthplace: Buffalo, N. Y. **Conversion:** 1884. **Former religion:** Congregationalist. **Education:** Public and private schools; Lawrence Coll., Appleton, Wis. **General:** Mr. Spearman established his reputation as a short story writer, and particularly stories of the railroad. After achieving success as a novelist, he spent much time traveling with his family—with Italy as a frequent goal. Spearman received the Laetare Medal from Notre Dame University in 1935 and was honored by other colleges and universities. **Authorities:** American Catholic Who's Who (1938-39); Guide to Catholic Literature, 1888-1940; Twentieth Century Authors; Curtis, G. P.: Some Roads to Rome in America. 1909; Donovan, F. P.: The Railroad in Literature; Spearman, E.: Memories. 1941; Titus, W. A.: Wisconsin Writers. 1930

Works

1900 The nerve of Foley and other railroad stories. Harper.
1901 Held for orders; being stories of railroad life. McClure, Phillips.
1901 The railroad (with others). McClure, Phillips.
1902 Doctor Bryson; a novel. C. Scribner.
1903 The daughter of a magnate. C. Scribner.

1904	The close of the day. D. Appleton.
1904	The strategy of great railroads. C. Scribner.
1906	Whispering Smith. C. Scribner.
1909	Adventures in field and forest (with others). Harper.
1910	Making good: stories of golf and other outdoor sports (with others). Harper.
1911	Robert Kimberly; illustrated by James Montgomery Flagg.
1912	The mountain divide. C. Scribner.
1913	Merrilie Dawes. C. Scribner.
1916	Nan of Music Mountain. C. Scribner.
1921	Laramie holds the range. C. Scribner.
1923	The marriage verdict. C. Scribner.
1925	Selwood of Sleepy Cat. C. Scribner.
1927	Flambeau Jim. C. Scribner.
1930	Spanish lover. C. Scribner.
1933	Hell's desert; a novel. Doubleday, Doran.
1935	Gunlock ranch; a novel. Doubleday, Doran.
1937	Carmen of the rancho. Doubleday, Doran.
n.d.	Boys book of big game hunting (with others). Harper.
n.d.	Your son's education. Ave Maria. pa.

SPOONER, MARY ANN (WETMORE) 1794-1877

Birthplace: New York City. **Former religion:** Her grandfather was a Presbyterian minister. **General:** Mrs. Spooner married Alden Spooner, editor of the Long Island Star, of Brooklyn, in 1831. A copy of the book listed below is in the Queens Borough Public Library, Jamaica, N. Y., and another is in the Long Island Historical Society, Brooklyn. **Authorities:** Catholic Builders of the Nation, v. 3. (Reference only); Sealock, R. B. and Seely, P. A.: Long Island Bibliography. 1940; Wetmore, J. C.: The Wetmore Family of America. 1861.

Works

| 1848 | Gathered leaves. G. P. Putnam. |

STAFFORD, WENDELL PHILLIPS, 1861-

Birthplace: Barre, Vt. **Education:** St. Johnsbury Acad.; Boston Univ. (LL.B., '83); Darmouth Coll. **General:** The author was a member of the Vermont state legislature in 1892, and became associate judge of the Supreme Court of that state in 1900. He assumed a like position in the Supreme Court of the District of Columbia a little later. Judge Stafford was honored by the Universities of Vermont, Georgetown, George Washington and Middlebury College. **Authorities:** American Catholic Who's Who (1942-43); Who's Who Among North American Authors (1933-36); Guide to Catholic Literature, 1888-1940.

Works

1902   North flowers, a few poems. Caledonian co.
1909   Dorian days; poems. Macmillan.
1910   Vermont. Elm Tree press. 14 leaves.
1913   Speeches of Wendell Phillips Stafford. A. F. Stone.
1915   Voices; a dramatic ode. Caledonian co. 12 p.
1916   The land we love. A. F. Stone.
1917   War poems. A. F. Stone. 15 p.
1934   A handbook of equity. National law book co.

STANCOURT, LOUIS J., 1900-

Birthplace: Brooklyn, N. Y. **Conversion:** 1934. **Former religion:** Although baptised a Catholic, renounced all faith. **Education:** Public schools of N. Y. C.; Alexander Hamilton High School (1913-14); Special courses in writing craft and wide reading. **General:** Mr. Stancourt, the son of Francisco and Assunta Stanco, became a secular member of the Oblates of St. Benedict after his conversion, and spent a year making his novitiate at St. John's Abbey, Collegeville, Minn. The author was a newspaper reporter from 1925 to 1939 and is now with the United States armed forces. **Authorities:** Letter from Mr. Stancourt, October 3, 1943; Stancourt, Louis: A flower for sign. 1937; Stancourt, Louis: Her Glimmering Tapers. 1943.

Works

1937 A flower for sign. Macmillan.
1943 Her glimmering tapers, a spiritual autobiography. Macmillan.

STARR, ELIZA ALLEN, 1824-1901

Birthplace: Deerfield, Mass. **Conversion:** 1856. **Former religion:** Unitarian. **Education:** Privately in Boston; also studied art in the same city (1896). **General:** Miss Starr, first woman to receive the Laetare Medal from the University of Notre Dame, taught art in her Boston studio and in private schools in Brooklyn and Philadelphia. She settled in Chicago about 1856 and became one of the first art teachers in that city, with many wealthy patrons contributing to her success. After her studio burned, she resided at St. Mary's Academy (now College) helping to organize the art department. **Authorities:** Catholic Encyclopedia, v. 14; Cyclopaedia of American Biography, v. 7; Dictionary of American Biography, v. 17; Guide to Catholic Literature, 1888-1940; Driscoll, A. S.: Literary Convert Women. 1928; Hayes, A. J.: A Convert's Reason Why. 1911; Catholic World, November, 1897; February, 1902.

Works

1867 Poems. H. McGrath.
1871-81 Patron saints (1st and 2d ser.) Catholic pub. soc.

1883	Pilgrims and shrines. Union Catholic pub. co. 2 v.
1887	Poems.
1888	Songs of a lifetime.
1889	Isabelle of Castile, 1492-1892. C. V. Waite.
1891	Christian art in our own age. Ave Maria.
1891	Christmastide. The author.
1891	What we see. The author.
1895	The three keys to the Camera della Segnatura in the Vatican. The author.
1896	Rafael's Vatican paintings. Chicago.
1898	The seven dolors of the Blessed Virgin Mary. The author.
1900	The three archangels and the guardian angels in art.

STAUNTON, JOHN ARMITAGE, father, 1864-

Birthplace: Adrian, Mich. **Conversion:** 1930. **Former religion:** Protestant Episcopal (minister, 1891-1930). **Ordained priest:** 1934. **Education:** Columbia Univ. (B.M.E.) **General:** The author began his career as a teacher of Latin and mathematics in the Fort Hill School in Rochester, N. Y. A few years after his ordination to the ministry he went to the Philippines as a missionary where he remained until 1926. After his conversion he became a professor at the University of Notre Dame and remained there until his retirement in 1934. **Authorities:** American Catholic Who's Who (1942-43); Guide to Catholic Literature, 1888-1940.

Works

1937 Scholasticism, the philosophy of common sense, with a foreword by the Reverend Charles C. Miltner, C.S.C. Garrison, N. Y.

STEAD, WILLIAM FORCE, 1884-

Birthplace: U. S. **Conversion:** 1933. **Former religion:** Anglican (minister, 1917-32) **Education:** Force School, Washington, D. C.; Friends' School, Washington, D. C.; Tome Institute, Md.; Univ. of Virginia (1904-08); Queen's Coll., Oxford, Eng. (B.A., '22; M.A., '25; B.Litt., '35). **General:** Between his two university careers, Mr. Stead was in the American Consular Service at Liverpool. Later he was Chaplain of Worcester College, Oxford, and from 1930 to 1933, Fellow at Worcester. "Uriel" is the author's chief work of poetry and "Shadow of Mt. Carmel" (showing approach to Catholicism) his best prose. **Authorities:** Letter from Mr. Stead, October 28, 1943; Guide to Catholic Literature, 1888-1940.

Works

1909 Moon flowers; a book of fancies. D. Nutt.
1911 Windflowers, a book of lyrics. E. Stock.
1917 Holy innocents, and other poems. Chiswick press. 20 p.
1920 Verd antiqua, poems. B. Blackwell.
1922 The sweet miracle, and other poems. R. Cobden-Sanderson.
1924 Wayfaring; songs and elegies. R. Cobden-Sanderson.
1926 The shadow of Mt. Carmel. R. Cobden-Sanderson.
1927 Festival in Tuscany, and other poems. R. Cobden-Sanderson.
1930 The house on the wold. R. Cobden-Sanderson.
1933 Uriel. R. Cobden-Sanderson.
1938 (ed.) The poetry of the Bible. R. Cobden-Sanderson.
1939 (ed.) Rejoice in the lamb; a song for bedlam, by Christopher Smart. J. Cape.

STEARNS, FOSTER WATERMAN, 1881-

Birthplace: Hull, Mass. **Conversion:** 1911. **Former reli-**

gion: Protestant Episcopal (minister, 1909-   ) **Education:** Amherst Coll. (A.B., '03; Harvard Univ. (A.M., '06); General Theological Sem. (grad., '09); Boston Coll. Graduate School (A.M., '15). **General:** Mr. Stearns began his career as librarian of the Boston Museum of Fine Arts, leaving in 1917 to become Massachusetts State Librarian. He served as a first lieutenant in the World War and received many decorations. After the war he entered the diplomatic service and was attached to the American embassies at Constantinople and Paris. From 1925 to 1930 he was librarian of Holy Cross College, Worcester, Mass. Pius XI honored him on two occasions. **Authorities:** American Catholic Who's Who (1942-43); Guide to Catholic Literature, 1888-1940; Who's Who in America (1942-43).

Works

1927   (tr.) Madeleine Semer, convert and mystic, 1874-1921, by Abbe Felix Klein, with a foreword by James J. Walsh. Macmillan.
1928   Edward Everett (American Secretaries of State series). Knopf.
1936   Blessed Adrian Fortesque, K.M.

STODDARD, CHARLES WARREN, 1843-1909

Birthplace: Rochester, N. Y. **Conversion:** 1867. **Education:** Unable to secure a college education because of poor health. **General:** Stoddard's first poem appeared in 1861, and for two years thereafter he contributed regularly to the Golden Era (San Francisco) under the pseudonym of "Pip Pepperpod." Mark Twain and Bret Harte were two of his fellow contributors. Because of the precarious state of his health it was necessary for the author to spend much time in a warm climate, and he chose the Hawaiian Islands and the South Seas. For a time he was in London as correspondent for the San Francisco Chronicle, but after his conversion Stoddard became successively, professor of English at the University of Notre Dame and lecturer at the Catholic University of America. **Authorities:** American Authors, 1600-1900; Book of Catholic Authors. 3d series; Catholic Encyclopedia, v. 14; Dictionary of American Biography, v. 18; Guide to Catholic Literature, 1888-1940; Who's Who in America (1908-09); Earls, Michael: Manuscripts and Memories. 1935; Ave Maria, May 15, 22, 1909; Catholic World, July, 1915; Harper's Monthly Magazine, December, 1917.

Works

1867 Poems of Charles Warren Stoddard, edited by Bret Harte.
1873 South-sea idyls. J. R. Osgood.
1874 Summer cruising in the South seas. Chatto & Windup.
1881 Mashallah! A flight into Egypt. D. Appleton.
1885 The lepers of Molokai. Ave Maria press.
1885 A trip to Hawaii. San Francisco, Oceanic steamship co.
1885 A troubled heart and how it was comforted at last. J. A. Lyons.
1894 Hawaiian life: being lazy letters from low latitudes. F. T. Neely.
1896 The wonder-worker of Padua. Ave Maria press.
1898 A cruise under the crescent. Rand McNally.
1899 Over the Rocky mountains to Alaska. B. Herder.
1901 Father Damien. Catholic truth soc. 30 p.
1902 In the footprints of the padres. A. M. Robertson.
1903 Exits and entrances; a book of essays and sketches. Lothrop.
1903 For the pleasure of his company. A. M. Robertson.
1904 The island of tranquil delight, a south sea idyl. H. B. Turner.
1907 Confessions of a reformed poet.

1909   Apostrophe to the skylark; the Bells of San Gabriel; Joe of
        Lahaina; An appreciation of Charles Warren Stoddard,
        by George Wharton James. Aroyo guild press.
1909   Passion play at Brixleg. Ave Maria press. pa.
1917   Poems; collected by Ina Coolbrith. J. Lane.
1933   Charles Warren Stoddard's diary of a visit to Molokai in
        1844, with a letter from Father Damien to his brother
        in 1873. San Francisco book club of California.

STODDARD, JOHN LAWSON, 1850-1931

Birthplace: Brookline, Mass. **Conversion:** 1922. **Former religion:** Congregationalist; later agnostic. **Education:** Public schools in Boston; Williams Coll. (grad., '71); Yale Divinity School. **General:** After deciding not to practice the ministry, Stoddard became an instructor in the classics at the Boston Latin School in 1873. Five years of teaching and traveling then preceded his career as a public lecturer. In an age of good speakers, Stoddard was outstanding, and his success permitted him to maintain a villa at various times in Europe. He had great personal magnetism, but his great vogue was chiefly due to the extreme care with which he prepared his addresses. **Authorities:** Dictionary of American Biography, v. 18; Who's Who in America (1930-31); Stoddard, J. L.: Rebuilding a Lost Faith. 1921; Catholic World, October, 1831; Hampton Magazine, October, 1910; Libraries, May, 1931; Guide to Catholic Literature, 1888-1940.

Works

1884   Red-letter days abroad. J. R. Osgood.
189-   Scenic America, the beauties of the western hemisphere.
        Werner.

196

1892	Glimpses of the world. R. S. Peale.
1894	Napoleon; from Corsica to St. Helena. Werner.
1894	Portfolio of photographs of our country and our neighbors. Werner.
1897-98	John L. Stoddard's lectures. Middlebrook. 10 v. (Originally published individually in The Travel Series. Werner, 1897)
1899	Famous parks and buildings.
1902	Beautiful scenes of America from Battery Park to the Golden Gate. Saalfield.
1910	(comp.) The Stoddard library: a thousand hours of entertainment with the world's great writers. G. L. Shuman.
1913	Poems. G. L. Shuman.
1914	Poems on Lake Como. G. L. Shuman.
1915	(comp.) The Stoddard library (supplement). G. L. Shuman.
1917	La decadence de l'Angleterre. F. Wyss. 40 p.
1921	Rebuilding a lost faith, by an American agnostic. P. J. Kenedy.
1924	(tr.) Christ and the critics, by Hilarin Felder. Burns, Oates and Washbourne. 2 v.
1926-27	(tr.) The theology of St. Paul, by Fernand Prat, S. J. Burns, Oates and Washbourne. 2 v.
1929	(tr.) St. Gregory the Great, by Mgr. Pierre Batiffol. Burns, Oates and Washbourne.
1930	(tr.) The evening of life (compensations of old age) by Monsignor Baunard. Bruce.
1930	Twelve years in the Catholic church. Burns, Oates & Washbourne.
1930	Yesterdays of an artist monk, by Dom Willibrord Verkade. P. J. Kenedy.

STONE, JAMES KENT (Father Fidelis, C.P.) 1840 1921

Birthplace: Boston, Mass. **Conversion:** 1869. **Former religion:** Protestant Episcopal (minister, 1863-69). **Ordained**

priest: 1872. **Education:** Attended E. S. Dixwell's Latin School, Boston; Harvard Univ. (grad.) **General:** For a short time Father Fidelis taught at Dixwell's Latin School, leaving to become a private in the Union army. In 1863 he began the study of theology, and following his ordination as a minister, became president of Kenyon College in Gambier, Ohio. In 1868 he was called to Hobart College in New York as president. After his conversion he became a Paulist but withdrew from this Order to join the Congregation of the Passion. Father Fidelis built many foundations for this Congregation both at home and abroad. **Authorities:** American Catholic Who's Who. 1911; Dictionary of American Biography, v. 18; Guide to Catholic Literature, 1888-1940; Curtis, G. P.: Beyond the Road to Rome. 1914; Smith, W. S.: Fidelis of the Cross. 1926; Ave Maria, October 31 to November 21, 1931.

Works

1870 The invitation heeded: reasons for a return to Catholic unity. Catholic pub. soc.
1920 Awakening and what followed. Ave Maria.

STORER, HORATIO ROBINSON, 1830-1922

Birthplace: Boston, Mass. **Conversion:** 1879. **Education:** Boston Latin School (1841-46); Harvard Univ. (A.B., '50); Tremont Medical School; Harvard Medical School (M.D., '53); Harvard Law School (LL.B., '68); studied medicine abroad for two years. **General:** Dr. Storer entered the medical field as assistant to his father at Harvard University. From 1865 to 1869 he was professor of obstetrics and medical jurisprudence at Berkshire Medical College.

When compelled to retire from active practice by ill health, he spent five years (1872-77) studying the fevers of southern Europe. Storer was an authority on medical numismatics and also one of the founders of the Journal of the Gynecological Society of Boston. **Authorities:** American Catholic Who's Who. 1911; Dictionary of American Biography, v. 18; Who's Who in America (1922-23); Toner, J. M.: A Sketch of the Life of Horatio R. Storer. 1878. (Contains bibliography); Harvard Graduate's Magazine, March 1923.

Works

1860 Criminal abortion in America.
1863 Eutokia: a word to physicians and to women upon the employment of anaesthetics in childbirth.
1866 Why not? a book for every woman. Lothrop.
1867 Is it I? A book for every man. Lothrop.
1868 Criminal abortion (with F. F. Heard).
1868 On nurses and nursing. Lothrop.
1871 The causation, course and treatment of reflex insanity in women.
1875 Southern Italy as a health station for invalids.
1931 Medicina in nummis. (Edited by his son).

STORER, MARIA (LONGWORTH) "Mrs. Bellamy Storer," 1849-1932

Birthplace: Cincinnati, O. **Conversion:** 1892. **Former religion:** Episcopalian "High Church." **General:** The author was the wife of Bellamy Storer, sometime ambassador to Belgium, Spain, and Austria-Hungary. As an artist in pottery decoration, Mrs. Storer achieved substantial success, winning honors at the Paris Exposition for an exhibit of twenty pieces of pottery mounted in bronze. She became one of the directors of the Van Briggle Pottery company of Colorado Springs, Colorado. **Authorities:** American Catholic Who's Who. 1911; Guide to Catholic Literature, 1888-1940; National Cyclopaedia of American Biography, v. 11; Curtis, G. P.: Beyond the Road to Rome. 1914; Curtis, G. P.: Some Roads to Rome in America. 1909.

Works

1891   (tr.) Tales for a stormy night. Translation from the French. R. Clarke.
1915   Sir Christopher Leighton; or, The Marquis de Vaudreuil's story. B. Herder.
1916   The Borodino mystery. B. Herder.
1916   Probation. B. Herder.
1918   The Villa Rossignol; or, The advance of Islam. B. Herder.
1923   In memoriam: Bellamy Storer. Merrymount press.

TABB, JOHN BANNISTER, father, 1845-1909
Birthplace: Near Richmond, Va. **Conversion:** 1872. **Former religion:** Protestant Episcopal. **Education:** Private tutoring; Episcopal Seminary, Alexandria, Va.; St. Charles (Cath.) Coll., Maryland. **General:** As a youth, the poet and priest was active during the Civil War on the side of the South as a blockade runner. While on the "Siren" in 1864, he was captured and imprisoned, and after his release taught at St. Paul's School, Baltimore, and at Racine College, Wisconsin. The conversion of his friend Alfred Allen Curtis (q.v.) hastened his own, and in 1881 he entered St. Mary's Seminary, Baltimore, to study for the priesthood. Father Tabb began teaching at St. Charles College even before he was ordained and remained there as a professor until shortly before his death. **Authorities:** American Au-

thors, 1600-1900; Dictionary of American Biography, v. 18; Guide to Catholic Literature, 1888-1940; Blair, Gordon: Father Tabb, Poet, Priest, Soldier and Wit. 1940; Finn, Sister M. P.: John Bannister Tabb. 1915; Heagney, H. J.: Blockade Runner. 1939; Litz, F. E.: Father Tabb; A Study of His Life and Works. 1923; Litz, F. E.: Father Tabb; A Study of His Poetry. 1924; Tabb, J. M.: Father Tabb, His Life and Work. 1921.

Works

1883	Poems. R. M. McBride.
1893	An octave to Mary. J. Murphy.
1894	Poems. Copeland & Day.
1897	Bone rules: or, Skeleton of English grammar. Benziger.
1897	Lyrics. Copeland & Day.
1899	Child verse. Small, Maynard.
1900	Two lyrics. Craftman's guild.
1902	Later lyrics. J. Lane.
1904	The rosary in rhyme. Small, Maynard.
1907	Quips and quiddits; ques for the qurious. Small, Maynard.
1910	Later poems. M. Kennerley.
1928	The poetry of Father Tabb, edited by F. E. Litz.

TAGGART, MARION AMES, 1866-

Birthplace: Haverhill, Mass. **Education:** Privately, at home. **General:** This extremely popular and voluminous author wrote chiefly for a young girl audience, beginning her writing career in 1882. In later years Miss Taggart also wrote fiction with a wider appeal. Besides her books she has contributed articles, stories and verse to magazines. **Authorities:** American Catholic Who's Who (1942-43); Guide to Catholic Literature, 1888-1940; Who's Who in America (1940-41); Catholic World, July, 1897.

1897 Aser, the shepherd. Benziger.
1897 Bezaleel. Benziger.
1897 Blissylvania post-office. Benziger.
1897 By Branscome river. Benziger.
1897 Three girls and especially one. Benziger.
1898 (ed.) The treasure of Nugget Mountain. Benziger.
1898 (ed.) Winnetou, the Apache knight. Benziger. (At head of title: Jack Hildreth among the Indiana).
1899 Loyal blue and royal scarlet. A story of '76. Benziger.
1900 Jack Hildreth on the Nile: adapted from the original of C. May. Benziger.
1902 In the days of King Hal. Benziger.
1902 Miss Lochinvar. D. Appleton.
1902 The Wyndham girls. Century.
1903 At Aunt Anna's. D. Appleton.
1903 The unravelling of a tangle. Benziger.
1904 The little grey house. McClure, Phillips.
1905 The little women club. H. Altemus.
1905 Nut-brown Joan. H. Holt.
1905 One afternoon, and other stories. Benziger.
1906 Daddy's daughters; il. by G. W. Break. H. Holt.
1906 Miss Lochinvar's return. D. Appleton.
1906 Pussy-cat town. L. C. Page.
1906 Six girls and Bob. W. A. Wilde.
1907 The daughters of the little grey house. McClure, Phillips.
1907 The doctor's little girl. L. C. Page.
1907 Six girls and the tea room. Illustrated by W. G. Stecher. W. A. Wilde.
1908 Six girls growing older. W. A. Wilde.
1909 Six girls and the seventh one. W. A. Wilde.
1909 Sweet Nancy; or, More about the doctor's little girl. Illustrated by A. B. Barry.
1910 Betty Gaston, the seventh girl. W. A. Wilde.
1910 The friendly little house and other stories. Benziger.
1910 Nancy Porter's opportunity. L. C. Page.
1911 Nancy, the doctor's little partner. L. C. Page.
1911 Six girls and Betty; a story. W. A. Wilde.
1912 Six girls grown up. Illustrated by W. F. Stecher. W. A. Wilde.

1913 Her daughter Jean. W. A. Wilde.
1913 The little aunt. M. C. Donohue.
1914 Beth's wonder-winter; a story, illustrated by W. F. Stecher.
1914 The elder Miss Ainsborough. Benziger.
1915 Beth's old home. W. A. Wilde.
1915 Nancy and the Coggs twins. L. C. Page.
1916 Beth of old Childton. W. A. Wilde.
1916 Hollyhock house. Doubleday, Page.
1918 Captain Sylvia. Illustrated by Clara M. Burd. Doubleday, Page.
1920 A pilgrim maid. Doubleday, Page.
1921 The Annes. Doubleday, Page.
1921 At greenacres. G. H. Doran.
1921 The bottle imp. G. H. Doran.
1921 Poppy's pluck. G. H. Doran.
1922 No handicap. Benziger.
1922 "Who is Sylvia?" Illustrated by Vera Clere. Doubleday, Page.
1922 Wonder story. Benziger.
1923 Wonder days. Benziger.

TARRY, ELLEN

Birthplace: Birmingham, Ala. **Conversion:** 1916. **Former religion:** Congregationalist. **Education:** Slater School (1912-19); Industrial High School, Birmingham (1919-21); St. Francis de Sales, Castle Rock, Va. (1921-23); Alabama State Teacher's Coll. **General:** Miss Tarry taught in the Birmingham public schools before becoming a feature writer on the Birmingham Truth in 1926. She left this work to become a free lance writer, most of her contributions going to the Catholic and Negro press. **Authorities:** American Catholic Who's Who (1942-43).

Works

1940 Janie Belle; illustrated by Myrtle Sheldon. Garden City pub. 30 p.

1942   Hezekiah Horton. Pictures by Oliver Harrington. Viking.
31 p.

TENNANT, JOHN ALEXANDER, 1868-

Birthplace: Darlington, Eng. **Conversion:** 1887. **Education:** Queen Elizabeth's School, Darlington; St. Francis Xavier Coll., N. Y. (Ph.B., '93). **General:** Mr. Tennant was a member of the publishing firm of Tennant and Ward. He wrote and published about fifty monographs, some of which are listed below. In 1908 he became editor of the American Annual of Photography and later edited Photo-Miniature, A Monthly Magazine. **Authorities:** American Catholic Who's Who. 1911.

Works

1899   (ed.) Hand camera work. Tennant & Ward.
1900   (ed.) Trimming, mounting and framing. Tennant & Ward.
1911   Photography at home; a handbook. Tennant & Ward.
1911   Photography out doors; practical suggestions. Tennant & Ward.
1912   Bromide printing and enlarging; a practical guide. Tennant & Ward.
1912   Dark room work; a practical dark room manual. Tennant & Ward.
1912   Developers and development; a practical survey. Tennant & Ward.
1912   Flashlight portraiture. Tennant & Ward.

TENNEY, SARA (BROWNSON) 1839-1876

Birthplace: Chelsea, Mass. **General:** Mrs. Tenney was the daughter of Orestes Brownson, the sister of Henry Brownson (qq.v.) and the second wife of William J. Tenney (q.v.)

Authorities: Appleton's Annual Cyclopaedia and Register of Important Events of the Year 1876. p. 625.

Works

1859 Marian Elwood, or, How girls live.
1865 At anchor.
1873 Life of Demitrius Augustine Gallitzin.

TENNEY, WILLIAM JEWETT, 1811-1883

Birthplace: Newport, R. I. **Conversion:** ca. 1840. **Former religion:** Congregationalist. **Education:** Yale Coll. (grad., '32); studied medicine, then law, and was admitted to the bar. **General:** Judge Tenney began the careers of medicine and law before deciding upon journalism in 1840. After some years as a reporter, he joined the staff of D. Appleton in 1853 and remained with this company for thirty years. Appleton's Annual Cyclopaedia, which he edited with Rossiter Johnson, was his greatest work although he was also at one time a criminal court judge in Brooklyn. He married the daughter of Orestes Brownson (q.v.). **Authorities:** Appleton's Annual Encyclopaedia (1883); Appleton's Cyclopaedia of American Biography, v. 6; Dictionary of American Biography, v. 18.

Works

1865 The military and naval history of the rebellion in the United States, with biographical sketches of deceased officers. D. Appleton.
1866 A grammatical analyzer. D. Appleton.

THAYER, JOHN, father, 1758-1815

Birthplace: Boston, Mass. **Conversion:** 1783. **Former re-**

ligion: Congregationalist (minister). **Ordained priest:** 1789. **Education:** Yale Univ. **General:** John Thayer was the first prominent New Englander to become a Catholic and the first to become a priest. His account of his conversion, translated in both French and Spanish, created a controversy both at home and abroad. He served as a Protestant chaplain during the Revolutionary War, later becoming a Catholic missionary. Thayer died in Ireland, leaving funds to found a convent in the United States. The Ursuline convent at Charlestown which was eventually built with these funds, was burned and sacked by an anti-Catholic mob in 1834. **Authorities:** Catholic Encyclopedia, v. 14; Guide to Catholic Literature, 1888-1940; Bridgett, T. E.: New England Convert. 1897; Merritt, E. P.: Bibliographical Notes on "An Account of the Conversion of Rev. John Thayer." 1923; Merritt, E. P.: Sketches of the Three Earliest Roman Catholic Priests in Boston. 1923.

Works

1787 An account of the conversion of the Reverend John Thayer.
1798 A discourse delivered, at the Roman Catholic Church in Boston. S. Hall. 31 p.

THOMPSON, CHARLES WILLIS, 1871-

Birthplace: Kalamazoo, Mich. **Conversion:** ca. 1890. **Education:** New York Univ. (LL.B., '92). **General:** Mr. Thompson began contributing satirical sketches to Judge at the age of thirteen on political subjects, and in 1897 took the stump for Henry George of Single Tax fame. In 1907 he was chief of the New York Times' Washington bureau and later, editor of the New York Times Book Review. Since 1924 the author has been a free lance writer, contributing principally to the American Mercury. **Authorities:** American Catholic Who's Who (1942-43); Guide to Catholic Literature, 1888-1940; Who's Who in America (1942-43); Catholic World, August, 1941.

Works

1906 Party leaders of the time. G. W. Dillingham.
1918 The new voter; things he and she aught to know about politics and citizenship. Putnam.
1929 Presidents I've known, and two near presidents. Bobbs-Merrill.
1931 The fiery epoch, 1830-1877. Bobbs-Merrill.

THOMPSON, THOMAS PAYNE, 1860-

Birthplace: Montgomery, Ala. **Conversion:** 1887. **Education:** Public schools in Montgomery and later private study. **General:** Mr. Thompson was a banker and civic leader, and particularly active in social reform. In 1910 his private library held six thousand volumes of Americana. **Authorities:** American Catholic Who's Who. 1911; Curtis, G. P.: Beyond the Road to Rome. 1914.

Works

1903 Catalogue of Americana. Consisting principally of books relating to Louisiana and the Mississippi Valley (Louisiana Purchase). Private print.
1904 Louisiana writers, national and resident. New Orleans.
n.d. Guide to the French Quarter of New Orleans.

TIERNAN, FRANCES CHRISTINE (FISHER) (Christian Reid, pseud.) 1846-1920

Birthplace: Salisbury, N. C. **Conversion:** "Early in life." **Former religion:** Father, Episcopalian; mother, Catholic. **Education:** At home. **General:** Mrs. Tiernan's father, a Confederate officer, was killed in the battle of Manassas in 1861. After his death the author lived in the family homestead until 1887 when she married James Marquis Tiernan of Maryland. She then went with her husband to Mexico where he had mining interests, and it was during this time that several of her novels of Mexican life were written. The author was devoted to the Church, and in 1909 was awarded the Laetare Medal by the University of Notre Dame. **Authorities:** American Catholic Who's Who. 1911; Catholic Encyclopedia, Supp. I (1922); Dictionary of American Biography, v. 18; Guide to Catholic Literature, 1888-1940; Donnelly, E. C. and others: A Round Table of the Representative American Catholic Novelists. 1897; Driscoll, A. S.: Literary Convert Women. 1928; America, April 24, 1920; Ave Maria, April 11, 1920.

Works

1870 Valerie Aylmer. A novel. D. Appleton.
1871 Mable Lee. A novel. D. Appleton.
1871 Morton House. D. Appleton.
1872 Ebb tide, and other stories. D. Appleton.
1873 Carmen's inheritance. Illustrated by W. J. Sheppard. To-day print. and pub.
1873 Nina's atonement, and other stories. D. Appleton.
1874 A daughter of Bohemia. D. Appleton.
1875 A gentle belle. D. Appleton.
1875 Hearts and hands. D. Appleton.
1875 A question of honor. A novel.
1876 The land of the sky. D. Appleton.
1877 After many days. A novel. D. Appleton.
1878 Bonny Kate. A novel.
1878 A summer idyl. D. Appleton.

1883	Hearts of steel. D. Appleton.
1884	Roslyn's fortune. A novel. D. Appleton.
1887	Miss Churchill: a study. D. Appleton.
1890	A cast for fortune.
1891	Carmela. H. L. Kilner.
1892	The lost lode. H. L. Kilner.
1892	A woman of fortune. Benziger.
1893	A comedy of elopement. D. Appleton.
1893	A little maid of Arcady. H. L. Kilner.
1894	The land of the sun. D. Appleton.
1896	The picture of Las Cruces. D. Appleton.
1897	Fairy gold. Ave Maria.
1897	The man of the family; a novel. G. P. Putnam.
1898	The chase of an heiress. G. P. Putnam.
1900	Under the Southern Cross. Capitol print. co.
1900	Weighed in the balance. Marlier, Callanan.
1903	A daughter of the Sierra. B. Herder.
1907	Vera's charge. Ave Maria.
1908	Princess Nadine. G. P. Putnam.
1911	The light of the visions. Ave Maria.
1911	The Wargrave trust. Benziger.
1913	The daughter of a star. Devin-Adair.
1915	The secret bequest. Ave Maria.
n.d.	Armine. Christian press.
n.d.	A child of Mary. Ave Maria.
n.d.	Phillip's restitution.

TINCKER, MARY AGNES, 1831-1907

Birthplace: Ellsworth, Me. **Conversion:** 1853. **Former religion:** Protestant. **Education:** Public and private schools; academy in Bluehill, Me. (1848-49) **General:** The novelist began teaching in the public school of Ellsworth when she was thirteen and later taught in its parochial school. At fifteen she began contributing sketches to the local newspapers and magazines. During the Civil War Miss Tincker became a volunteer nurse and was active in Washington, D. C. in that capacity for a short time. After the war she resumed her writing, contributing to Harpers and Putnam's magazine. Her first novel "The House of Yorke" shows the strong imprint of her Catholicity. **Authorities:** Catholic Encyclopedia, v. 14; Cyclopaedia of American Biographies, v. 7; Dictionary of American Biography, v. 18; Baker, E. A.: Guide to the Best Fiction in English. 1913; Driscoll, A. S.: Literary Convert Women. 1928; Ave Maria, July 24, 1909.

Works

1872 The house of Yorke. Catholic pub. soc.
1873 The winged word.
1874 (tr.) Grapes and thorns; or, A priest's sacrifice (from the French).
1878 Six sunny months. Catholic pub. co.
1879 Signor Monaldini's niece. W. F. Roberts.
1881 By the Tiber. W. F. Roberts.
1884 The jewel in the lotus. A novel. Illustrations by Thomas and Helen C. Hovenden. J. B. Lippincott.
1886 Aurora. J. B. Lippincott.
1889 Two coronets. Houghton, Mifflin.
1892 San Salvador. Houghton, Mifflin.
1889 Autumn leaves, verse and story. W. H. Young.

TWINEM, LEO LEONARD (Leonard Twynham, pseud.) 1890-

Birthplace: Fairmont, W. Va. **Conversion:** 1937. **Former religion:** Protestant Episcopal (minister, 1917-37). **Education:** Wooster Coll.; Columbia Univ.; Union Theological Sem. **General:** During the World War Mr. Twinem was a chaplain in the U. S. Navy and afterward spent some years teaching. From 1927 to 1937 he was rector of St. John's Episcopal Church, Flushing, Long Island. He is an occasional contributor to periodical literature. **Authorities:** American Catholic Who's Who (1942-43); Guide to Catholic Literature, 1888-1940.

Works

1932   Maria Monk's daughter of Sharon and Amenia: the true story of Lizzie St. John Eckel Harper and her church on the hill, by Leonard Twynham. Flushing, N. Y.

VAN STOCKUM, HILDA, (Mrs. Ervin Marlin), 1908- **Birthplace:** Rotterdam, Netherlands. **Came to U. S.:** 1934. **Conversion:** 1939. **Former religion:** Parents, agnostics, but author became an Episcopalian. **Education:** Very early schooling at home; attended art school in Dublin and later in Amsterdam. **General:** Mrs. Ervin Marlin is the daughter of an Irish mother and a Dutch father, and although born in Holland, her first language was English. Her husband, whom she met in Dublin, is a native American. The author's principal career is that of mother and wife to a growing family. The Marlins have four children. **Authorities:** Book of Catholic Authors, 2d series; Catholic Library World, October, 1942; American Catholic Who's Who (1944-45).

Works

1934   A day on skates, the story of a Dutch picnic; with illustrations by the author. Harper.
1936   (tr. and illus.) Afke's ten, by Mevrouw Troelstra. J. B. Lippincott.
1937   (tr. and illus.) Tilio, a boy of Papua, by Rudolph Vanhoeve. J. B. Lippincott.
1938   The cottage at Bantry Bay. (Illustrated by the author). Viking.

1939 Francie on the run. (Illustrated by the author). Viking.
1940 Kersti and St. Nicholas. (Illustrated by the author). Viking.
1941 Pegeen. (Illustrated by the author). Viking.
1942 Andries. (Illustrated by the author). Viking.

VINCENT, JOHN, pseud., **See** Huntington, Jebediah Vincent, 1815-1862

WAKEFIELD, PRICILLA, pseud., **See** Learned, Ellin (Craven) "Mrs Frank Learned," 1850-1940

WALLACE, SISTER MARY IMELDA, 1884-

Birthplace: Sanilac County, Mich. **Conversion:** 1898. **Former religion:** Methodist Episcopal. **Education:** Northern Arizona Teacher's Coll. (1903); Loretto Heights Coll. (B.A., '34). **General:** Except for three lengthy visits to Canada, the author lived in Arizona from the age of four until she became a Sister of Loretto in 1908. Sister Imelda taught in the Arizona mining camps of Congress, Iron King, and Jerome from 1903 to 1908. After entering the convent she resumed teaching, this time in the parish schools of St. Louis, Missouri, Auburn, Nebraska, Denver, Colorado, and Loretto, Kentucky. Her artistic talent has been utilized in illustrating some of her works. **Authorities:** Letter from Sister M. Imelda, January 10, 1944; American Catholic Who's Who (1942-43); Boyer, M. G.: Arizona in Literature, a Collection of the Best Writings of Arizona Authors. 1934.

1923 The outlaws of Ravenhurst. Illustrations and initials by the author. Franciscan Herald press.
1924 The lure of the West. J. H. Meier.
1935 Learning my religion (with M. A. Schumacher). Benziger.
1938 The story beautiful. Benziger.
1942 Living my religion (Books I-IV). The questions and answers of the revised Baltimore catechism (with others). Benziger. (Books III and IV have not yet been published).

WALTER, EUGENE, 1874-1941

Birthplace: Cleveland, O. **Conversion:** 1941. **Education:** Cleveland public schools. **General:** As a newspaper reporter, Mr. Walter was a correspondent for the Cleveland Plain Dealer, Detroit News, New York Sun, and other papers. He left this work however, and for some time was a business manager for theatrical companies and other amusement enterprises. In 1898 he served with the United States Army. Besides writing for the legitimate stage, the author wrote numerous scenarios and a series of lectures, published under the title, "How to Write a Play." **Authorities:** Who Was Who in America (1897-1942); Who's Who in America (1928-29); Who's Who in the Theatre. 1936.

Works

1901 Sergeant James.
1905 The flag station.
1907 Paid in full.
1907 The undertow.
1908 The easiest way; an American play. Goerck art press.
1908 Inside the circle.
1908 The wolf; founded on the play by Charles Somerville. G. W. Dillingham.

213

1910 Boots and saddles (from Sergeant James).
1910 Homeward bound. (Mrs. Maxwell's mistake).
1910 Just a wife.
1911 Fine feathers.
1911 The trail of the lonesome pine.
1914 A plain woman. (The better way).
1916 Just a woman.
1916 The little shepherd of Kingdom Come.
1917 The assassin.
1917 The knife.
1917 The small town girl (with Cronin Wilson).
1918 The heritage.
1918 Nancy Lee.
1919 The challenge.
1919 Poor little sheep.
1920 The toy girl.
1921 The man's name (with Marjorie Chase).
1921 Under Northern stars.
1927 Different woman.
1928 Jealousy (from the French).

WALWORTH, CLARENCE AUGUSTUS, father (C.S.P.) 1820-1900

Birthplace: Plattsburg, N. Y. **Conversion:** 1845. **Former religion:** Protestant Episcopal. **Education:** Albany Acad., and Sloan School, Williamstown, N. Y.; Union Coll., Schenectady (grad. '38); Studied law and admitted to bar (1841); studied for ministry at General Theological Sem., but became a Catholic before ordination. **Ordained priest:** 1848. **General:** Father Walworth practiced law for a year before his conversion, but reaching for a higher career, studied for the ministry. This in turn failed to satisfy him and he turned to the Catholic Church. With Isaac Hecker (q.v.) he went to St. Trond College in Belgium to study theology, and in 1858 returned to the United States to help in the founding of the Congregation of St. Paul. **Authorities:** Dictionary of American Biography, v. 19; Guide to Catholic Literature, 1888-1940; Burton, Katherine: In No Strange Land. 1942; Walworth, E. H.: Life Sketches of Father Walworth. 1907.

Works

1863 The gentle sceptic. D. Appleton.
1873 The doctrine of hell.
1888 Andiatorocte; or, The eve of Lady-day on Lake George, and other poems. G. P. Putnam.
1893 Reminiscences of Edgar P. Wadhams, first bishop of Ogdensburg. Benziger.
1895 The Oxford movement in America; or, Glimpses of life in an Anglican seminary. Catholic book exchange.
1897 The Walworths in America. Weed-Parsons.
1911 Early ritualism in America. 3d ed. Christian press.

WALWORTH, ELLEN (HARDIN) 1832-1915

Birthplace: Jacksonville, Ill. **Conversion:** 1852. **Education:** Jacksonville Acad., and private tutors; New York Univ. (grad. in law) **General:** Mrs. Walworth was the daughter of Colonel John J. Hardin who was killed at Buena Vista. From 1872 to 1887 she was principal of a school for young ladies, maintaining at the same time an active interest in historic shrines. She contributed to the Magazine of America History, and from 1892 to 1894, edited the National Historical Magazine. Previously, in 1890, she founded with others, the national society of the Daughters of the American Revolution. **Authorities:** American Catholic Who's Who. 1911; Appleton's Cyclopaedia of American Biography, v. 6; Cyclopaedia of American

Biographies, v. 7; Guide to Catholic Literature, 1888-1940; Who Was Who (1897-1942).

Works

1877   Saratoga, the battle—battle ground—visitor's guide, with maps. American news co.
1891   Battles of Saratoga, 1777. Munsell.
1897   Parliamentary rules for the use of societies, clubs, chapters, etc. J. J. Little.

WALWORTH, MANSFIELD TRACY (Hotspur, pseud.) 1830-1873

Birthplace: Albany, N. Y. **Former religion:** Presbyterian. **Education:** Union Coll. (grad., '49); Harvard Law School (grad., '52). **General:** Walworth began the practice of law in Albany but abandoned this profession in favor of a literary career, writing chiefly for the Home Journal. His tragic death at the hands of his son, later declared insane, precipitated a trial famous in the annals of American law. The author was the brother of Clarence A. and husband of Ellen Hardin Walworth (qq.v.). **Authorities:** Appleton's Cyclopaedia of American Biography, v. 6; Walworth, F. H.: The Walworth parricide! 1873; Young, Alfred: Catholic and Protestant Countries Compared. 1903 (Reference only).

Works

1853   The mission of death: a tale of the penal laws of New York. Sadlier(?)
1863   Lulu: a tale of the National Hotel poisoning. G. W. Carleton.
1864   Hotspur: a tale of the old Dutch manor. G. W. Carleton.
1866   Stormcliff: a tale of the highlands. G. W. Carleton.

1869   Warwick; or, The lost nationalities of America. A novel.
       G. W. Carleton.
1871   Delaplane; or, The sacrifice of Irene. A novel. G. W. Carle-
       ton.
1872   Beverly; or, The white mask. A novel. G. W. Carleton.
1882   Twenty questions. H. Holt. (Attributed in Cushing's "Ini-
       tials and Pseudonyms" to M. T. Walworth).
1888   Married in mask. (Published in 1890 by Street and Smith)
1888   Zahara; a leaf from empire. A novel. G. W. Dillingham.

WARD, ARTEMUS, pseud., See Browne, Charles Farrar, 1834-1867

WARD, JUSTINE BAYARD (CUTTING) 1879-

Birthplace: Morristown, N. Y. **Conversion:** 1904. **Former religion:** Father, French Huguenot; mother, Scotch Presbyterian. **Education:** Privately, and at Brearley School, N. Y.; music with Hermann H. Wetzler (1918-21); Gregorian chant with R. Dom André Mosquereau, O.S.B. (1921-29). **General:** As a musician, Mrs. Ward is active in the propagation of Gregorian chant and was made an honorary doctor in 1925 by the Pontificia Instituto di Musica Sacra of Rome. She is president of the Dom Mosquereau Schola Cantorium Foundation and delivers frequent lectures on Church music. **Authorities:** American Catholic Who's Who (1911; 1942-43); Guide to Catholic Literature, 1888-1940; Driscoll, A. S.: Literary Convert Women. 1928.

Works

1914   Music, first-year (with E. W. Perkine). Catholic educa-
       tional press.
1914   William Pardo of the Company of Jesus. Longmans,
       Green.

1916   (comp.) Searchlights of eternity. Encyclopedia press.
1930   The chant of the Church (with others). Liturgical press.
         40 p.
1930   Hymnal. New edition with rhythmic signs; a supplement
         to Music, first and second year. Catholic education press.
1935-38 Music . . . Teachers' manual. Catholic education press.
1936   Frances Delehanty. Catholic educational press.
1936-38 Music . . . Children's manual. Catholic education press.
1943   Gregorian chants sung by a group of clerics under the
         direction of Sister Mary Agnesine, S.S.N.D. and con-
         ducted by Justine Ward. Washington, U. S. recording
         co., for Catholic educational press.
n.d.   Ward method of musical education for schools.

WHITCHER, FRANCES MIRIAM (BERRY) 1811-1852

Birthplace: Whitesboro, N. Y. **Former religion:** Protestant Episcopal. **Education:** Local schools. **General:** Mrs. Whitcher was one of a family of thirteen children. She first attracted attention as the author of "The Widow Spriggins" sketches, written in colloquial dialect. Later she contributed many sketches of like nature to Neal's Gazette and Godey's Lady Book. Her deeply religious nature, exhibited in the author's hymns and devotional poems are in sharp contrast to the satirical sketches which made her literary reputation. **Authorities:** American Authors, 1600-1900; Appleton's Cyclopedia, v. 2; Dictionary of American Biography, v. 20; Whitcher, F. M. B.: The Widow Bedott Papers, With Introd. by A. B. Neal. 1856; Young, Alfred: Catholic and Protestant Countries Compared. 1903. (Reference only).

Works

1856 The Widow Bedott papers . . . With an introduction by
      Alice B. Neal. Phillips, Sampson.

1867　Widow Spriggins, Mary Elmer, and other sketches. Edited with a memoir, by M. L. Ward Whitcher, with comic illustrations. G. W. Carleton.

WHITE, CAROLINE (EARLE) 1833-1916

Birthplace: Philadelphia, Pa. **Conversion:** 1857. **Education:** Nantucket (Mass.) High School. **General:** Mrs. White was the daughter of Thomas Earle, candidate for the Vice-Presidency in 1840. From 1892 to 1916 she edited, with others, The Starry Cross, a magazine devoted to antivivisection and to the prevention of cruelty to animals. She had large humanitarian interests, and founded two organizations for the prevention of cruelty. The author was a contributor to Harpers and the Forum. **Authorities:** American Catholic Who's Who. 1911.

Works

1890　Love in the tropics, a romance of the South Seas. J. B. Lippincott.

1893　A modern Agrippa. Patience Barker; a tale of old Nantucket. J. B. Lippincott.

1895　A holiday in Spain and Norway. J. B. Lippincott.

1903　An ocean mystery. J. B. Lippincott.

WHITELEY, ISABEL (NIXON) 1859-

Birthplace: New York (state). **General:** Mrs. Whiteley was the daughter of Rev. J. Howard Nixon and the sister of Mary F. Nixon-Roulet (q.v.). Besides her writings in book form she contributed short stories to Harper's Bazaar and articles to the Records of the American Catholic Historical Society. The author was one of the founders of the

Confraternity of St. Gabriel, and made her home in Italy for a considerable time. **Authorities:** American Catholic Who's Who. 1911; Guide to Catholic Literature, 1888-1940; Who's Who in America (1906-07).

Works

1897   The falcon of Langeac. Copeland & Day.
1898   For the French lilies (A.D. 1511-12). J. B. Lippincott.
1903   Wanted: a situation, and other stories. B. Herder.

WILBUR, RUSSELL IGNATIUS JONES, father, 1876-1940

Birthplace: Omaha, Nebr. **Conversion:** 1908. **Former religion:** Protestant Episcopal (minister, —1908). **Ordained priest:** 1912. **Education:** Williams Coll. (1893-97); Northwestern Univ. (A.B., '99); Western (P. E.) Theological Sem. (1900-03); Pontifical Coll., Rome (1908-13; S.T.B. '10). **General:** As a Protestant minister, Father Wilbur served in various parishes from 1906 to 1908. Since 1928 he has been pastor of Notre Dame de Lourdes Church in Wellston, Mo. He has contributed to various national periodicals, including the Fortnightly Review, Commonweal, Atlantic Monthly and others. **Authorities:** American Catholic Who's Who (1940-41).

Works

1919   Theodore Roosevelt; a verse sequence in sonnets and quatorzains. Houghton, Mifflin.
1940   Essays and verses. Sheed and Ward.

WILLIS, RICHARD STORRS, 1819-1900

Birthplace: Boston, Mass. **Education:** Hale Coll. (grad.,

'41) **General:** The author, a brother of the poet Nathaniel Parker Willis, studied music in Frankfort and Leipsic and counted Mendelssohn among his friends. The latter revised some of his musical compositions. Willis edited the Musical Times, which later consolidated with the Musical World, and founded the magazine, Once a month. **Authorities:** American History and Encyclopedia of Music. 1908, v. 6; Appleton's Cyclopaedia of American Biography, v. 6; Catholic Builders of the Nation. v. 3. (Reference only)

Works

1854	Church chorals and choir studies.
1856	Memorial of Jessie Willis: prepared for her little daughters, Annie, Blanche and Jessie, by their father. J. F. Trow.
1856	Our church music. W. R. Dana.
1860-61	Carols and music poems. T. Nourse.
1883	Pen and lute. T. Nourse.
1900	Night song. F. F. Lovell.

WIRRIES, MARY MABEL (CABANA) 1894-

Birthplace: South Bend, Ind. **Conversion:** 1902. **Former religion:** Church of Christ (Campbellites); a tradition of Catholicism on both sides of the family. **Education:** St. Ursula's Acad., Toledo, O. (grad., '13); Detroit Commercial Coll. (1915); Bowling Green (Ohio) State Normal Coll. (1916-17). **General:** Mrs. Wirries entered the business world in 1913 and was variously employed in office work and photography until 1916. Besides writing her many books the author has raised a large family, and continues to write "The Weekly Postscript" for the Ave Maria magazine. She is completing an historical juvenile, "Juan of San Bruno," which is expected to be finished in 1944. **Authorities:** Letter from Mrs. Wirries, September 5, 1943; American Catholic Who's Who (1942-43); Guide to Catholic Literature, 1888-1940; Who's Who in America (1942-43).

Works

1924 Mary Rose. Benziger.
1924 Mary Rose at boarding school. Benziger.
1925 Mary Rose keeps house. Benziger.
1925 Mary Rose, Sophomore. Benziger.
1926 Mary Rose, graduate. Benziger.
1928 Mary Rose at Rose gables. Benziger.
1929 Paula of the drift. Benziger.
1930 Mary Rose at Friendville. Benziger.
1931 The Barrys at Briarhill. Benziger.
1932 Mary Rose's sister Bess. Benziger.
1932 Praying pines.
1934 Patsy goes to the mountains. Benziger.
1936 Gay witch April, and other poems. Keddington-Mission.
1937 Shadows on Cedarcrest. Benziger.
1939 Wayside idyls. Ave Maria.
1940 The road is long. Ave Maria.

WOODMAN, CLARENCE EUGENE, father (C.S.P.) 1852-1924

Birthplace: Saco, Me. **Conversion:** 1875. **Former religion:** Anglican. **Ordained priest:** 1879. **Education:** Saco public schools; Monson Acad.; Trinity College, Hartford, Conn. (B.A., '73); Amherst Coll. (M.A., '77); Manhattan Coll. (Ph.D., '84). **General:** Father Woodman studied for the ministry before his conversion but left after two years of study. From 1877 to 1892 he made various trips to Central America, Morocco and Spain and was knighted by the monarch of the latter country for his contributions to the science of astronomy. In 1892 he became an assistant in the observatory at the Catholic University of America, holding that position for two years. In 1900 he assumed a like post at the Smithsonian Institution. **Authorities:** American Catholic Who's Who. 1911; Guide to Catholic Literature, 1888-1940; National Cyclopaedia of American Biography, v. 19; Catholic World, January, 1925.

Works

1887   Manual of prayers.
1888   The bridal wreath.
1890   Civil and religious liberty.
1892   Poets and poetry of Ireland.
1906   Perpetual ecclesiastical calendar. Columbus.

WRIGHT, CUTHBERT, 1899-

Birthplace: Elmira, N. Y. **Conversion:** 1936. **Former religion:** Episcopalian. **Education:** Kent School, Connecticut (1911-14); Harvard Univ. (A.B., '18; 1931-32); Univ. of Paris (Cert., '29-'30). **General:** Professor Wright is a teacher of history at Assumption College, Worcester, Mass. He served in the World War from 1917 to 1918 and received the Major Campaigns decoration. The author, whose father was a Protestant minister, contributes occasional articles to the New York Times, America, and other periodicals. **Authorities:** American Catholic Who's Who (1942-43); Guide to Catholic Literature, 1888-1940.

Works

1916   One way of love. Brentano.
1926   The story of the Catholic church. A. & C. Boni.

WYMAN, HENRY H., father (C.S.P.) 1849-1929

Birthplace: Westminster, Mass. **Conversion:** 1871. **Former religion:** Congregationalist. **Ordained priest:** 1876. **Education:** Brown Univ. (grad., '71) **General:** The veteran Paulist missionary was famous as a confessor and writer. He contributed many articles to the Catholic World and other Catholic periodicals. **Authorities:** Guide to Catholic Literature, 1888-1940; Catholic World, April, 1929.

Works

1906 Certainty in religion. Columbus press.
1921 Story of my religious experiences. International Catholic truth soc.

YOUNG, ALFRED, father (C.S.P.) 1831-1900

Birthplace: Bristol, Eng. **Came to U. S.:** 1832 (?) **Conversion:** 1850. **Former religion:** Protestant Episcopal. **Ordained priest:** 1856. **Education:** Princeton Univ. (grad., '48); City of N. Y. Medical School (1852); studied theology at Sulpician Sem., Paris, France. **General:** While completing his studies in medicine, Father Young became a Catholic and was soon studying theology in France. After his ordination he became instructor in the classics at Seton Hall College, and in 1862 joined the Congregation of St. Paul. He is remembered as a controversialist and a skilled musician. In the former role his disputes with Robert G. Ingersoll are memorable. In 1873 he founded the famous Paulist choir. **Authorities:** Cyclopaedia of American Biographies, v. 7; Dictionary of American Biography, v. 20; Guide to Catholic Literature, 1888-1940.

1863   The complete sodality manual and hymn book.
1869   The office of vespers.
1884   Catholic hymnal. Columbus.
1885-86   Carols for a merry Christmas and a joyous new year. 2 v.
1890   Carols for the month of May; music by Father Young. Catholic pub. soc.
1895   Catholic and Protestant countries compared in civilization, popular happiness, general intelligence and morality. Catholic book exchange.

CHRONOLOGY OF AUTHORS

1821-1865   MacLeod, Xavier Donald, father
1822-1898   Johnston, Richard Malcolm
1823-1903   Deshon, George, father
1824-1871   Miles, George Henry
1824-1871   Cary, Phoebe
1824-1891   Preston, Thomas Scott, monsignor
1824-1901   Starr, Eliza Allen
1825-1898   Dahlgren, Madeleine (Vinton)
1827-1899   Howarth, Ellen Clementine (Doran)
1827-1859   Fairbanks, Charles Bullard
1828-1890   Hemenway, Abby Maria
1829-1919   Emmet, Thomas Addis
1829-1885   Cooke, Nicholas Francis

1830-1839

1930-1922   Storer, Horatio Robinson
1830-1873   Walworth, Mansfield Tracy
1830-1897   Bliss, George
             Cecil, Elizabeth Frances Nash
1831-1858   Caldwell, Howard Hayne
1831-1900   Young, Alfred, father
1831-1904   De Costa, Benjamin Franklin, father
1831-1907   Tincker, Mary Agnes
1831-1908   Curtis, Alfred Allen, bp.
1832-1899   Garland, Augustus Hill
1832-1915   Walworth, Ellen (Hardin)
1833-   Cary, Emma Forbes
1833-1916   Hilgard, Eugene Woldemar
1833-1916   White, Caroline (Earle)
1834-1867   Browne, Charles Farrar
1834-1925   Harris, Miriam (Coles)
1835-   Corbin, Caroline Elizabeth (Fairfield)
1835-1913   Brownson, Henry Francis
1836-   Adams, Charles Collard
1936-1888   Hassard, John Rose Greene
1837-   Martin, Elizabeth Gilbert
1837-1923   Hardin, Martin D.
1838-   Copeland, Charles Carroll
1838-1916   Hill, James Jerome
1839-1876   Tenney, Sara (Brownson)

1839-1918	Searle, George Mary, father
1839-1921	Spalding, James Field

1840-1849

1840-1914	Bandelier, Adolph Francis Alphonse
1840-1921	Stone, James Kent (Father Fidelis)
1840-1928	Coleman (Charles) Caryl
-1910	Nealis, Jean Elizabeth (Wilkinson)
-1911	Bull, George Joseph
	Maire, Frederick
	Richards, Jarrett Thomas
1843-	Sloan, William Hill
1843-1909	Stoddard, Charles Warren
1843-1911	Dwight, Thomas
1843-1915	Greene, Edward Lee
1843-1924	Keyes, Edward Lawarence
1845-	Fairbanks, Hiram Francis, father
1845-1909	Tabb, John Bannister, father
	Smith, Sara Trainer
1846-	Robins, Julia Gorham
1846-1916	Gallagher, Sister Mary Antonio
1846-1920	Tiernan, Francis Christine (Fisher)
1846-1923	Emery, Susan L.
1846-1923	Goodyear, William Henry
1847-1923	Brown, Edward Osgood
1848-1908	Harris, Joel Chandler
1848-1927	Grierson, Francis
1849-	Parker, William Thornton
1849-1929	Wyman, Henry H., father
1849-1932	Storer, Maria (Longworth)
1849-1921	Barnum, Francis Aloysius, father

1850-1859

1850-1909	Henderson, Isaac Austin
1850-1923	Mackin, Sarah Maria Aloisa
1850-1931	Stoddard, John Lawson
1850-1940	Learned, Ellin (Craven)
-1942	Richards, Jarrett Thomas
1851-	Fraser, Mary (Crawford)
1851-1898	Lathrop, George Parsons
1851-1925	Ford, Henry Jones

1851-1926	Lathrop, Mother Mary Alphonsa
1851-1929	Avery, Martha Moore
1852-1924	Woodman, Clarence Eugene, father
1853-1879	Russell, Irwin
1854-1924	Nicholls, Charles Wilbur de Lyon
1854-1909	Crawford, Francis Marion
1854-1915	Copus, John Edwin, father
1854-1916	Hedges, Samuel Colahan, father
1854-1926	Pope, Sir Joseph
1854-1934	Beach, Charles Fisk
1855-	Battle, Jesse Mercer
1855-	Sener, Samuel Miller
1855-1920	Hayes, Alice Jeannette
1856-1932	Schultz, Charles Henry
1857-	Sargent, Henry Leonard, father
1857-1916	Shipman, Andrew Jackson
1857-1928	Skinner, Henrietta Channing
1859-	Whiteley, Isabel (Nixon)
-1930	Roulet, Mary F. Nixon
1859-1937	Spearman, Frank Hamilton

1860-1869

1860-	Thompson, Thomas Payne
1860-1916	Seawell, Molly Elliot
-1939	Hewetson, George Benson
1861-	Heggie, Cora M.
1861-	O'Malley, Sallie Margaret (Hill)
1861-	Stafford, Wendell Phillips
1861-1905	Harland, Henry
1861-1924	McGarvey, William, father
1862-	Chanler, Margaret (Terry)
1862-	Kobbe, Carolyn Therese (Wheeler)
1862-	MacKintosh, Hugh Fraser
1862-1926	Hunt, Gaillard
1863-1927	MacNutt, Francis Augustus
1864-	Kite, Elizabeth Sarah
1864-	Staunton, John Armitage, father
1866-	Taggart, Marion Ames
1866-1942	Merrill, William Stetson
1867-	Keasbey, Lindley Miller
1867-	Portuondo, Josephine B.

230

1867-	Shepperson, Sister Mary Fides
1867-1906	Craigie, Pearl (Richards)
1867-1935	Baldwin, Charles Sears
-1937	Baldwin, Gratia Eaton (Whithed)
1868-	Kinsman, Frederick Joseph
1868-	Moody, John
1868-	Tennant, John Alexander
1869-	Converse, Mary Teresa Evelyn
1869-1929	Logan, John Daniel

1870-1879

1870-	Buck, Jacob Reverdy, father
1870-	Goldstein, David
1870-	Hayword, William Leete, father
1870-	Bret Harte, Geoffrey
1870-1919	Mitchell, John
1871-	Bolling, George Melville
1871-	Hilliard, Marion Pharo
1871-	Thompson, Charles Willis
	Sholl, Anna McClure
1874-	Mosby, Thomas Speed
1874-1935	Delany, Selden Peabody, father
1874-1941	Walter, Eugene
1876-1940	Wilbur, Russell Ignatius Jones, father
1878-1938	Hard, William
1878-	Hawks, Edward William, monsignor
1878-	Small, James Louis
1879-	Ward, Justine Bayard (Cutting)
1879-	Berry (Elwood) Sylvester, father

1880-1889

1880-	Olf, Lillian (Browne)
1880-1936	Reeve, Arthur Benjamin
	Mills, Philo Laos, father
1881-	Bell, Herbert Clifford Francis
1881-	Stearns, Foster Waterman
1882-	Hayes, Carlton Joseph Huntley
1882-	Peck, Theodora Agnes
1883-	Arent, Leonora
1883-	Cory, Herbert Ellsworth
1884-	Chapman, Michael Andrew, father

231

1884-	Holsapple, Lloyd Burdwin
1884-	Hunt, Duane Garrison, bp.
1884-	Stead, William Force
1884-	Wallace, Sister Mary Imelda
1885-	Keyes, Frances Parkinson (Wheeler)
1885-	Lord, Robert Howard, father
1886-	Lawrence, Raymond P., father
1886-	Millar, Moorhouse Francis Xavier, father
1886-1918	Kilmer, (Alfred) Joyce
1887-	Campbell, Thomas Bowyer
1887-	Gamble, Anna Dill
1888-	Bregy, Katherine Marie Cornelia
1888-	Carver, George
1888-1931	Rockne, Knute Kenneth
1888-1939	Broun, Heywood Campbell
1888-1941	Kilmer, Aline (Murray)
	Farmer, Francis Xavier, father
1889-	Levy, Rosalie Marie
1889-	Musser, Benjamin Francis
1889-	Palmer, Benjamin Whipple
1889-	Quirk, Charles Joaquin, father
	Atkinson, Samuel

1890-1899

1890-	Burton, Katherine (Kurz)
1890-	Criss, Mildred
1890-	Eliot, Ethel (Cook)
	MacGill, Caroline Elizabeth
1890-	Mahan, Bruce Ellis
1890-	Maynard, Theodore
1890-	Sargent, Daniel
1890-	Savage, Courtenay
1890-	Twinem, Leo Leonard
	Fiske, A. Longfellow
	Nichols, Anne
1891-	Colby, Elbridge
	Ford, (Julia) Lauren
1892-	Bagger, Eugene Thomas Schoen
1892-	Hull, Robert Reuel
1892-	Kernan, William Fergus
1892-	Murfey, Etta Josephean

232

1892-1936	Moon, Parker Thomas
	Browne, Anita Maria
1894-	Wirries, Mary Mabel (Cabans)
1895-	Burbank, Addison
1895-	Clark, Eleanor Grace
1896-	Bedier, Julie (Sister M. Juliana)
1896-	Grein, Ludwig
1896-	Monroe, Nellie Elizabeth
1898-	Beebe, Catherine (Herman)
1898-	Lane, James Warren
1899-	Chamberlin, Edward Hastings
1899-	Day, Dorothy
1899-	Dorsey, Theodore Hooper
1899-	Wright, Cuthbert

1900-1909

1900-	Grant, Dorothy (Fremont)
1900-	Johnston, Sister Mary Francis
1900-	Nutting, Willis Dwight
1900-	Stancourt, Louis J.
1901-	Forbes, Clarence Allen
1901-	Larsson, Raymond Ellsworth
	Cook, Frederick
	Hoare, Sister Mary Regis
1902-	Hoffman, Ross John Swartz
1902-	Gurian, Waldemar
1903-	Baldwin, Marshall Whithed
1903-	Eustace, Cecil John
	Landreth, Helen
1905-	Lynn, Jeannette (Murphy)
1905-	Pegis, Anton Charles
	Tarry, Ellen
1906-	Magaret, Helene
1907-	Pegis, Jessie (Corrigan)
	Brown, Beatrice Bradshaw
1908-	Newcomb, Covelle
1908-	Haas, Rosamond
1908-	Van Stockum, Hilda
1909-	Adams, Elizabeth Laura
1909-	MacLean, William Michael Stanley
1915-1938	Fields, Maurice C.

CHRONOLOGY OF CONVERSION

Ellet, Elizabeth Fries (Lummis)
Howarth, Ellen Clementine (Doran)
Mason, Emily Virginia
1851 Deshon, George, father
1851 Hassard, John Rose Greene
Whitcher, Frances Miriam (Berry)
1852 Fairbanks, Charles Bullard
1852 Ives, Levi Silliman
1852 Richards, Henry Livingston
Walworth, Ellen (Hardin)
Walworth, Mansfield Tracy
1853 Tincker, Mary Agnes
1853 Richards, William
MacLeod, Xavier Donald, father
1855 Cary, Emma Forbes
1855 Dwight, Thomas
Hilgard, Eugene Woldemar
1856 Starr, Eliza Allen
Dahlgren, Madeleine (Vinton)
Hemenway, Abby Maria
1857 White, Caroline (Earle)

1860-1869

1861 Nealis, Jean Elizabeth Ursula
Parker, William Thornton
Tiernan, Frances Christine (Fisher)
1862 Searle, George Mary, father
Barnum, Francis Aloysius, father
Cary, Phoebe
Gallagher, Sister Mary Antonio
1863 Fairbanks, Hiram Francis, father
1864 Hardin, Martin D.
1865 Copeland, Charles Carroll
1867 Browne, Charles Farrar
1867 Emmet, Thomas Addis
1867 Stoddard, Charles Warren
Harris, Miriam (Coles)
Keyes, Edward Lawrence
1868 Coleman, (Charles) Caryl
1869 Brown, Edward Osgood
1869 Stone, James Kent (Father Fidelis)

236

1870 Hedges, Samuel Colahan, father
1870 Martin, Elizabeth Gilbert
      Russell, Irwin
      Willis, Richard Storrs
1871 Wyman, Henry H., father
1872 Curtis, Alfred Allen, bp.
      Tabb, John Bannister, father
1874 Sener, Samuel Miller
1875 Cooke, Nicholas Francis
1875 Emery, Susan L.
1875 Johnston, Richard Malcolm
1875 Pope, Sir Joseph
1875 Woodman, Clarence Eugene, father
1876 Bolling, George Melville
1876 Copus, John Edwin, father
1876 Shipman, Andrew Jackson
1878 Seawell, Molly Elliot
1878 Skinner, Henrietta Channing (Dana)
1879 Storer, Horatio Robinson
      Heggie, Cora

1880-1889

1880 Crawford, Francis Marion
1880 Goodyear, William Henry
      Fraser, Mary (Crawford)
      Smith, Sara Trainer
1881 Bendelier, Adolph Francis Alphonse
1883 Adams, Charles Collard
1883 Chanler, Margaret (Terry)
1883 MacKintosh, Hugh Fraser
1883 MacNutt, Francis Augustus
1884 Bliss, George
1884 Spearman, Frank Hamilton
1885 Greene, Edward Lee
1885 Portuondo, Josephine B. (Thomas)
1886 Converse, Mary Teresa Evelyn
1886 O'Malley, Sallie Margaret (Hill)
1886 Richards, Jarrett Thomas
1886 Shepperson, Sister Mary Fides

1887 Maire, Frederick
1887 Tennant, John Alexander
1887 Thompson, Thomas Payne

1890-1899

1891 Lathrop, George Parsons
1891 Lathrop, Mother Mary Alphonsa
       Thompson, Charles Willis
1892 Bull, George Joseph
1892 Craigie, Pearl (Richards)
1892 Merrill, William Stetson
1892 Spalding, James Field
1892 Storer, Maria (Longworth)
1894 Mackin, Sarah Maria Aloisa
1894 Roulet, Mary F. Nixon
       Buck, Jacob Reverdy, father
       Taggart, Marion Ames
       Whiteley, Isabel (Nixon)
1896 Berry (Elwood) Sylvester, father
1896 Henderson, Isaac Austin
1897 Millar, Moorhouse Francis Xavier, father
1898 Harland, Henry
1898 Wallace, Sister Mary Imelda
1899 De Costa, Benjamin Franklin, father
1899 Mosby, Thomas Speed
1899 Nicholls, Charles Wilbur de Lyon
1899 Robins, Julia Gorham

1900-1909

1901 Hunt, Gaillard
1902 Beach, Charles Fisk
1902 Wirries, Mary Mabel (Cabana)
1903 Cook, Mercer
1904 Avery, Martha Moore
1904 Hayes, Carleton Joseph Huntley
1904 Schultz, Charles Henry
1904 Ward, Justine Bayard (Cutting)
       Mills, Phila Laos, father
1905 Goldstein, David
1905 Quirk, Charles Joaquin, father

238

1906 Battle, Jesse Mercer
1906 Bregy, Katherine Marie Cornelia
1906 Kite, Elizabeth Sarah
1907 Corbin, Caroline Elizabeth
1907 Mitchell, John
1908 Harris, Joel Chandler
1908 Hayword, William Leete, father
1908 Wilbur, Russell Ignatius Jones, father
1908 Hawks, Edward William, monsignor
1908 McGarvey, William, father
1908 Curtis, Georgina Pell
1908 Musser, Benjamin Francis
      Sloan, William Hill
1909 Bagger, Eugene Thomas Schoen
1909 Bret Harte, Geoffrey
1909 Sargent, Daniel
1909 Sargent, Henry Leonard, father
      Hayes, Alice Jeannette

1910-1919

1911 Stearns, Foster Waterman
1912 Lawrence, Raymond P.
1912 Levy, Rosalie Marie
      Small, James Louis
1913 Kilmer, (Alfred) Joyce
1913 Kilmer, Aline (Murray)
1913 Mahan, Bruce Ellis
1913 Maynard, Theodore
1913 Palmer, Benjamin Whipple
      Hilliard, Marion Pharo
1914 Bedier, Julie (Sister M. Juliana)
1914 Colby, Elbridge
1914 Hewetson, George Benson
1914 Moon, Parker Thomas
1915 Farmer, Wilmoth Alexander, father
      Hunt, Duane Garrison, bp.
1916 Hill, James Jerome
1916 Sholl, Anna McClure
1916 Tarry, Ellen
1917 Gamble, Anna Dill

1917	Grierson, Francis
1918	Chapman, Michael Andrew, father
1918	Logan, John Daniel
1919	Ford, Henry James
1919	Kinsman, Frederick Joseph

1920-1929

1920	Peck, Theodora Agnes
1921	Forbes, Clarence Allen
	Hoare, Sister M. Regis
	Stafford, Wendell Phillips
1922	Arent, Leonora
1922	Carver, George
1922	Hull, Robert Reuel
1922	Stoddard, John Lawson
	MacGill, Caroline Elizabeth
1923	Beebe, Catherine
1925	Clark, Eleanor Grace
1925	Eliot, Ethel (Cook)
1925	Rockne, Knute Kenneth
1925	Newcomb, Covelle
	Keasbey, Lindley Miller
1926	Grein, Ludwig
1926	Lord, Robert Howard, father
1926	Reeve, Arthur Benjamin
1927	Criss, Mildred
1927	Day, Dorothy
1927	Learned, Ellin (Craven)
	Gurian, Waldemar
1928	Nichols, Anne
1928	Fiske, A. Longfellow
1929	Adams, Elizabeth Laura
1929	Eustace, Cecil John

1929-1939

1930	Baldwin, Marshall Whithed
1930	Burton, Katherine (Kurz)
1930	Delany, Selden Peabody, father
1930	Nutting, Willis Dwight

1930	Pegis, Anton Charles
1930	Staunton, James Armitage, father
	Cook, Mercer
	Dorsey, Theodore Hooper
	Ford, (Julia) Lauren
	Lynn, Jeannette (Murphy)
1931	Baldwin, Gratia Eaton (Whithed)
1931	Campbell, Thomas Bowyer
	Chamberlin, Edward Hastings
1931	Hoffman, Ross John Swartz
1931	Holsapple, Lloyd Burdwin
1931	Lane, James Warren
1931	Kernan, William Fergus
1931	Moody, John
	Larsson, Raymond Ellsworth
	Johnston, Sister Mary Frances
1932	Kobbe, Caroline Teresa (Wheeler)
1933	Cory, Herbert Ellsworth
1933	Haas, Rosamond
1933	MacLean, William Michael Stanley
1933	Monroe, N(ellie) Elizabeth
1933	Stead, William Force
1934	Baldwin, Charles Sears
1934	Bell, Herbert Clifford
1934	Brown, Beatrice Bradshaw
1934	Grant, Dorothy (Fremont)
1934	Hard, William
1934	Stancourt, Louis
1935	Murfey, Etta Josephean
1936	Wright, Cuthbert
1937	Savage, Courtenay
1937	Twinim, Leo Leonard
	Atkinson, Samuel
	Cook, Frederick
1938	Fields, Maurice C.
1938	Olf, Lillian (Browne)
1939	Broun, Heywood Campbell
1939	Browne, Anita Maria
1939	Keyes, Frances Parkinson
1939	Landreth, Helen
1939	Van Stockum, Hilda

1941 Burbank, Addison
1941 Walter, Eugene
1942 Magaret, Helene

AUTHORS ERRONEOUSLY CONSIDERED
CONVERTS

ADAMS, HENRY AUSTIN, 1861-1931 (Ex-Convert)
ALLEN, HUGH ANTHONY, 1892-   (Catholic)
BARRY, JOSEPH GAYLE HURD, 1858-1931 (Non-Catholic)
CAMPBELL, JAMES MARSHALL, father, 1895-   (Catholic)
CURTIS, GEORGE DE CLYVER (Non-Catholic)
DUNNE, FINLEY PETER, 1867-1936 (Catholic)
FARROW, JOHN, 1904-   (Catholic)
LILJENCRANTZ, CARL JOHAN (Ex-Convert)
LOCKWOOD, ELEANOR STANLEY (Non-Catholic)
LONG, VALENTINE, father (O.F.M.) (Catholic)
MAURIN, PETER (Catholic)
MAYNARD, SARA, 1890-   (Catholic)
O'HARA, MARY (Mary Alsop Sture-Vasa) 1885-   (Non-Catholic)
PISE, CHARLES CONSTANTINE, father (S.J.) 1802-1866 (Catholic)
RICHARDS, JOSEPH HAVENS COWLES, father (S.J.) 1851-1923 (Catholic)
RIGGS, THOMAS LAWRASON, father, 1888-1943 (Catholic)
RUFFIN, MRS. MARGARET ELLEN (HENRY) d. 1941 (Catholic)
STERLING, GEORGE, 1869-1926 (Ex-Convert)
THOMPSON, NEWTON WAYLAND, father, 1882-   (Catholic)
WALWORTH, ELLEN HARDIN, 1858-   (Catholic)
WECTER, DIXON, 1906-   (Ex-Convert)
WILLIAMS, MICHAEL, 1878-   (Catholic)

BIBLIOGRAPHY OF WORKS CONSULTED

Alexander, Calvert. Catholic literary revival; three phases in its development from 1845 to the present. Bruce, Milwaukee. c1935.

Allibone, S. A. Critical dictionary of English literature and British and American authors, living and deceased, from the earliest accounts to the latter half of the nineteenth century. Philadelphia, Lippincott, 1858-91. 5 v.

American authors, 1600-1900; a biographical dictionary of American literature. Ed. by Stanley J. Kunitz and Howard Haycraft. N. Y., Wilson. 1938.

American catalog of books, 1876-1910. N. Y., Publishers weekly, 1876-1910. 9 v. in 13.

American Catholic who's who. Ed. by Georgina Pell Curtis. 1911.

American Catholic who's who (1934/35—) Detroit, Walter Romig, 1934-

Appleton's annual cyclopaedia and register of important events, 1861-1902. N. Y., Appleton, 1862-1903. 42 v.

Appleton's cyclopaedia of American biography. Ed. by J. G. Wilson and John Fiske. N. Y., Appleton. 1887-1900. 7 v.

Association of research libraries. A catalog of books represented by Library of Congress printed cards. Issued to July 31, 1942. Ann Arbor, Mich., Edwards Bros., 1942-   30 v.

Book of Catholic authors. (1st, 2d and 3rd series). Informal self-portraits of famous modern Catholic writers. Edited by Walter Romig. Detroit, Walter Romig & co. c1942-44.

Bregy, Katherine. Poets and pilgrims; from Geoffrey Chaucer to Paul Claudel. N. Y., Benziger. 1925.

Burton, Katherine. In no strange land. N. Y., Longmans. 1942.

Catholic builders of the nation. Boston, Continental press inc., 1923. 5 v.
Volume 3 contains a lengthy classified list of American Catholic converts.

Catholic encyclopedia. N. Y., Catholic encyclopedia press. c1907-22. 17 v.
Includes Supplement I.

Catholic periodical index. 1930-   N. Y., Wilson. c1940-

Curtis, G. P. Beyond the road to Rome. St. Louis, Herder. 1914.

Curtis, G. P. Some roads to Rome in America; being personal records of conversions to the Catholic Church. St. Louis, Herder 1909.

Cyclopaedia of American biographies comprising the men and women of the United States. Edited by John Howard Brown. Boston, The Cyclopaedia pub. co. 1897-1903. 7 v.

Dictionary of American biography. Edited by Allen Johnson and Dumas Malone. N. Y., Scribner. 1928-35.

Donnelly, E. C. (and others). A round table of representative American Catholic novelists. 2d ed. N. Y., Benziger. 1897.

Driscoll, A. S. Literary convert women. Magnificat. 1928.

Earls, Michael. Manuscripts and memories; chapters in our literary tradition. Milwaukee, Bruce. c1935.

Encyclopedia Americana. N. Y., Encyclopedia Americana corp. 1931-32. 30 v.

Encyclopedia of social sciences; editor-in-chief, E. R. A. Seligman, assoc. ed., Alvin Johnson. N. Y., Macmillan. 15 v.

Evans, Charles. American bibliography; a chronological dictionary of all books, pamphlets and periodical publications . . . down to and including the year 1820. Chicago, Columbia press. 1903-35. 12 v.

Great American lawyers, edited by William Draper Lewis. Philadelphia, Winston. 1907-1909. 8 v.

Guide to Catholic literature, 1888-1940; edited by Walter Romig . . . Detroit, Walter Romig & co. c1940.

Kelly, James. American catalogue of books published in the United States from Jan. 1861 to Jan. 1871. N. Y., Wiley. 1866-71. 2 v.

Manly, J M. and Rickert, Edith. Contemporary American literature. N. Y., Harcourt. c1922.

Moulton, C. W. Library of literary criticism of English and American authors. Buffalo, Moulton pub. co. 1901-05. 8 v.

Musser, B. F. Outside the walls. St Louis, Herder. 1914.

National Catholic almanac. Paterson, N. J., St. Anthony's guild. 1943.

National cyclopedia of American biography. 1892-   N. Y., White, 1893-

New international encyclopedia. N. Y., Dodd, 1922-30. 27 v.

New York Times index. 1913-   N. Y., New York Times. 1913-

Parsons, Wilfrid. Early Catholic Americana; a list of books and other works by Catholic authors in the United States, 1729-1830. N. Y., Macmillan, 1939.

Roorbach, O. A. Bibliotheca Americana. 1820-61. N. Y., 1852-61. 4 v.

Sargent, Daniel. Four independents. N. Y., Sheed and Ward, 1935.

Shea, J. G. A history of the Catholic church within the limits of the United States from the first attempted colonization to the present time. 1886-88. N. Y., John G. Shea. 4 v.
Title varies with vol. 1 and 2.

Stedman, E. C., and Hutchinson, E. M., eds. Library of American literature. N. Y., Webster, 1891. 11 v.
Vol. 11 is a biographical dictionary.

Twentieth century authors; a biographical dictionary of modern literature. Edited by Stanley J. Kunitz and Howard Haycraft. N. Y., Wilson, 1942.

Union list of serials in libraries of the United States and Canada. 2d edition. Edited by Winifred Gregory. N. Y., Wilson, 1943.

United States catalog; books in print 1899-   N. Y., Wilson. 1900-   Includes supplements, i.e., the Cumulative book index . . .

Universities and their sons. Boston, Herndon. 5 v.

Who was who in America (1897-1942). Chicago, Marquis, 1942.

Who's Who among North American authors. 1921-   Los Angeles, Golden syndicate pub. co., c1921-

Who's who in America, a biographical dictionary of notable living men and women of the United States (1899-   ). Chicago, Marquis, 1900-

Who's who in New England. 1st ed. Chicago, Marquis, 1909.

Young, Alfred. Catholic and Protestant countries compared. 12th ed. N. Y., Catholic book exchange, 1903.
Contains lengthy classified lists of American converts.

Periodicals

America. N. Y., 1899-

American anthropologist. Washington, N. Y., Lancaster, Pa., 1888-

American Catholic historical society. Records. Philadelphia, 1894-

American Catholic quarterly review. Philadelphia, 1876-1924. v. 1-49. The July, 1893 and January, 1894 issues contain lengthy unclassified lists of American converts.

Ave Maria. Notre Dame, Ind., 1865-

Catholic bookman. Detroit, 1937-

Catholic library world. Scranton, Pa., 1929-

Catholic mind. New York, 1903-

Catholic world. New York, 1865-

Commonweal. New York, 1924-
Ecclesiastical review. Philadelphia, 1889-
Extension magazine. Chicago, 1906-
Fortnightly review. St. Louis; Techny, Ill.
American Irish historical society. Journal. Boston, 1898-
Magnificat. Manchester, N. Y., 1907-
Missionary. Washington, 1924-
Saturday review of literature. N. Y., 1924-
Theatre, an illus. weekly magazine; drama, music, art. N. Y., 1886-
1893. v. 1-9.
Thought. New York., 1926-
Truth. Raleigh, N. Y.; New York., 1897-

INSTITUTIONS CONSULTED

Gallery of living Catholic authors. Sister M. Joseph, S.L., Director. Webster Groves, Mo.
Library of Congress. Washington, D. C.
Pacific Northwest bibliographic center. Doctor John Van Male, Director. University of Washington, Seattle, Washington.

DIRECTORY OF PUBLISHERS AND PRINTERS

A

Adams-Cannon, St. Paul
Ainsworth & company, Chicago
G. Allen, London
Henry Altemus company, inc., Philadelphia
America press, ptg., New York
American book company, New York
American book and Bible house, Philadelphia
American management association, New York
American news company, New York
American Unitarian association, Boston
W. H. Anderson company, Cincinnati
Angel Guardian press, Boston
Angelmodde press, Loretto, Pa.
D. Appleton & company, New York
D. Appleton-Century company, inc., New York
Edward Arnold & company, London
Associated Publishers, Washington, D. C.
Austin publishing company, Los Angeles
Ave Maria press, Notre Dame, Ind.

B

Richard G. Badger (The Gordan press) Boston
Walter H. Baker company, Boston
Baker, Voorhis and company, New York
Baker and Scribner, New York
Baker and Taylor company, New York
Balch brothers, Boston
Baltimore City printing and binding company, Baltimore
Baltimore publishing company, Baltimore
M. Bancroft, New York
Bancroft-Whitney company, San Francisco
Barnard & Gunthrop printers, Chicago
A. S. Barnes and company, New York
Beacon press, Boston
Belford, Clarke and company, Chicago
Belford, Middlebrook & company, Chicago
Bengalese press, Washington, D. C.

Benziger brothers, New York
Drexel Biddle, San Francisco
Henry Bill publishing company, Norwich, Conn.
Bernice Pauahi Bishop Museum, Honolulu, Hawaii
Basil Blackwell and Mott, Oxford, England
Blanchard & Mohun, Washington, D. C.
Bobbs-Merrill company, Indianapolis
Albert & Charles Boni, New York
Boni incorporated, New York
Boni & Liveright, New York
Book Club of California, San Francisco
Booklovers' Library, Philadelphia
Bosqui engraving and printing company, San Francisco
Bowen-Merrill company, Indianapolis
Bozart press, Oglethorpe university, Atlanta
A. Bradley, Boston
J. Bradley, Philadelphia
Milton Bradley, Springfield, Mass.
Bradstreet press, New York
Brentano's, New York
Broadway publishing company, New York
Brook and company, Toronto
Bruce publishing company, Milwaukee
F. M. Buckles, New York
Burns, Oates & Washbourne, limited, London
A. L. Burt company, inc., New York
E. H. Butler and company, Philadelphia
Thornton Butterworth, limited, London
J. Byrne & company, Washington, D. C.

C

Caledonia company, St. Johnsburg, Vt.
Jonathan Cape and Robert Ballou, inc., New York
Capitol publishing company, Washington, D. C.
E. L. Carey and A. Hart, Philadelphia
George W. Carleton & company, New York
Carnegie institution of Washington, D. C.
Carswell company, ltd., Toronto
Cassell publishing company, New York
Catholic book company, Wheeling, W. Va.
Catholic educational press, Washington, D. C.

Catholic standard and times publishing, Philadelphia
Catholic truth society, Toronto, London, etc.
Caxton press, New York
Central law journal company, St. Louis
Century company, New York
J. B. Chandler printer, Philadelphia
Chapman and Grimes, Boston
G. Chase, New York
Chatto and Windrup, London
Chicago literary club, Chicago
The Chiswick press (C. Whittingham & company) London
Christian press association publishing company, New York
Clarendon press, London
Arthur H. Clarke & company, Cleveland
R. Clarke and company, Chicago
R. Cobden-Sanderson, limited, London
R. Coddington, New York
Colburn, London
P. F. Collier & son, New York
T. K. and P. G. Collins, Philadelphia
W. Collins sons and company, limited, New York
Constable and company, London
Continental publishing company, New York
Copeland and Day, incorporated, New York
Cordon company, New York
Cosmopolitan book corporation, New York
Coward-McCann, incorporated, New York
F. S. Crofts & company, New York
Thomas Y. Crowell company, New York
Crown publishers, New York
Cubery and company, San Francisco
Peter F. Cunningham and son, Philadelphia

D

Dana & company, New York
G. S. Davis, Detroit
J. D. Denison, New York
Derby & Jackson, New York
Devin-Adair company, New York
Dial press (Lincoln McVeagh) incorporated, New York
Charles T. Dillingham, New York

G. W. Dillingham, New York
Dodd, Mead & company, incorporated, New York
Dolphin press, Philadelphia
George H. Doran company, Chicago
Dorance & company, incorporated, Philadelphia
Doubleday, Doran & company, incorporated, Philadelphia
Doubleday, Page & company, Garden City, New York
Frederick J. Drake and company, incorporated, Chicago
Driftwind press, North Montpelier, Vt.
Duckworth and company, London
E. Dunigan, New York
E. P. Dutton, New York
J. E. Dubal printing company, Mobile, Ala.
Evert Duyckinck, New York

E

Editions de l'arbre, Montreal
George H. Ellis, Boston
Emmet press, New York
Encyclopedia press, New York
S. Engles, Pittsburgh
Exposition pr., New York

F

Farrar and Rinehart, incorporated, New York
Federal book company, New York
Fergus printing company, Chicago
W. P. Fetridge and company, Boston
T. H. Flood & company, Chicago
Flood and Vincent, Chicago
Thomas J. Flynn and company, Boston
Thomas Foley, Ebensburg, Pa.
Foote and Davis company, Atlanta
B. C. Forbes publishing company, New York
J. T. Ford, Baltimore
Four seas company, Boston
The Franciscan press, St. Bonaventure, N. Y.
Franciscan Herald press, Chicago
Samuel French, incorporated, New York
Frye publishing co., New York
Funk & Wagnalls company, New York

G

Garden City publishing company, incorporated, New York
Jacob Gideon, junior, Washington, D. C.
Ginn & company (Athenaeum press), Boston
L. J. Gomme, New York
Edwin S. Gorham, New York
Government printing office, Washington, D. C.
Grafton press, New York
W. O. Graham, Art Craft, Kansas City, Mo.
Gross & Delbridge, Chicago
Grosset & Dunlap, incorporated, New York

H

Harcourt, Brace & company, incorporated, New York
G. Harjes, New York
Harper & brothers, New York
Henry Harrison, publisher, New York
A. Hart, Philadelphia
E. Hartsock, The Bozart press, Atlanta
W. P. Hazard, Philadelphia
Hearst's international library company, New York
D. C. Heath & company, Boston
Hedian & O'Brien, Baltimore
B. Herder book company, St. Louis, Freiburg, etc.
C. Hertzog, El Paso
Historical printing club, Brooklyn
Hodder & Stoughton, London
M. L. Holbrook & company, New York
Henry Holt & company, New York
H. O. Houghton & company, Cambridge, Mass.
Houghton Mifflin company (The Riverside press, Cambridge)
   Boston
John Howell, San Francisco
Bruce Humphries, incorporated, Boston
Hurd and Houghton, New York
Hutchinson & company, limited, London

I

Inquirer printing and publishing company, Lancaster, Pa.
Intermountain Catholic truth society, Salt Lake City
International Catholic truth society, Brooklyn, N. Y.

J

W. Jacobs & company, Philadelphia
Jansen, McClurg and company, Chicago
T. & J. W. Johnson & company, Philadelphia
Judd & Detweiler, Washington

K

Kahoe & company, Yellow Springs, Ohio
L. Kehoe, New York
Kelly, Hedian & Piet, Baltimore
Kelly, Piet and company, Baltimore
P. J. Kenedy & sons, New York
Mitchell Kennerley, New York
Key & Biddle, Philadelphia
J. B. Kirker, New York
The Knickerbocker press, New York
Knight & Millet, Boston
Isaac A. Kollock, Elizabethtown, N. J.

L

John Lane (The Bodley Head) limited, New York, London
Henry C. Lea, Philadelphia
Lee and Shepard publishers, Boston
F. D. Linn & company, Jersey City, N. J.
J. B. Lippincott, Philadelphia
Little, Brown & company, Boston
Liturgical press, Collegeville, Minn.
Liveright publication corporation, New York
G. Long & brother, New York
John Long, limited, London
Ray Long and Richard R. Smith, New York
Longmans, Green & company, New York
Lothrop company, Boston
Lothrop, Lee & Shepard company, Boston
A. Lovell & company, New York
Frank F. Lovell & company, New York
John W. Lovell company, New York
W. H. Lowdermilk, Washington
F. Lucas, junior, Baltimore

M

The Macaulay company, New York
W. Macbeth, New York
Robert M. McBride & company, New York
McClelland & Stewart, limited, Toronto
McClure, Phillips & company, New York
A. C. McClurg & company, Chicago
Arthur MacDonald, Washington
T. F. McGrath, Cleveland
McGraw-Hill book company, incorporated, New York
David McKay company, Philadelphia
The Macmillan company, New York
John Joseph McVey, Philadelphia
Magnificat press, Manchester, N. H.
Marlier & company, Boston
Marlier and Callanan, Boston
Marsh, Capen, Lyon & Webb, Boston
Martin & Hoyt company, Atlanta
Masson, Paris
Meals printing company, Gardener, Mass.
J. Meichel, Philadelphia
Andrew Melrose, limited, London
The Merriam company, New York
Merrymount press, Boston
Message publishing company, Jefferson City, Mo.
J. Messner, incorporated, New York
Methodist book concern, New York
Methuen & company, limited, London
P. Miller & son, Philadelphia
Mission press, Techny, Ill.
Mohawk press, incorporated, New York
J. W. Moore, Philadelphia
Morehouse publishing company, Milwaukee
Morrison & Gibb, Limited, Edinburgh
William Morrow, New York
C. V. Mosby company, St. Louis
George Munro's sons, New York
James Monroe company, Boston
Joel Munsell's sons, South Norwalk, Conn.
John Murphy company (Metropolitan press) Baltimore

Murphy & Bechtel, Trenton, N. J.
John Murray, London

N

J. H. Nash, San Francisco
National law book company, Chicago
Walter Neale, New York
Thomas Nelson & sons, New York
New York history company, New York
T. Nourse, Detroit
D. Nutt, London

O

James W. O'Brien, New York
Order of Bookfellows, Chicago
James R. Osgood & company, Boston
P. O'Shea, New York
Otis, Broaders & company, Boston
Our Sunday Visitor, Huntington, Ind.
Oxford book company, New York
Oxford university press, New York

P

L. C. Page & company, Boston
A. N. Palmer company, New York
Parnassus press, New York
Parish Visitors of Mary Immaculate press, New York
Park City publishing house, Chicago
H. B. Parsons, Albany, N. Y.
O. F. Parsons, New York
Paulist press, New York
Payson and Clarke, limited, New York
Peace book company, London
R. S. Peale company, Chicago
Pegasus press, London
J. Penington, Philadelphia
Phillips, Sampson & company, Boston
J. B. Piet, Baltimore
Pilot press, Los Angeles
Pitman publishing corporation, New York
The Poets press, New York

James Potts & company, New York
The Preservation of the Faith press, Silver Spring, Md.
Press of Chase brothers, Haverhill, Mass.
Press of Commercial printing company, St. Louis
Press of Piercy and Reed, New York
Press of the western painter, Chicago
Preston & Rounds company, Providence, R. I.
The Primavera press, Los Angeles
Frederick Pustet company, incorporated, New York
G. P. Putnam's sons, New York

Q

The Quartermaster association, Washington

R

Radio replies press, St. Paul
Rand McNally and company, New York
Anson D. F. Randolph and company, New York
J. S. Radfield, New York
Reformed Church publisher's board, Philadelphia
The Peter Reilly company, Philadelphia
Reilly & Lee company, Chicago
M. T. Richardson company, New York
The Ridgway company, New York
P. S. Ridsdale, Washington, D. C.
John C. Riker, New York
Riverside press, Cambridge
W. F. Roberts company, Washington
A. M. Robertson company, San Francisco
Runford press, Concord, N. H.
Herbert Russell, London
Ryerson press (United Church publishing House) Toronto

S

Saalfield publishing company, Akron, O.
J. Sabin & sons, New York
D. & J. Sadlier, New York
W. H. Sadlier, New York
St. Anthony guild press, Paterson, N. J.
St. Xavier's convent print, Beatty, Pa.
Salem Gazette office, Salem, Mass.
Salem Press, Salem, Mass.

Saitary publications company, Chicago
W. R. Scott, New York
Charles Scribner's sons, New York
J. H. Sears and company, incorporated, New York
Sheed & Ward, New York, London
Sheldon press, London
Shepard, Clark & Brown, Boston
C. Sherman & son, Philadelphia
G. L. Shuman & company, Boston
Smelter, Pittsburg, Kans.
Richard R. Smith, New York
Society for Promoting Christian Knowledge, London
Society of the Divine Word, Techny, Ill.
Christopher Sower company, Philadelphia
W. V. Spencer, Boston
Stanford and Swords, New York
Hugh Stephens ptg. and stationery company, Jefferson City, Mo.
Eliot Stock (Sidney Kiek & son, limited) London
Frederick A. Stokes company, New York
Stratford company, Boston
Street & Smith, New York
Stringer and Townsend, New York
L. K. Strouse and company, New York
Sunwise Turn, incorporated, New York
Swift, London

T

H. Taylor, Baltimore
J. A. Taylor and company, New York
Tennant & Ward, New York
Thomas, Cowperthwait and company, Philadelphia
Three worlds press, Huntington, Ind.
Tichnor and company, Boston
Tichnor, Reed and Fields, Boston
Transatlantic publishing company, New York
J. F. Trow, New York
G. A. Tuttle and company, Rutland, Vt.

U

The Union news league, incorporated, Boston
Unique press, incorporated, Detroit
United crafts, Syracuse, N. Y.

United States book company, New York
University publishing company, Lincoln, Nebr.
T. Fisher Unwin, London
S. C. Ustick, Washington

V

C. Van Benthuysen, Albany, N. Y.
D. Van Nostrand, New York
Vanguard press, incorporated, New York
C. F. Vent company, Chicago
Viking press, incorporated, New York
Virtue and Yorston, New York

W

C. V. Waite and company, Chicago
J. P. Walsh, Cincinnati
Webb publishing company, St. Paul
Charles L. Webster and company, New York
Weed-Parsons printing company, Albany, N. Y.
E. S. Werner, New York
West publishing company, St. Paul
Whittemore, Niles and Hall, Boston
Whittet and Shepperson, Richmond, Va.
Wickersham printing company, Lancaster, Pa.
W. A. Wilde company, Boston
John Wiley and sons, incorporated, New York
Wiley and sons, incorporated, New York
Willett, Clark and company, Chicago
Willey & Danforth, Vermillion, S. D.
Williams and Wilkins company, Baltimore
John Wilson and son, Cambridge, Mass.
M. H. Wiltzius and company, Milwaukee
J. A. Wineberger, Washington
J. W. Winterich, incorporated, Cleveland
William Wood and company, New York
A. S. Woodburn, Ottawa, Canada
F. Wyss, Berne

Y

J. H. Yewdale and sons company, Milwaukee
William H. Young and company, New York
Young Churchman company, Milwaukee